Ecological Migrants

ECOLOGICAL MIGRANTS
The Relocation of China's Ewenki Reindeer Herders

Yuanyuan Xie

berghahn
NEW YORK · OXFORD
www.berghahnbooks.com

Published in 2015 by
Berghahn Books
www.berghahnbooks.com

English-language edition
© 2015, 2020 Yuanyuan Xie
First paperback edition published in 2020

Chinese-language edition
© 2010 Peking University Press
生态移民政策与地方政府实践

本作品原由北京大学出版社于 2010 年出版。
英文翻译版经北京大学出版社授权于全球市场独家出版发行。
保留一切权利。未经书面许可，任何人不得复制、发行。

The Chinese edition is originally published by Peking University Press in 2010. This translation is published by arrangement with Peking University Press, Beijing, China. All rights reserved. No reproduction and distribution without permission.

Publication of this book is supported by the
Chinese Fund for the Humanities and Social Sciences.

Library of Congress Cataloging-in-Publication Data

Names: Xie, Yuanyuan (Sociologist) author.
Title: Ecological migrants: the relocation of China's Ewenki reindeer herders / Yuanyuan Xie.
Other titles: Sheng tai yi min zheng ce yu di fang zheng fu shi jian. English
Description: New York: Berghahn Books, 2016. | Includes bibliographical references and index.
Identifiers: LCCN 2015034304 | ISBN 9781782386322 (hardback: alk. paper) | ISBN 9781782386339 (ebook)
Subjects: LCSH: Migration, Internal--China--Inner Mongolia. | Evenki (Asian people)--China--Inner Mongolia--Migrations. | Evenki (Asian people)--China--Inner Mongolia--Economic conditions--21st century.
Classification: LCC HB2114.I56 X5413 2016 | DDC 305.894/1--dc23
LC record available at http://lccn.loc.gov/2015034304

British Library Cataloguing in Publication Data
A catalogue record for this book is available from the British Library

ISBN 978-1-78238-632-2 (hardback)
ISBN 978-1-78920-790-3 (paperback)
ISBN 978-1-78238-633-9 (ebook)

Dedicated Sincerely to All Who Love Me and Whom I Love

Contents

Illustrations

Figures

All photos were taken by the author

Tables

Charts

Foreword

It will be a great contribution to the world anthropology that Dr Yuanyuan Xie's book about Aoluguya Ewenki will be published in English. I was delighted to write the foreword for her Chinese version published in 2010, and this time I am again delighted to do it for the English book.

As the initiator of the Peking University Aoluguya Ewenki Ecological Migrants Research Project, I visited the Aoluguya Ewenki Township, Genhe County, Inner Mongolia—the place where Dr Xie would later undertake her anthropological fieldwork. The project had its origins in a chance opportunity during a work trip in 2003. I witnessed the living conditions of the locals, who had undergone the ecological migration move. The living conditions were arduous and poor; the newly built homes were humid and chilly; and their indoor toilets were not ready for use. The local people's psychological state was depressed and stood in sharp contrast to what we might normally expect to see from a people jubilant about relocating to a new and better place. Therefore, as soon as I returned to Peking University, I immediately initiated such a research project.

Later I knew that a doctoral student had set off alone to the faraway and unfamiliar mountainous region to conduct field research. Throughout the winter she endured snowy conditions and bitter, piercing cold; throughout the summer she suffered an ongoing onslaught of insect bites, and assorted threats of infectious diseases like meningitis and tuberculosis. She lived in the underdeveloped small countryside area for one year. Several of our professors who had been to the Aoluguya region were quite aware of the living conditions at that time; therefore, we were all greatly impressed by the courage with which Dr Xie undertook this project and the determination that she exhibited during her long, independent field research. She successfully overcame all obstacles and completed the daunting research task that this project entailed.

Dr Xie was widely popular among the local people and she still keeps in frequent contact with them. She lived and ate together with the locals, and at times lived in the hunters' tents in the hilly forests, where conditions were extremely harsh. The local people think highly of her, and praised her as adept at enduring hardships of every kind. I am deeply impressed by the vigorous, optimistic and enduring spirit she has exhibited through the course of her work.

As far as I know, the materials recounted in Dr Xie's book are accurate descriptions based on solid fieldwork, including the collection of the precious historical archives, the first-hand data and materials, long-term participant observation, and in-depth communication with the local people. Her writing is lively, thorough, and makes for very good reading.

This work of ethnography is both eloquently written and thought provoking. Through detailed recounting of a minority group's ecological migration process, the author reflected on China's modernization and social developments since 1949. This is a typical case that focused on a slice of life in the past development stage in China. This research, with merits in both its theme and methodology, could be worth sustained attention from national and international peers.

Any written research paper does not merely describe the object being studied, but also expresses the author's attitudes and beliefs. Upon finishing reading this book, readers will readily come to acknowledge that the author is a scholar who possesses compassion toward the society and writes with the wisdom of rationality and careful reflection. Through her work, she was sharply aware of the various complaints voiced by the local people; sensitively perceived the subtle psychological states among Ewenki people, and found the key problem of how to understand the Ewenki Hunters' identity. Having obtained in-depth understandings of the social reality as experienced by the local people, she engaged in conscientious reflection on the conflicts among the different subjects and creatively revealed the discourse trap in the implementation of the governmental policy. Some of her research findings have proven to be very useful for re-evaluating and improving policies. For example, her work revealed an internal division within the Aoluguya Ewenki Hunters' group. This information served as a significant and timely alarm that clearly demonstrated the problem with the government's implementation of a catch-all policy solution that had considered them as a united group.

Since her book was published in Chinese in 2010, positive comments have come successively. I know two mentionable details. One reader wrote in a public blog: "Yuanyuan Xie's book—the most caring anthropological work—has aroused persistent thinking . . . She is like a dancer on the cutting edge. I can feel that she was using incomparably cautious and euphemistic words to display her seeing and thinking with great care." Another mentionable incident is that when her Chinese book was sent back to Aoluguya, the local people thought it was honest and respectable. Especially, the local venerable scholars thought that her book was very genuine and authentic. One of them even broke into tears for the touching comprehension in her book. I think such feedback is the best reward for the author.

I believe that the upcoming international concern with this book will arouse broader comparative research and profound reflection, which will promote knowledge innovation. Constant knowledge innovation enables us to breach self-imposed prejudices and barriers, and encourages us to see people and issues in a more forgiving, caring and generous fashion. Altogether, this provides individuals and society with increased possibilities for creating a more congenial and harmonious social environment.

Ping Hao
Summer 2014

Preface

This book is about an event of ecological migration regarding a unique minority group in China that was called the Aoluguya Ewenki Hunters. Before the event happened in 2003, this group was not as well known. In history it was called Yakut, while in Chinese academic circle today it is called Reindeer Ewenki or Ewenki Reindeer-Using Tribe. It belongs to one of three branches of the Ewenki ethnic minority in China; the other two branches were historically called Solon and Tungus. Because of the ecological migration event, the Aoluguya Ewenki Hunters was called "the last hunting tribe in China" in the news coverage. China's last hunting tribe became ecological migrants in August 2003. Soon after, they were relocated to a new place as the ecological migrants. I went there to conduct my fieldwork.

I called that event Aoluguya Ewenki Ecological Migration. Aoluguya, which means a place with lush poplar woods, is the name of a river. At the same time, Aoluguya is the name of a township located in Genhe County, Inner Mongolia Autonomous Region—a northern province in China. Aoluguya became the landmark and brand name for this place of the "last hunting tribe" upon the event of ecological migration. It was a small town with no more than 300 people. Because it was a village-sized town, it was easy for me to get acquainted with everyone there, and I soon became familiar with all the things happening around.

Any small social setting could reflect larger issues of politics and identity, so such an unusual ecological migration event that happened in the small county where the Ewenki Hunters were forced to give up hunting to be relocated in the suburb to begin city life is worthy of rethinking by more people in the multicultural context. The event itself is worthy of being recorded and is of profound historical value.

Peking University Press published this research in Chinese (my native language) in 2010. For the publishing opportunity, I am indebted to Professor Ngai Pun. When I worked as a visiting scholar at the University of Oslo, Norway, in 2009, I met Professor Ngai Pun from the Hong Kong

Polytechnic University, who gave a lecture at an academic seminar. She was in charge of the compilation of the Chinese book series "Social Development Theory and Practice." When she finished reading my manuscript she recommended it to the Peking University Press, who had it published.

I feel fortunate that my book will be published in English and can reach a wider audience. I am hugely grateful to Dr Marion Berghahn and Berghahn Books, whose interest in international social science issues and my research greatly facilitated the publication of my English book.

This book originates from my Chinese book *The Ecological Migration Policy and Its Application by Local Authorities: A Case Study of the Aoluguya Ewenki Ecological Migration* (2010). However, it has been substantially reworked for a wider audience. I hope readers can enjoy reading a story that was composed of facts. I know that despite my best efforts to maintain a researcher's attitude of impartiality, my perspectives are still limited. It is my hope that through the publication of this book I will be able to deliver my gratitude to the Aoluguya Ewenki people and perhaps be of some use to them in their endeavors to improve their lives. Usually, more readers and more attention benefit the local people. In addition, I realize that when the feeling for the events and people are transformed into written words, there is always the possibility of regret. To avoid the possibility of unintended harm to those kind people, I have changed all the names in the book—only pseudonyms are used. Please try not to identify the various people in the book with the people currently holding positions in government. Countless changes have taken place in the years since I finished the fieldwork. It is important to note that the various time references and ages of people described in the main body of the book use the year 2004 as the baseline, and data without specific reference is from my fieldwork research.

Acknowledgments

As for the premier translation from Chinese to English, I extend my heartfelt gratitude to two translators: Pei Zhang-Miller and Raymond Ambrosi. Pei, my dear sister in the United States, conducted the first-round translation. Raymond, a Canadian gentleman and Ph.D. in anthropology of Peking University, made meticulous revisions and added numerous annotations as well as explanatory notes. They both supplemented relevant materials that would be helpful for my adaption, for which I am deeply grateful. During the adaption process while I was at the University of Illinois at Urbana-Champaign, with the help of Max Fisher, I received a lot of advice from Chelsea Coronel and Jill Tschopp Huang. I am very grateful for their help, and I also owe many thanks to Professor Jesse Ribot for his hospitality and support. In addition, I feel honored that this work is supported by the Chinese Fund for the Humanities and Social Sciences; and my thanks also go to the anonymous assessment panel.

Here, I must express my gratitude to those people who gave me powerful help with this book. I am grateful to Professor Bingzhong Gao of the Institute of Anthropology and the Department of Sociology of Peking University. Under his influence, I realized that scholars should make those voices heard that have been overlooked by policymakers, and should be able to provide the necessary theoretical support to help various groups adopt appropriate practices.

I must express my thanks to Professor David Anderson of the University of Aberdeen who took time to go over my manuscript and provided me with valuable insights. I also appreciate the incisive opinions from the anonymous reviewers, whose profound suggestions were very helpful. Especially, my sincere gratitude goes to the editors of the press. Berghahn Books offered me its excellent editorial assistance for publishing my work. I must mention that Max Fisher provided the maps. I thank him for his outstanding work and warm help.

I thank heartily all of the Aoluguya people, who embraced me and shared their life stories with me. They provided continuous support and care like my family. I remember an exciting scene in April 2009 when I attended the Fourth World Reindeer Herders' Congress at Kautokeino in the Sami region in northern Norway. While attending the conference, I was elated to meet the delegation from China's Aoluguya Ewenki. When they told me that Ewo ("Auntie" in local Ewenki language), who had hosted me during my stay in Aoluguya, still frequently mentioned me and hoped I would return for a visit with my young daughter, I could not hold back my tears. To me, Aoluguya is more than an experience in my life journey. In June 2011, in July 2013 and in July 2014 I returned to Aoluguya and found that the local Ewenki people's lives had gradually returned to a more peaceful, regular routine, and saw that cultural tourism is becoming an important part of the regional economy. Maybe it is time for all parties to revisit that period of history with calm impartiality.

Lastly, I would like to dedicate this poem to those people always in my mind:

Years apart,
A period neither long nor short,
My thoughts of longing are like a song,
Weeping in a quiet whisper,
Drawing me back to distant memories.

At one time wishing to give up,
Flashed this selfish thought,
But you quietly endured despite it all,
And a profound shame
Encouraged me to persevere.

Amidst growing shame, I prayed to be worthy of your ardent hope.
Before my eyes, obscured and vague,
Are those faces so familiar yet so far away.
Once again, unable to hold back tears that fall like misty rain.

Maps

Map 1 Reindeer Ewenki historical migration

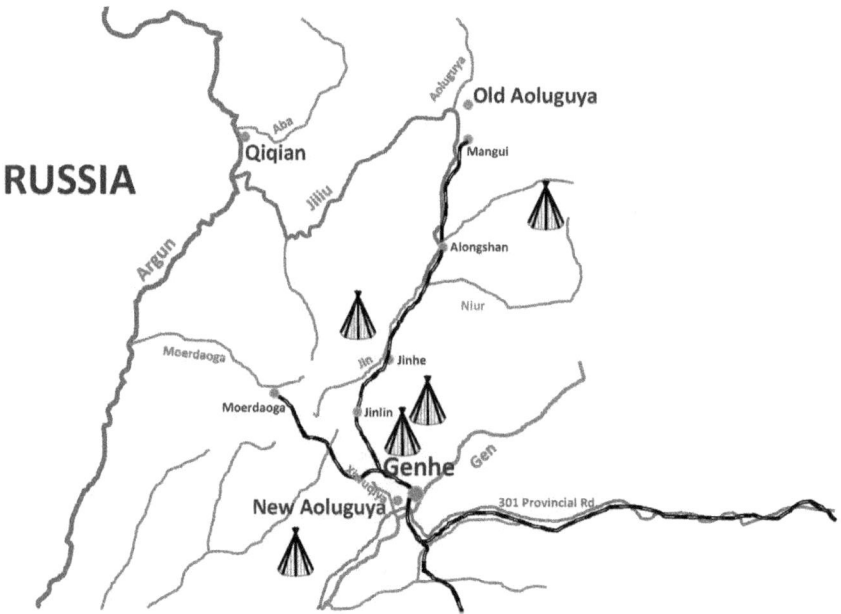

Map 2 Location of main fieldwork in China

Introduction

$\Longrightarrow \cdot \Longleftarrow$

On 11 August 2003, *The People's Daily*[1] ran a news report entitled "Nation's Last Hunting Tribe Moving from Mountains to New Residence" in its Important News Special Delivery column. It briefly reported that on 10 August 2003, in the forest of the Greater Khingan Range in Genhe County of Inner Mongolia, the Aoluguya Ewenki Hunters[2] called "China's last hunting tribe," who lived a lifestyle of hunting and reindeer herding, started packing household items early in the morning. They took down the *cuoluozi*,[3] herded reindeer out of the woods, and began preparing for the relocation to a new residence comprised of rows of newly constructed brick and concrete houses 260 km away. The Chinese Central TV was so eager to report this move that it gave a live broadcast of news coverage. All of a sudden, the Aoluguya Ewenki Ecological Migrants/Migration[4] had garnered ongoing attention from the Chinese and overseas media, generating tremendous interest from the general public. Driving this interest were a range of factors: myths and legends about the Aoluguya hunters; the government's hype about this move as a historic significant leap from "primitivism" to "modernization"; the tremendous monetary investment in the relocation as part of an overall ecological migration[5] program of the state; and the debate among scholars over "preserving people" or "preserving culture."

In general, when an event is exaggerated by the media and results in a wide social response, different voices easily arise. Although these different voices can broaden people's thinking, they can confuse those people who lack perceptual understanding of the actual situation. In the end, the focus of the debate often relates to how much information is in hand about the facts, and how well people know and understand the parties involved. In an unfamiliar cultural environment, a considerable amount of time and shared experience are required for people to mutually know and understand each other further. Anthropological fieldwork provides a practical pathway to achieve such knowing and understanding. I took twelve months from 2003 to 2004 to closely observe, feel, experience and contemplate Aoluguya Ewenki ecological migrants' life.

According to historical documents, prior to the establishment of the People's Republic of China in 1949, the reindeer-herding Ewenki hunters had lived in the forests of the Greater Khingan Range for over three hundred years. They sustained their livelihoods by collecting plants and herbs, hunting animals, and herding reindeer. Although they had undergone several dynastic changes, there had been no significant change to their roaming and hunting lifestyle for centuries. Since 1949, the new central government has become highly concerned with the welfare of this minority group, so two residential relocation projects were planned for them: the first one took place between 1957 and 1959 when the Ewenki hunters were moved from the hilly woods to Qiqian[6] alongside the Argun River; the second took place in 1965 when they were moved from Qiqian to old Aoluguya (the Ewenki habitat prior to the ecological migration in 2003). Local researchers familiar with Aoluguya Ewenki history defined the two relocation projects as "settling down without occupancy" and "occupancy without settling down" respectively. The use of these terms showed that the two residential relocation programs organized by the government did not truly achieve their goal—that is to say, Ewenki hunters' hunting and reindeer-herding lifestyle continued. The ecological migration move began on 10 August 2003 was indeed the third residential relocation program that the government planned for the Ewenki hunters.

When the ecological migration move was carried out, the government no longer allowed the Ewenki hunters to hunt. This was very much unlike the period from the early 1950s to the late 1970s, when the government encouraged the Ewenki hunters to hunt and even supplied them with more advanced guns and bullets. This time, on the eve of the ecological migration move, the hunters' guns were confiscated and their hunting behavior was no longer legal. According to media reports, the hunters put down their guns, walked out of the forests, then started new lives as modern urban dwellers. Shortly after the move there appeared seriously sentimental reactions from the ecological migrants, which were completely different from the reactions after the previous two relocations—this time there was an unusually large number of complaints and abundant discontent among the various groups. Fierce clashes at new Aoluguya were something hitherto unheard of.

During my fieldwork, both the county and township officials in charge of the ecological migration project displayed their goodwill and efforts to improve the lives of Ewenki ecological migrants. They did take some measures and actions in order to help these migrants adapt to so-called modern lives. The officials acknowledged the migrants' complaints about the governmental resettlement—this was deemed normal and unavoidable in the process of modernization. With regard to the outbursts of wrath from the migrants, the local officials gave two explanations: one was that the migrants were not well educated and lacked the ability to match the modern life; the other was that the migrants were so anxious to step into modernization and were impatient about the tough adjustment process. The local government implemented several povertywrelief policies to help the migrants more rapidly adjust to their new environment in order to settle down and enjoy their new lifestyle. However, the migrants did not appreciate their efforts. Why did the government's well-intended relocation arrangement and series of assistance policies fail to achieve the expected results? These conflicts prompted me to ask: what is indeed the cause of the problem?

I had a clear sense of the depressed spirit of the Aoluguya community during my stay from September 2003 to October 2004. When the migrants told me of their past lives filled with joy that now only existed in memories, I believed that their persistent complaints were worthy to investigate—why did they feel so unhappy? It is true that life is not always perfect and complaints are unavoidable. However, when almost everyone in a community is complaining continuously for years at a time, regardless of whether they are average people or government officials, and it is apparent that many people are full of regret, bitterness, and pain, then such a problem is worthy of our consideration. The persistent complaints became a starting point for me to observe and reflect the ideas and practices of all parties involved.

Since 1949, the central government has adopted the perspective of nationwide regulation and had persisted in sending the Ewenki hunters along a path of resettlement. In each of the different historical periods, was there a difference in the way that Ewenki hunters perceived these planned relocation initiatives? Did they perceive the government and nation in different ways? And what was the basis behind the government's implementation of planned relocation policies? I will address these questions through a historically thick, ethnographic description—detailed and thorough—of the Ewenki ecological migrants, providing an analysis of the Aoluguya Ewenki ecological migration case. Let us start with the following questions: who are the Ewenki hunters and where did they come from?

Ewenki Hunters and Aoluguya

The Ewenki, a small ethnic minority group in north China, has a total population of 30,505 people according to the year 2000 census data, and 30,875 people according to the year 2010 census data. As one of the branches of Ewenki, today the Reindeer Ewenki or Ewenki Hunters have a population of approximately 200. According to the Chinese historian Guangtian Lü (1962), Chinese Ewenki were composed of three tribes called, respectively, Solon, Tungus, and Yakut, and today's Aoluguya Ewenki are the descendants of the Yakut, who led a traditional life-style and were a mixture of reindeer herders and hunter-gatherers—they domesticated the wild reindeer for milk and transport, and hunted other animals for meat. Existing historical records have indicated that the population has always fluctuated around several hundred.

S.M. Shirokogoroff, a Russian anthropologist, did the first influential ethnographic study on northern China. In his research, Chinese Reindeer Ewenki were called Reindeer Tungus (Shirokogoroff 1966[1929]).[7] Moreover, he pointed out: "The study of the anthropology of Northern China shows that the same anthropological (somatological) types can be observed among very different ethnical groups, viz. Chinese, Koreans, Turcs, Mongols and Tungus. These ethnical groups form so peculiar and distinct anthropological complexes that they cannot be united by any but a purely geographical generalization" (Shirokogoroff 1923: 114). Obviously, Reindeer Tungus belonged to the complex of northern Tungus. The northern minorities from the complex shared a similar lifestyle, although they were scattered throughout different countries or regions, and included the Khant, who lived traditionally by hunting and freshwater fishing, and the reindeer-herding groups such as the Nenets, Evenk, Eveny, Buryats, Sami, and the Eskimo, etc. (Ingold 1976, 1980; Beach 1981, 1993; Vitebsky 1990; Humphrey 1990; Anderson 1991, 1999, 2000; Omura 1998; Inoue 2001; Lavrillier 2010; Ulturgasheva 2012).

The earliest descriptions of the reindeer-herding group in China are found sporadically in various Chinese antiquarian books, such as *New Book of Tang* (1060), *History of Ming* (1739), and *Factual Record of Qing Dynasty* (1930), and it was called the Reindeer-Using Tribe (Pinyin: *shi lu bu*) (Kalina 2004). According to the Chinese historians' research findings (Lü 1962), the Reindeer-Using Tribe's ancestors originally lived around Lake Baikal and the upper reaches of the Nerchinsk River, north-east of Lake Baikal, about four thousand years ago. From the sixteenth century to the mid seventeenth century, they followed wild reindeer herds to the area near the Vilyuy River and Vitim River, both of which are tributaries of the Lena River, northwest of Lake Baikal. Around the eighteenth century, this Reindeer-Using Tribe followed the Shilka River and arrived at the Greater Khingan Range on the east bank of the Argun River. The wide range of animals living in the Greater Khingan Range, like birds, land animals, and a wide range of fish, became the tribe's sources of food and clothing. Over the long passage of history, this tribe created and developed reindeer domestication, birch bark handicrafts, animal skin tanning, and bear veneration beliefs.

Beginning in 1956 and continuing in the years that followed, China's central government organized experts in ethnology, history and linguistics to conduct broad and thorough social and historical investigations into the Reindeer Ewenki. Some historical records were compiled; a number of authentic reliable research papers and academic writings were published. Reports like "Social Conditions of the Reindeer Ewenki of Argun Banner in the Inner Mongolia Autonomous Region" compiled by the National People's Congress Ethnic Group Committee Office (1958), and "Ewenki Conditions in Argun Banner" jointly compiled by the Inner Mongolia Minority Social & Historical Investigation Group and the History Research Institute, Inner Mongolia Branch, Chinese Academy of Sciences (1960), were both investigative reports focused on the status of the Reindeer Ewenki. These reports contained detailed records of the Ewenki historical situation, economics, social organization, and spiritual culture. *Ewenki Primitive Society Status* (1962) by Pu Qiu was the first book in China that focused on the Ewenki. It discussed their production methods, social organization, and how the tribe made the direct transition from primitive life to socialism. During this period of time, ethnological and historical research on the Reindeer Ewenki began to use the discourse that relied on the Marxian stage of development theory and saw the Reindeer Tribe as living in a stage of primitive society. This popular opinion showed that the modernization notion—in which time and space were disconnected—had already been widely accepted. At the same time, it also hinted at the scholars' viewpoint of historicism (Popper, 1987[1957]: 2).

Since Reform and Opening Up in 1978, several specialized Chinese works on Ewenki and Oroqen have been published in succession, including some novels, picture albums, and research papers (Tian 1981; Manduertu 1981; Chaonang 1981; Wang and Wang 1988; Du 1989; Chaoke 1992; Ning 1992; Suritai 1992, 1997; Kong 1994, 1995;

Wuyundalai 1998; Wureertu 1998; Chen 1999; Wang 2000; Song 2001; Chaoke and Wang 2002). These works were helpful to my research in three respects. Firstly, the works showed the authors' understanding of nomadic minorities, which reflected the authors' overall view of history as evolving through stages of development—a notion that guided national modernization practice at that time (Yang 1994). The descriptions in these books became the materials for me to reflect upon the notion on which their texts were based. Secondly, through these works, I could learn much about many traditional reindeer-herding and hunting life practices, which are hard to find today and include traditional knowledge and experience, which I consider a type of life wisdom accumulated from living in a natural environment and embodying concepts such as how to live harmoniously with nature, how to deal with natural risks and disasters, how to solve conflicts between groups, and other related cultural practices. Thus, I could learn about the Reindeer-Using Tribe's rich cultural practices and spiritual world; obtain their sense of their self-esteem and self-confidence as a distinct ethnic group. Thirdly, these works were a valuable reference for me to learn about Ewenki living conditions at different times, their customs and habits, and changes in their religious beliefs. However, few studies on the Ewenki have attempted to look at the interconnectedness of the national modernization programs and the ethnic groups' cultural change. Therefore, it is necessary to bridge the gap between anthropological reflections on modernization and Ewenki studies.

As the name of the Aoluguya Ewenki Ethnic Township, Aoluguya refers to two township sites: one is the site before the ecological migration; the other is the site after the ecological migration. In order to make it clear, the former is called old Aoluguya and the latter is called new Aoluguya. For simplicity, the local people shortened the official name Aoluguya Ewenki Ethnic Township to Ao Township. From the name of a small river as shown on the map, Aoluguya has become famous and has developed—especially since the ecological migration event in 2003—to a specific indication to represent the mysterious and ancient nomadic hunting and reindeer-herding culture.

The following three factors are the possible reasons for its fame. First, because of the TV and Internet broadcast of the ecological migration event, Aoluguya attracted a large amount of tourists from all over the world. Second, it aroused attention from the Association of World Reindeer Herders (WRH) and the International Center for Reindeer Husbandry (ICR). Hence, the Ewenki group at Aoluguya was invited to attend the Fourth World Reindeer Herders' Congress in Norway in 2009; moreover, the Congress unanimously decided to hold the next Congress in Aoluguya. In 2013, the Ewenki Reindeer Herders at Aoluguya hosted the Fifth Congress and the Aoluguya Declaration was announced during the conference. Third, with the development of the tourism industry in recent years, the local reindeer products, such as antlers, penis, heart blood, reindeer jerky and semi-fluid extract of reindeer fetus, have been registered with the trademark of Aoluguya. Artistic creations such as documentaries and musical dramas with the theme of "Aoluguya" have won international prizes.

Historical Modernization Policies in China

It is impossible to investigate the development of the Ewenki people without putting them in the context of world history. Since World War II, before the Cold War ended, social planning programs on a grand scale were rolled out throughout the Third World. These plans were carried out in the name of modernization (Luo 2004), and were based on an assumption of Western superiority (Parsons 1966, 1971, 1977); namely, the Western political, economic and value systems were superior to those of the non-Western world. In the face of pressure from powerful Western forces of modernization, China initiated a series of planned modernization programs.

With the founding of New China in 1949, the new government under the leadership of Chairman Mao wanted to realize China's modernization from an agricultural nation in a very short time. The ultimate goal was to build up powerful modernized industry, modernized agriculture, modernized transportation, and modernized national defense, based on socialism, just like the Soviet Union at that time. The First Five-year Plan (1953–1957) which manifested the Soviet approach to economic development, did achieve much success. The administration structure, law system, and various public services, such as the collective farm and food ration system were imitated from the socialist power—i.e., the Soviet Union.

However, with the deterioration of Soviet-China relations, which climaxed in 1964, as reflected in the second relocation of Ewenki people, and the addition of the three years of great Chinese famine (1958–1961) and policy catastrophe of the culture revolution, China was looking for an opportunity to develop on its own and was slowly changing to a market-oriented economy under the leadership of Deng Xiaoping with so-called Chinese characteristic socialism, especially after the collapse of the Berlin Wall and the end of the Soviet Union. With the market opening further during Jiang Zemin's tenure, and the concentration on economy, China gained much progress with their gross domestic product

(GDP) and average income, particularly after joining the World Trade Organization (WTO) in 2001.

In 2002, China officially acknowledged, firstly, that "the urban and rural dual structure"—the socioeconomic differential development in urban and rural regions—was a serious economic and social problem. The goal to achieve "the integrated and coordinated development of urban and rural regions" was also raised. In 2003 the government further clearly emphasized the Comprehensive Development Concept—i.e., there would be no more blind emphasis on growth of GDP. It embraced the coordinated plans for urban-rural development, regional development, economic-social development, more harmonious human-nature development, and for domestic economic growth and an opening-up policy. In 2004, the Scientific Development Concept was developed. During this time, the main guiding principle of the Scientific Development Concept as people-orientated was emphasized yet again, and sustainability was introduced as a new guiding concept.

After the Scientific Development Concept, the government then raised the goal of the construction of a socialist, harmonious society, which demonstrated an important strategic decision to impel harmonious social construction based on practical implementation. The government under the leadership of Hu Jintao fully addressed the main content of this important strategic change and emphasized the importance of constructing a socialist harmonious society. In 2005, the Party Central Committee's view underwent strategic modifications from first emphasizing modernization and later emphasizing comprehensive development; their policy was continuously refined, deciphered and gradually evolved to become governmental policy.

It can be seen from policy documents that the central government has stepped away from the original strategic goal of modernization. The reason is that modernization theory today is in deep crisis (Nash 1979; Marglin 2001[1996]). Many factors have contributed to the crisis. The most obvious one is the extreme unbalance (such as polarization of the rich and poor) and the ever-increasing ecological disasters related to modernization (damage to tropical forests and mountainous region hydrology; possible damage to ecological systems by giant dams and large-scale hydraulic engineering). These issues have led to the awakening of non-Western social, cultural and political movements in the Third World, which grow day by day and receive increasing levels of support. There is appearing an increasingly accepted tendency to return to local value systems (Eisenstadt 1988; Escobar 2000[1998]; Evans 1979). Chinese central government's strategic change from emphasis on modernization to comprehensive development demonstrates a clear shift in value assumptions.

In recent years, from a strategic level, the government's transition from modernization to comprehensive development, combined with a focus on sustainability, has led to the formulation of an ecological migration policy, with the express purpose of saving and preserving the highly sensitive and badly damaged ecology of western China. This shift has entailed considerable difficulties and setbacks, and exploration remains for the future. As national policy was undergoing this transition, under the leadership of local government, the Aoluguya Ewenki hunters were relocated to a new site as part of the local government's ecological migration plan.

As far as I have observed, Aoluguya town was infused with tension and resistance from the people's narratives and the considerable deject and agitation in their behavior. What troubled me most were the complaints and conflicts stemming from a wide range of people—Ewenki and other local people. I could not help but be curious about the Aoluguya Ewenki ecological migration project planned by the local government and why goodwill yielded a disaster. From every detail gleaned during fieldwork, I gradually discovered that the mistake was following a mistaken train of thought, which proved to be far more lethal than any lack of professional skill in the implementation of the relocation project. Once being set on the wrong direction, even the possession of great skills will only ever result in an ever-greater deviation from the original goal. Here the mistaken train of thought was, in fact, the original modernization notion, which should have been replaced by the new Scientific Development Concept. The type of discourse employed by the government in the case of the Ewenki hunters' ecological migration was precisely the above-mentioned original modernization, which I shall more accurately term as planned modernization. It was the inevitable use of planned modernization by the government in its implementation of the relocation that led to unavoidable conflicts and complaints by all parties involved. By undertaking fieldwork, I was able to identify the conflict between new ideologies in the form of comprehensive development and new practices in the form of the ecological migration event, and then proceed to analyze this conflict and provide plausible explanations.

It is well known that the central government's investment in poverty-relief efforts in remote and ethnic minority areas has increased greatly during the last four decades. I found that the governmental modernization programs to improve living conditions in underdeveloped areas did indeed achieve some success in a short time, but, later on, the programs did not yield ideal effects. During the rapid development of the market economy, large monetary investments in minority areas often resulted in a vicious cycle of social issues. Some ethnic minorities could not live on their own like before in such a new market economy, thus they have had to be sustained by the government. These ethnic minorities were entitled to governmental preferential treatment. This has caused concern about social unfairness on a large scale.

This type of dependent-development has led to a shortage of self-reliant local institutions, which in turn has caused the central government to increase investment in the region year after year, without seeing much improvement. That is to say, the government's transfusion of investment into the region did not succeed in stimulating economic and social self-reliance in the region. This is a common phenomenon in the marginal minority regions of China, but it has not been thoroughly reflected upon. By researching this ecological migration project related to modernization and urbanization, we can gain more information and a better understanding of this phenomenon.

Summary of the Book

This book will be presented in the form of ethnography. This is a complicated case study. Its main content is an examination of the Aoluguya Ewenki ecological migration event, including the proposal of the ecological migration plan, its implementation, and the short-term consequence one year after the relocation. Providing a clear description of this case will not only show the developmental ideology and implementation of the planned modernization that preceded the Scientific Development Concept, but will also provide a foundation for discussion and future reflection on planned modernization.

One of the main purposes of this research is to engage in reflection, then explore and discover solutions to the problem. In order to analyze and reflect on the implications of modernization in China, I have used the concept of planned modernization—a term that serves to summarize the defining characteristics of the government's implementation of the relocation. In addition, the term serves as a theoretical summary of the government's long-term mode of thinking regarding modernization and practical implementation. The term "planned" represents certain characteristics of the state's developmental concept regarding modernization and thus can serve as a conceptual tool with which we can reflect on modernization from the perspective of critical thinking.

I focus closely on the country's holistic historical narrative that forms the backdrop for the vicissitudes and changes that have taken place with this ethnic minority's living conditions, as well as on the linkages between the holistic historical narrative and the local historical narrative. My work especially focuses on the voice of the Ewenki people and my personal fieldwork experiences. In this narrative of the ecological migration event, I present the voices of various players in the text. At the same time, by reflecting on my participation in community life, I strive to reveal the differences among a diversity of players with different value systems and thinking perspectives, and show how my mode of thinking and perspectives changed over time. With this in mind, my ultimate aim is to promote mutual understanding and forgiveness among different groups.

The book is divided into five chapters. In Chapter One, I present my fieldwork experience. I want to introduce the reader to the Ewenki Township with interest, and let the reader know what the situation was like there. I pay attention to my first-hand experience and original documents and the culture shock of facing the new, exotic culture. I introduce the fact that the Aoluguya Ewenki ecological migration event is an example of a modernization project, which appears to have been guided by the Chinese state's new Scientific Development Concept, but in reality it was carried out by using the old strategy of planned modernization.

Chapter Two provides background information on the ecological migration project, which includes a description of the complicated kinship networks in the Aoluguya Township and of the Ewenki Hunters' traditional living conditions, as well as historical government policies that directly affected the Ewenki Hunters' lifestyle. This chapter serves as a preparatory backdrop against which the rest of the ecological migration story can be more easily understood. Chapter Three gives the details about the process of ecological migration, including the policies and guidelines from official documents. It presents how the government made the relocation decision, how they planned the migration project, and how they executed the relocation finally. Township resident identities changed after the relocation.

Chapter Four provides a detailed ethnographic description of the entire Aoluguya Ewenki ecological migration event after the relocation. The description is full of dramatic incidents. Through these incidents, I present all parties' voices and show the conflicts in their notion and practice, the solutions provided by the government, and the status of the local reindeer antler economy. Finally, in Chapter Five, I discuss the issue of "preserving people" or "preserving culture," analyze the discourse trap of the ecological migration event, and provide reflection on the process of modernization in China. Also, I present possible approaches in the future to some problems that have been presented.

Notes

1. *The People's Daily* (Pinyin: *ren min ri bao*), the most important and most authoritative newspaper in China.
2. Here "Hunters" is a political identity, since they were forced to give up hunting in 2003. When in the book it means their identity prior to 2003—their actual hunting life—I do not capitalize the first letter of "hunters."
3. *Cuoluozi* (in the Ewenki language: *djiu*) is a type of simple and convenient tent in the shape of an umbrella, made with a frame of 20–30 stripped pinewood poles. The outside of the tent is covered with birch skins. In winter the tent is covered with more layers of animal skins. On top there is a hole for ventilation and light. Experienced hunters can set it up without any nails or pins. This unique structure is the material embodiment of the Ewenki people's wisdom and talent.
4. In Chinese, *sheng tai yi min* (生态移民) can refer to both the people who are required to move (the ecological migrants) and the policy regarding migration (ecological migration).
5. In order to change and improve the unbalanced development between eastern and mid-western China, in 2000 the Party Central Committee proposed the Grand Western Development Plan. When developing the western region, people face an extremely fragile ecological environment caused by natural and historical factors. To improve the ecological environment in the western region, the government deems it is necessary to change the aboriginal lifestyles led by the pastoralists and hunters. The goal is to reduce human damage to the environment. So the government wants to move those people and animals out of the areas where the ecological environment suffers seriously, and at the same time enclose the area to nurture plantation through artificial cultivation. The government thinks this kind of human effort is the only way to gradually improve the environment. Under this guideline, the governmental ecological migration policy was made in 2001. Ecological migration as a concept appeared earlier.
6. Qiqian was named Ust-Urov in Russian.
7. Dr Ethel John Lindgren-Utsi was one of very few Western anthropologists to carry out research in Northeastern China in the 1930s. She also used Reindeer Tungus to refer to the local reindeer herding people (Lindgren 1930, 1935, 1936). In addition, the local reindeer herding people were also called Reindeer Oroqen by the Japanese researcher Haruka Nagata (Nagata 1985[1939]).

Chapter 1

Living with Ewenki Hunters

⋙•⋘

First Arrival at Aoluguya

At the beginning of the ecological migration event, all media reports were quite positive. The message they sent out was that the Ewenki hunters were satisfied with the relocation. However, different voices started to appear shortly afterward—on 14 August 2003, the newspaper *Beijing Youth* ran a report entitled "How far is the road out of mountains for the Ewenki?" When this news clip was reprinted on the top official website Xinhua News Network and other websites with the title "The nation's last hunting tribe, Ewenki, return to mountains just one day after relocation," more people became aware of the ecological migration event, and more people began to further contemplate the issue. Soon there appeared online a signed article "Cannot civilization tolerate tradition?" that criticized this ecological migration relocation. After that, on 19 August, the Xinhua News Network again reprinted a news clip from Genhe News Online entitled "Interview notes of the hunters' new village." In the article, the head of the Ao Township defended the ecological migration project, saying the *Beijing Youth* reporters did not understand the circumstances, so "their report was nonsense."

Before embarking on my fieldwork, I had already been drawn to these conflicting reports. Where on earth lies the truth? These reports greatly aroused my curiosity and desire to seek the truth. After briefly browsing through books about Ewenki history and their local traditions and customs, I packed up my things and began my journey to Aoluguya. There was no direct transportation from Beijing to Aoluguya. I first boarded a cross-prairie train from Beijing, arriving in the Hailar area in the Hulun Buir City jurisdiction in Inner Mongolia after over 30 hours (the same trip by air takes 1 hour and 50 minutes). Then I transferred to a long-distance bus, which set off down the rugged asphalt mountain roads. The bus traversed unpaved roads constructed of sand and pebble, and finally reached Genhe County. If everything goes smoothly, this drive in summer takes over three hours. But in winter when it is freezing cold and the road is covered with ice and snow, sometimes for long stretches, the drive takes about four hours.

It was the most beautiful season when I arrived. From Hailar to Genhe the mosaic color was everywhere. There were deep and light greens, bright and dim yellows, dazzling and faint purples, vague and hazy blues; yet the colors of an exuberant palette would not have been enough to paint the striking beauty of nature that appeared before my eyes. From yellowish-green prairie to emerald green and violet-red bushes; from yellowing pine trees to birch trees with red and yellow leaves, and the evergreen camphor woods—these rich landforms of the northern frontier were on display as the bus sped along the road in the autumn light. It was such a feast for the eyes. Deep blue rivers that reflected the crystal blue sky flowed around the roads and bushes. They added the spirit of movement to the quiet mountains and woods. Awestruck by the pure and clean colors, I could not stop myself from blurting out loud my amazement at the beauty of the land. It truly felt like I had entered a mystical land that existed only in fairy tales. I could not help but envy the people living on this land.

When I was about to enter the west suburb of Genhe County, suddenly, among the dusty grayish houses, there appeared a bright zone of a new development—rows of red, white and blue triple-colored single-story houses lined up neatly and orderly. These were the new residences for the Ao Township Hunters after their relocation. A Russian-style two-story building with similar colors and a pointed roof caught my eye. It was the Ao Township museum. In such a pocket-sized town with a population of less than 300, the existence of a museum was indeed a rare thing.

The first person to receive me in Genhe County was Mr Kong. He had spent much of his career time and spare time on conducting research on the Aoluguya Ewenki group. He had published two books and was considered an expert in this area. During our first meeting he cautioned me:

Sipsongpanna[1] was famous in the south, while Aoluguya was famous in the north. The most distinguishing feature of Aoluguya is its Ewenki hunters.

Figure 1.1 Ao Township museum in the new Aoluguya

Because the total number of Aoluguya Ewenki hunters is very small, they are exempt from capital punishment. This is the only place in the nation where the death penalty is not carried out. If you want to conduct research on this Ewenki tribe you need to remember three principles—schedule most of your visits in the morning, fewer visits in the afternoon, and do not go there in the evening. The reason is that in the morning their drinking has not yet started, by the afternoon drinking has already begun but it is not so serious, but by the evening they are all drunk and your visits will be a waste of time.

Initially I thought Mr Kong was joking and I laughed out loud. Later he realized that I had not taken him seriously, so he repeated the "three principles" again and even used several "horror stories" to try to scare me: "hunter so-and-so shot his wife in the head with a gun, and so-and-so stabbed his own brother to death." Mr Kong had worked in Genhe for over thirty years, and was familiar with the Ao Township. Before the ecological migration, the Ao Township was located about 260 km from Genhe County, in a valley about 17 km from Mangui Town. Although it was quite distant and the roads were hard to travel, he had visited frequently. Because of his familiarity with the Ao Township and his vivid and colorful descriptions, I was inclined to believe what he had told me, and I became increasingly concerned about the situation. He tried his best to persuade me to stay in the county town rather than living in the Ao Township. When I agreed, he breathed a sigh of relief and kindly helped me to find a small inn for the night. The inn was a privately owned one-story inn near the Genhe railroads. A middle-aged couple was in charge of it. They greeted me warmly when they learned I was from afar and would stay there for quite some time to do research. They offered me a double room, and though there was no writing desk, they brought a small round table as a substitute. They also provided several other items, such as a multiple-outlet power plug and a hot-water boiler. They were very considerate and helped arrange things that I had not thought of, which would make my stay more comfortable. New in town, I immediately felt the local people's warmth, sincerity, and kind-heartedness.

The front of the inn faced onto the street. It consisted of a front and back row of buildings, and in between was a small courtyard. At the end of the back row of buildings, there was a wood-sheltered restroom that was shared by hosts and guests. Each building had four rooms, and the door of each room faced the one across from it. In the narrow hallway there was a coal-burning furnace against the wall, with a large iron bucket on top. It was used to warm up the cold water that the host brought in from outside for the guests to wash with. At the end of the hallway was an open washroom without any faucet. It was a tiled sink area with several plastic tubs. Each room was about five to six square meters and had a single bed near the north wall. There was an old-style wooden window in the south wall, with a light blue translucent curtain. The north wall was plastered quite rough, which made me curious. I looked around but did not find any heater. Just when I was wondering how to handle the freezing cold of the northeast, the hostess came over to check on me. She was wearing only a woolen vest, whilst I was bundled up in a sweater and a warm coat. She smiled, "you southerners are not used to cold. I will run the firewall for you right now."

I was thought of as a "southerner?" "Firewall?!" As a native from Shandong Province, I had always regarded myself as a northerner, and this was the first time in my life I had ever heard of a firewall. I had thought they would use a *kang*—a heated brick bed like that in my hometown. Now I realized the rough and bumpy north wall was the firewall. The door of the furnace was in the wall of the hallway outside of the room. The hostess opened it and stuffed in a pan of coal, which sparked as it began to burn. Before long the firewall became warm; after a while it was burning hot. No wonder the bed was not placed immediately against the wall—it might light the bedding on fire. The entire room became warm from the heat radiated from the wall. In the evening I crawled into the warm bed, savoring the new experience and looking forward to more. Excitement and the faint unpleasant smell from the washroom made me toss and turn the whole night.

Fairly early next morning I was woken up by the startling sound of rumbling trains. Coming out into the hallway, I picked a relatively clean washbasin, scooped two dippers of water from the large iron bucket, and quickly washed. Using the restroom was quite a hassle. This was a single wooden stall with a deep pit covered with several wood boards. I was always nervous when stepping on those boards, afraid that they would break and send me plunging into the pit. Though the owners cleaned it as often as possible, with eight to nine people sharing just one toilet, it is not hard to imagine the smell and unpleasant environment.

The hostess attentively asked me, "How was your night? Is there anything you are not comfortable with?" I replied, "Everything is quite good, and the room is fairly warm." She said happily, "How nice! I did not expect you adapt to this well. Many people are not used to the heat from the firewall, saying that the dry heat causes rough and scratchy throats." Indeed, it is not easy for people to feel at home wherever they are. Most people cannot easily get used to the transition from modern to backward; I guess maybe it is quite easy to step from backward to modern.

Rushing through breakfast, I set off for the Ao Township. It took only a 10 minute cab ride from my inn. The cost was 5 RMB for the 2.5 km distance. As the cab approached, I spotted rows of brightly colored houses under blue skies and white clouds. Surrounding on three sides there were hilly woods, and asphalt roads extended in all directions. It was a beautiful picture of post-modernism.

Everything was quiet in the new Ao Township. There was hardly anyone on the roads. Surrounding each house there were 1.3 meter high black iron fences. Large aluminum window frames reflected the bright light of the autumn sun. From outside I could see people walking about inside their houses, while other houses had the curtain drawn completely. Having just arrived, I did not want to intrude by going directly to the Ewenki houses, and so, instead, I first went to the Ao Township ethnic elementary school. My thought was to start building connections with parents through their children—the students. After all, children are friendlier, more accepting, and relatively easier to get close to.

The Ao Township elementary school was one of the new buildings erected as part of the relocation project. It was a cream-colored two-story flat-roofed building, located to the west of the majority of the residential houses and to the south of several other houses. The asphalt roads separated the school from the houses, and while the school's style was different from other buildings, the buildings all complemented one another quite harmoniously. I found the office director, who was soon to be the school principal, and introduced myself. When I volunteered to teach the students English she was very excited and quickly arranged my class schedule. In the afternoon I would start teaching the children.

I went to the teachers' office afterward and chatted with them. Almost all the teachers were local people, and most between twenty and thirty years old. Maybe because I was from the same generation they talked with me warmly and casually. They all showed surprise after learning I would stay here for one year. My plan to stay in a small community for such a long time greatly aroused their interest. Following the first thoughts that came to mind, I said:

> The Ao Township ecological migration is a great event. It marks a fundamental change in the lifestyle of an ethnic minority. Ecological migration is based on national policy, and its practical implementation is the result of a transition in the nation's views on development—a transition from the over-exploitation of natural resources to a focus on ecological environment preservation, which would make us achieve more sustainable development. Recording such an event is very significant. Also, I have read many controversial reports about this relocation. I sincerely want to learn about what indeed happened, and how local people view this relocation.

A tall male teacher laughed upon hearing my words. "You were fooled—You just read those reports and believe that the people's lifestyle changed. If you really believed that, they fooled you." I was baffled at his words. He continued, "There is not much change in our lifestyle. Moving down the hills only means: firewood has been replaced by bottled gas, telephones by beepers; outhouse toilets have been replaced by flushing toilets; fire-beds and firewalls have been replaced by heaters; however, reindeer are still herded in the forests and the hunters still camp in tents up in the mountains." During our chat, I learned that this male teacher was an Ewenki by the name of Ajun; his mother was a pure blood Ewenki hunter and could speak the Ewenki language. Pleased to have made his acquaintance, I asked him to take me to his mother for a visit. Ajun said his mother was not home at the moment—she had gone to the campsite to herd reindeer. During the class break, he invited me to visit his mother's new house and have some tea, and offered to introduce his older sister to me.

Ajun's older sister has an Ewenki name, Xueyina. She can speak the Ewenki language and her Mandarin is also very fluent. She studied at an art college and has published a number of literature essays. From Ajun's words I could sense his admiration for his sister. In his eyes Xueyina was an important person among the Ewenki.

Chatting along the way, we soon came to his home. His sister was home alone, and she made me a cup of black tea. With her permission, I had a look around the house. On the sunny side of the apartment was the living room with an area of eleven to twelve square meters, and a narrow restroom. On the shady side was a bedroom a bit smaller than the living room, and a kitchen about five to six square meters. Just outside the rooms was a storage room with a lower ceiling that was about five to six square meters. The floor was covered with smooth light-pink ceramic tiles, and every room in the house had a radiator that had already been turned on, so it was very warm. The kitchen was equipped with an air vent and a bottled-gas stove, as well as running water and a sink made of white ceramic. There was a square dining table and one dish cabinet. In the restroom there was a squat-style toilet and a sink with a faucet. There were double beds in both the living room and the bedroom. Also in the living room there were two sofas and one color TV. There was one dresser in the bedroom, and several leather containers. The furniture was not cluttered, but rather quite modern. I secretly compared it with the small inn I was boarding in and thought, "Would not it be nice if I could move to the hunters' new house?" However, Xueyina seemed dissatisfied with the house and commented:

> The house is too small. My father measured it. The house's actual usage area is less than thirty-five square meters, not including the storage room. This is much smaller than our old house in the Ao Township. Before the relocation the government promised houses that were eighty square meters. What is more, although the houses were built for the hunters, none of them like the houses. My mother dislikes the cold tile floor, which easily becomes dirty. She cannot bring herself to sit on the cold hard floor. This is truly not as good as our old house in Aoluguya[2]—that house had tall ceilings, a walled yard, and a wood floor. Now, you can see this yard is not only small, but there are no walls around it. The fence is too low and can block nothing. Living in such a house I dare not keep the curtains open. This design simply regards us as items for display. It may look nice from the outside when shown on TV, but it is not practical for living in at all.

Xueyina also told me that she and her brother were both employed by the Ao Township. In the old Ao Township the houses were big enough for a family and their adult children to live together. However, the new houses were much smaller and could not accommodate so many people. The new cramped accommodation precluded a family's adult children from living in their parents' house. Making matters worse, people with jobs like Xueyina and Ajun were not provided with houses. As a result, both of them now live in the Hunters' house (Pinyin: *lie min fang*) that was assigned to their mother. Many Ewenki hunters sarcastically joke about their cramped accommodation by referring to it as *Juehufang*—the family lineage will surely fade into extinction because their houses are too small to provide the room for children.

Xueyina soon learned that I would be staying here for one year and plan to learn to speak the Ewenki language. She expressed her surprise, but her reply surprised me as well when she explained, "Very few people here can speak the Ewenki language now. Young people in their twenties can hardly understand it. In daily life they all speak Mandarin. You would have no problem communicating with them. Except for my mother, my two aunts, and another older woman, Maruia Suo, at the Alongshan hunters' site, who cannot speak much Mandarin, all the other elders basically can." Before I could ask her any questions, she asked my opinion of this relocation. My first response was, "It is a great thing." She looked down seemingly deep in thought, and then she looked at me and said: "In the past, many domestic and international scholars have come here to visit. Some were doing work on history, others on anthropology. There also came well-known writers. They have been to the old Aoluguya many times. They all care about our development. After learning about this relocation, they expressed their concerns in private. Some people's attitudes were quite tough. Some of them even cried after learning we would move to Genhe."

Xueyina added: "Our tribe is different from those Ewenki in other places. Do you know this?" I remembered that when I first came to Hailar I made a special trip through the vast Hulun Buir grassland to visit the Nantun Ewenki Autonomous Banner Museum near Hailar. I had a clear memory of the museum interpreter, who pointed out an exhibit that introduced three types of different Ewenki tribes. The figures of the men and women were life-sized wax figurines. Their ethnic clothing, accoutrements and decorations were quite different. Each of the figurines represented a member of each of the three Ewenki tribes: Solon, Tungus, and Yakut.

According to the introduction offered by the museum, the Ewenki hunters at Aoluguya had historically lived in the hinterland of the forest of the Greater Khingan Range for several hundred years. These people—nomadic hunters living in the forests—were known as the Yakut or the Reindeer-Using Tribe. The Solon people inhabited the Nantun and Chenbaerhu Banner (part of the Hailar district)—a geographic area famous for the Hulun Buir grassland. Historically they made a living from agriculture and raising livestock. There are no members of the Tungus tribe currently living within the borders of China;[3] they now live entirely within Russian territory.[4]

Xueyina continued: "Our tribe has the fewest number of people and we are the only reindeer herders in our country. Reindeer are designated as China's second-class protected animals. The Solon and Tungus Ewenki have long since given up so-called primitive life; among us some people still live the primitive hunting lifestyle in the mountains. Only our tribe still preserves its traditional lifestyle. The scholars I mentioned are all concerned that our relocation would cause the loss of cultural traditions— and then we as an ethnic branch would no longer exist. Therefore, they are all worried. They actually do not support the ecological migration."

I asked: "Then do you have a favorable opinion about the ecological migration?" She smiled in hesitation, possibly feeling that my question was difficult to answer, since she had multiple identities that drew her in different directions. Do we take the position of preserving ethnic cultural traditions? Or shall we pursue the life of modern civilization? For most people, these two positions would be polar opposites. Maybe she also needed to think. Eventually she answered:

> We as an ethnic minority indeed often move our households around. Reindeer love to eat lichen. When they are about to finish all the lichen in one place, we need to move to a different area. Lichen grows slowly— usually five years to wait. In regard to this ecological migration, we have moved from the north dense hinterland of the forest to the south forest to grassland crossover patches—the old site Aoluguya and the new site Sanchejian[5] are both within the Genhe County area. However, we had thought about this move naively. I am a salary worker and the relocation has little impact on me, but to those hunters without jobs, the impact is different. You will understand this in time.

At my request, Xueyina taught me several simple Ewenki words. After a while, her father returned. He was an ethnic Han Chinese, nearly seventy years old with hair that was completely gray. He had come to the old Aoluguya region in the 1960s as part of a government resettlement program that transferred large numbers of ethnic Han Chinese to borderland regions. He had worked at the bank in the Ao Township and had retired decades ago. These days he just did household chores. He could not speak Ewenki, but was able to understand it. I called him elder uncle in Chinese, instead of using the Ewenki term of address, *Heke*. In the Ewenki language, I referred to Xueyina's mother, Linda, as *Ewo* (elder aunt). Ewo Linda went to herd the reindeer in the mountains. I had thought she herded reindeer on the mountainside close by and that she returned in the evenings for dinner and spent the night at home. But it turned out that Linda had to live in the mountains for a lengthy period of time, although the campsite where she herded reindeer was only 20 km from the house and in fact was rather close to the new Aoluguya community in comparison to other hunters' campsites. I desperately wanted to go and see what kind of life it was as soon as possible.

It so happened that 28 September 2003 was the date commemorating the completion of the Ao Township ecological migration. In order to provide a more interesting experience and show Ewenki culture to the outside visitors, the township leaders decided to erect a *cuoluozi*—the unique style of tent used by Ewenki hunters—at the reindeer herding sites in the mountains. Ajun was appointed to set up a *cuoluozi* at his mother Linda's campsite.

At about one o'clock in the afternoon on 25 September, Ajun and I took a half-hour bumpy ride in a taxicab before finally arriving at the hunters' campsite (Pinyin: *lie min dian*). When we got out of the taxi, I heard the barking of a large hunting dog. A military green canvas tent stood in an empty area in the woods. The tent occupied an area of about twelve to thirteen square meters. Encircling the campsite was a wood stockade fence—very similar to the ones used by ranchers in western Canada and the United States—consisting of vertical wooden fence posts and three horizontal wooden poles connecting one post to the next. Two meters away from the tent entrance was a pile of firewood that had been cut to length about 70–80 cm. In the middle of the tent there was an iron stove, and a long curving chimney stuck out from one side at the top of the tent. This was the main apparatus for cooking and heating. Circled around the iron stove were four one-meter wide beds—one on the left and one on the right side and the others against each other at the back. All four bed frames were made of coarse stripped pine wood. On top of each frame there were the wood bed boards, on top of which there was earth-colored bedding rolled up at one end of the bed. Over the stove there was an aluminum kettle, blackened from use over many fires and emitting a shrill whistling sound.

There were mainly two households at this campsite; Ajun's mother and uncle were counted as one household, and the other household was Uncle Xiren and Aunt Marusya and their second son Keli. I wondered how the four beds accommodated five people and boldly asked Uncle Xiren. He answered casually, "Add one board to the bed inside there, and then your aunt and me would share it." I had seen both Xiren and Marusya on television. The news of the Aoluguya ecological migration move had made nearly everyone in the Ao Township a "star." All five people at this site were Ewenki, but Xiren's ancestors were of the Solon tribe. As far as I could see, he and the Reindeer Ewenki shared the same physical traits—long slender eyes, high and full cheeks. Their skin color was relatively light, though their faces and hands had darkened into a healthy tan due to sweat and labor under the sun.

Both Xiren and Marusya were barely over fifty years old, but Xiren had just been drinking liquor and was walking unsteadily, so he looked older than his actual age. Ajun's mother Linda was over sixty years old, but she did not know exactly how old she was. She explained, "We Ewenki do not record our birthdays." Ajun said the township government had calculated her age as sixty-five. Her older brother Lengei was a slim and small man—by assumption he was over seventy years old, but he looked physically fit and tough. He also had a Russian name, Grishka. He said that when he was a boy at school, all the teachers were Russians. Keli was one year younger than me and he was the youngest professional hunter at that time.

All five hunters at the campsite were very friendly to me. I greeted them with my newly learned Ewenki language, and they were all pleased and smiled kindly, especially Uncle Xiren. When he learned that I—a young girl far from home and my parents—would stay here for an extended period to conduct research, he was truly touched. He held my hand and took me to the tent. I smelt a strong liquor smell. Xiren's face was red; he walked unsteadily, swaying from side to side. He had me sit down on the bed to the left of the stove, and then he sat down on another bed next to me. With a serious face he told me that in Ewenki tents there were particular taboos; the place behind the stove was reserved for the Malu god, and I—a female adult—must neither go there, nor circle around the stove. I had to exit the tent from the same place I had entered.

Xiren was not clear about the research I had come here to do. At my request for him to tell his stories, he replied as if being interviewed by the reporters: "My family was the first household to move to Sanchejian [the place name of the new Ao Township site]. I was the 'lead goose.' Long live the Communist Party!" The alcohol made his speech somewhat incoherent. After a while, he continued, "I have met your university president, we are sworn brothers, and we took photographs together shoulder to shoulder. Whatever you want to research here, I will tell anything you want to know." Then, all of a sudden, he yelled out to his wife Marusya: "Hey, Keli's Mother, quickly bring my ethnic clothing. I need to put them on, quick!" He had noticed that I was beginning to point my camera in his direction, and wanted to be accommodating. I sincerely liked this adorable uncle.

We had only had several sips of reindeer-milk tea after arriving at the campsite when Ajun started to work on the *cuoluozi* with Keli and Lengei. Keli was in charge of selecting slender pine trees of the right size,

Figure 1.2 A picture of Chairman Mao hangs where the Malu god was originally placed

then chopping them down, stripping them and carrying the poles to the place where the *cuoluozi* would be set up. Lengei and Ajun were respon- sible for refining the pine poles and building the *cuoluozi* frame. The only tool they used was the Ewenki traditional hacking knives, used primarily for chopping, and they were made by the hunters themselves. Xiren told me that currently only one old hunter was able to make this kind of knife, and his name was Ningdao. When working, the three men did not speak at all, but simply immersed themselves in labor. Keli walked around in the woods, selected the appropriate pine trees, then with just a few deft and

Figure 1.3 Malu god fetish

agile strokes, chopped them down cleanly, and effortlessly carried them over to the others all by himself. Watching him work so hard with such ease and smoothness, I found his execution of this work to be cool and impressive. Lengei was thin and light, in spite of his advanced age, and I could tell he was skilled and capable to work at many tasks. He worked together with Ajun, and before long they located the point where the poles would all balance and support one another, and set up the frame of the *cuoluozi*.

Marusya was busy calling to the reindeer and cooking, and with a thick iron needle and reindeer tendon thread, Linda was sewing laboriously the bridle used for pulling reindeer. Xiren seemed embarrassed that he was the only person not working on something. He explained to me: "Something is wrong with my hands. They shake constantly, and I only feel better after drinking liquor. But a couple days ago I accidentally burned my hands." I took a look. It was true—his right forearm was covered with a large pink scar. He continued proudly, "Several days ago I was a little drunk and got burned by the stove. I went to the hospital but the doctor could not help much. In the end your aunt Marusya gathered some herbs known by the Ewenki hunters and they worked." He then proceeded to show me the herbs, but I could not see how the plant might be identified as a healing herb. This made me admire the Ewenki hunters' acumen in recognizing nature's treasures. I could only hope that these amazing secrets would never be lost.

At about 3:30 in the afternoon the sunlight suddenly fell away from the tree branches and the sky turned dim in seconds. The bright light from the stove fire penetrated the darkness outside of the tent, and the temperature in the woods began to fall. One *cuoluozi* had already been built. Ajun explained to me that they did not fully adhere to the traditional construction process when building it. To simplify the process, they skipped several stages and had actually used some nails when setting it up—outsiders would not be able to tell by viewing it from the exterior. He explained, "The *cuoluozi* and the circling fence built by old hunters were so cleverly designed with self-supporting wood poles without using any steel nail." When the *cuoluozi* was completely set up, Lengei built a fire inside it. White smoke rose up out of the hole specially left open at the top of the *cuoluozi*. He told me that the rising smoke meant "The Ewenki people's life goes on and on."

It was getting darker by the minute, and Marusya cried out in a special voice and tone to call the reindeer back for the night. The reindeer were huge—far bigger than I had imagined, and they looked almost like bulls.

Figure 1.4 *Cuoluozi*

Marusya held a reindeer's neck like a mother hugging her child, and I found the entire scene greatly moving. Marusya had made dinner and set up the table. The table was made of two thick logs that had been laid horizontally on the ground to serve as the base, on top of which a round table top was laid. Xiren and the others either sat on the ground or on a wood bench, but they had me sit on a more comfortable wood bench covered with roebuck skin. They said only honored guests were allowed to sit there. They were treating me like a daughter coming back to her parents' home, and I felt an intense sense of warmth and gratitude run through my heart. Marusya cooked two dishes; stir-fried eggplant with pork and green pepper, and Chinese cabbage mixed with meats. It was almost 6:00 P.M. when we began to eat dinner. There was no other light except for the glow of the fire. Xiren lit a candle, and as we sat down and bumped the table, there was a loud buzzing sound as a large swarm of flies that had been covering the cutting board and dining table were startled and took to the air. In the dim light, I could not see the color of the dishes, and I was not sure if the chopsticks were clean, but I ate just like everyone else. Maybe because I was hungry, the food seemed delicious. Before we had finished, the taxicab arrived to take us back. It was completely dark by that time, even though it was only around 6:30 P.M.

Upon returning to the small inn, the hostess and several merchant guests who frequently stayed there came over and greeted me warmly. They chatted for quite some time and were clearly interested in learning my insights and feelings about my visit to the hunters' campsite. I was quite astounded when they brought up questions like—"Do the hunters there in the mountains eat raw meat?" Not knowing how exactly to respond, I said in reply: "You have never been to the hunters' campsite, have you?" They all shook their head; they had never been there before, and, they added, did not dare to go. Their knowledge about the Ewenki hunters was all based on hearsay, rumors, and legends. Even more surprising to me was that the couple who owned the inn had never been to the hunters' campsites either, despite the fact they had lived in Genhe for over forty years. They told me that probably in the entire Genhe region, the number of people who had been to the hunters' campsites could be counted with two hands. One of the guests, who was involved in the trade of reindeer antlers, seemed to know quite a bit about the Ao Township. He told me in a caring fashion that in the Ao Township there was one common disease shared by both humans and animals—tuberculosis. Because nearly all reindeer carried the tuberculosis bacteria, he warned me to be careful when having food at the hunters' campsite—especially in the beginning when I did not know how I might physically adjust to the local area.

The head of the Ao Township said to me: "Now you have been to the hunters' campsite and have seen the backward living conditions up in the mountains. Compared with the brand new facilities here at the Hunters' houses, the vast difference is like heaven and earth. Nevertheless, some hunters are still backward in their mindset. All they want is to stay at the hunters' campsites, and are unwilling to move down." I was intrigued. So there were people willing to return to the hilly woods and live such tough lives? Assuming Ewenki hunters did not know about the existence of such wonderful living conditions in the outside world, it would be easy to understand how they could feel content with their hard life in the mountains. But now with the new settlement, it was obvious—the conditions down here in the settlement were much better than that of up in the mountains. Why then would people want to return to the woods and live there? This seemed to be beyond my comprehension. I decided that whenever an opportunity arose I would go to the campsites and try to find out what on earth it was that the hunters liked so much about their community in the mountains. My encounter with the hunters dismissed any concerns about safety issues. It seemed clear that they did not constitute any threat to me at all. Quite contrarily, I felt relaxed and at ease around them.

The next morning Ajun said he needed to go up to the hunters' campsite again to set up one more *cuoluozi*. I followed the local customs and went to the market to buy some liquor and meat as presents. The township government sent a red Jeep to take us to the campsite. Along the way I was immersed in the beautiful view and suddenly wished that the Jeep could continue forever along the lovely route. My daydream came to an abrupt end when half an hour later we arrived at Uncle Xiren's tent. He was quite sober because he had not yet begun to drink. He taught me how to count in the Ewenki language.

Figure 1.5 Ao Township

That morning I only wanted to learn the language from Xiren, so did not ask him any questions. Shortly after arriving at the Ao Township I was able to sense the ongoing irritation the hunters felt toward the media reporters. I could tell they were extremely unhappy about outsiders' onslaught of curious questions. Some people told me flatly, "We do not like all kinds of questions asked like those reporters. What is so strange about our life? We live just as it is!" Later Xueyina explained to me: "We Ewenki are actually very hospitable. But because of the ecological migration, too many reporters came, and the news reports were terribly exaggerated and had no truth behind them. They treated the hunters as weirdoes. The hunters got upset, and that is why they are unfriendly toward the reporters." With this in mind, I was very discreet when I first arrived at the campsite and did not take the initiative to ask about the most sensitive subject—the ecological migration. However, Uncle Xiren voluntarily mentioned the reason why the hunters moved back to the mountains after the relocation: "We moved down in the rain on 10 August, but only stayed down there for one week before moving back to the mountains. We did so because the reindeer had nothing to eat down in the lowlands. They lost weight quickly and many of them died."

Close to noon, the main frame of the second *cuoluozi* was completed. We began to eat lunch. The big hunting dog—named Pengpeng (meaning "friend")—rubbed against me with the hope I would throw him some tasty treat. I imitated Xiren and fed him the roast chicken bones; he wagged his tail with satisfaction. On the two trips to the campsite I did not have the chance to try wild game. To be honest, I was not particularly keen on eating wild game at all. Very thoughtfully, my Ewenki hosts at the campsite had already thought about this for me and made apologetic comments on not having any special food at hand that would be suitable for serving to guests from afar. Xiren felt a bit guilty and he explained:

Because the new residence is too close to the city, all of the hunters' guns were confiscated. Before the ecological migration move, our guns were confiscated because as part of the overall resettlement plan, reindeer would be brought down from the mountains and kept in pens. But that did not work out and we still needed to return to the mountains to raise reindeer. To enable us to defend the reindeer from wild animal attacks, the township distributed a small caliber gun to each hunters' campsite. Altogether we have five hunters' campsites now. But all of the semi-automatic guns were confiscated. Those small caliber guns cannot do much. It is cold now, and the wild animals' skin grows thicker. A single shot from a small caliber gun cannot kill a wild animal, but rather just drives them off more quickly.

Several of us finished eating quickly, leaving only Xiren and Lengei to continue eating, all the while continuing to drink alcohol. This time we had brought two bottles of white liquor to the camp, but before the meal had even begun, Xiren had emptied an entire bottle while snacking on salted pickles. During the meal, he opened the second bottle, gave some to Lengei, and finished the rest himself. Soon, Xiren was drunk and wanted more liquor. In the beginning, no one responded to his requests so he started cursing, some in Mandarin and some in the Ewenki language. He appeared to have become really very angry and even kicked the furnace in the tent. His wife Marusya entered the tent; she also ignored the uncle's cursing and refused to give in to his demands. Her behavior made him even angrier—he could not endure this any longer and really began acting up. To put an end to this, his wife pinned him to the ground by sitting on top of him and then slapped him lightly. She was irritated and amused, and at the same time scolded him in the Ewenki language— roughly translated she was saying that when he got drunk like this, he lost face in front of guests. Despite being pinned down by her, he would not stop yelling. Here and there I was able to catch the odd words. What he said shocked me: "Nobody wants to live like this!", "Who wants to live in this shabby tent?", "I am nobody's fool!" and "Just shoot me!"

I was a bit shaken by the scene, and could not help eyeing the small-caliber rifle lying against the bed leg at the back of the tent. But the others all remained calm. Maybe people who used guns often had the habit of using words like "shoot." Was Xiren really drunk? I was not sure. While his wife still had him pinned down, he turned to me, called my name, and said, "Do not be afraid." Slowly, Xiren calmed down. When Marusya got up, Xiren remained on the ground. The small incident was over, but for quite a long time my heart could not find peace. I could understand the pain beneath Xiren's violent behavior when he was drunk; I had a profound sense of the sadness, rage and frustration that was embodied in his yelling.

After several days of close contact with the hunters, I felt that the horror stories that Mr Kong had talked about would not happen to me. So I made plans to move to the township to live. I first went to the township government in the hope that they might help me find a rental place in the Ao Township. At the same time, I asked Ajun to help me check around to see if anyone had a place for rent. Frequent contact with Xueyina and her family led to a friendship that became increasingly close and trusting. Linda's nephew Qinglin was a single young man and had been allocated a house right next to Linda's house. Because he herded the reindeer at the most remote campsite in the Alongshan region, he was often out of town. Therefore, most of the time, Xueyina lived in Qinglin's house by herself.

The township government did not come up with a solution to my request. They explained that there were really no extra houses in the township. Government employees had to rent accommodation in downtown Genhe County and even the township head was boarding at the Hunter Trading Shop. The officials in the township government tried their utmost to persuade me not to live in the township, because they were afraid that I would meet some type of accident. Before long, Ajun had a response to my request. He said I could live with his sister. All I needed to do was to inform the township leaders. When I moved out of the small inn, the hostess looked very concerned about me. She felt sympathy for me, a young girl living in an unfamiliar place by myself, and she was also worried about my safety because she had heard so many bad rumors about the hunters. Despite these worries expressed by others, with Ajun's help I soon smoothly moved everything from the small inn to Qinglin's house. The arrangement of this house was similar to Linda's. I slept in the bedroom while Xueyina slept in the living room. This was the beginning of my life in the Ao Township. In this pocket-sized community of just sixty-two households, they soon learned about me. When Linda came down from the hunters' campsite she often took me to visit people. Slowly over time, people began to see me in a different light, and began to accept my presence in their community. When the first snowfall came in less than one month of arriving there, Linda chose for me a beautiful Ewenki name—Yimanna, which means white snow.

Aoluguya's Four Seasons

Life at the new Aoluguya was monotonous during the long cold winter. The lowest temperature in the Genhe County area was 40 to 50 degrees centigrade below zero. The people living at the new Aoluguya realized the advantage of central heating over burning firewood. It was much easier to enjoy the comfort of a heated house than to split firewood outdoors. During the three coldest winter months (from mid December to mid March), the hunters who engaged in reindeer herding normally did not stay at the hunters' campsites. This was because during the cold season, reindeer seldom required tending to; they roamed everywhere and grazed on lichen under the snow. The hunters only needed to go up and track the reindeer every fortnight to ascertain their location. This would make it easier to find the reindeer when snow melted after the arrival of spring. During their trips every two weeks, the hunters also checked to see if the snow was too thick over the lichen, which was reindeers' favorite food, and if there was any trace of the "white disaster."[6] With the outside temperature reaching minus 50 degrees in the Greater Khingan Range, how could shabby tents and log-burning ironclad furnaces compare with the modern apartment with the central heating system? Despite this, the old hunter Maruia Suo preferred living in the Alongshan hunters' campsite rather than coming down to the city. Her daughter picked her up from the hunters' campsite 200 km away and brought her to the new-bought house in Genhe for the Spring Festival. I longed for the warm season when the snow would melt and the flowers would reach out to the sun in bloom. Then, the hunters would stay in the mountains for long periods at a time, and I would be able to go with them in the green forests and deep mountains.

In April before the ice and snow completely melt, the hunters stay up in the mountains for long periods of time. This busy period of time was soon to arrive. The hunters' work would begin with selecting a place to build a large reindeer pen[7] for the pregnant reindeer. The chosen site should be an easily accessible area sheltered from the wind; at the same time, it should possess a clean water supply, rich lichen growth, and plenty of sunshine. The forest in April is steeped in the chill of spring, with ice and snow starting to melt, and the creeks beginning to swell with water that carried floating blocks of ice. All living things in the forests had awakened to a new cycle; everything green was about to sprout to new life.

Figure 1.6 Reindeer pen at mountain campsite

April, May, June and July were the busiest months for the hunters to attend to the reindeer. During these four peak months, hunters were occupied birthing reindeer and cutting antlers. To help out with the extra work, any family member who was able to lend a hand came up to the hunters' campsites; hence, during this period, more people arrive on mountains and the hunters' campsites are bustling with noise. The township sent cars to each of the campsites and helped to transport the collected reindeer antlers to the antler-processing workshop in the Ao Township. The beautiful reindeer antlers were large and thick. When piled together, they looked like large coral reefs on an ocean bed. Expectations ran high during the antler-cutting season that the antlers would be sold at a high price and help to compensate for the economic loss that incurred when the Ewenki had been forced to give up hunting after the ecological migration.

Viewing the grand forests from afar, one is awed by their eternal and enchanting beauty. However, after having spent only half a day in the forest in the summer, I became agitated, like some weeds had sprung up in my heart, and I was anxious to flee from the forest. Beginning in April, small insects as tiny as a grain of sand begin to come alive in the forest. Local people call these "caopazi," which is a type of wood tick. The horrifying thing was that some ticks carried the forest meningitis virus. A person bitten by an insect with this virus, without treatment, could die within half an hour. Even if a bite victim was treated immediately, they could possibly suffer aftereffects like speech disorders and memory loss.

During this dangerous season, I covered myself from head to toe in the fear that the ticks would find me an easy target. But the hunters said to me: "It is no use you wrap up so tightly. The bugs can still crawl into your clothes, or into your hair. You have no way to find them." Although I was in a panic, the hunters were all at ease. One day, the elderly woman Maruia Suo took off her coat and there in the folds and on her skin were many ticks. I was terrified, but Maruia Suo paid no attention to the insects whatsoever and continued working on the task at hand. She said caopazi had never hurt her. Yet every year in Genhe there were people who were bitten by the ticks and died. For this reason, in recent years, the Ewenki hunters have received immunization injections to protect against forest meningitis. The old hunters lamented: "Now even the caopazi have transformed. In the past the hunters were bitten, but did we ever hear of anyone dying from this? This is the karma for the human ruination of nature."

In June and July the danger of the forest meningitis ended to my great relief. But this was the very season that mosquitoes and flies began to appear and multiply. Every manner of insect was beginning to appear— flies, mosquitoes, gadflies. These insects were bigger in size and made quite a lot of noise. When attacked, people could really feel their bite. Little bugs like ceratopogonidae or biting midges made no noise when they were around, and their sneaky attacks and bites with no warning signs deprived me of any way to defend myself. The hunters could immediately tell what type of bug had bitten me by simply looking at the wound. Each time I went into the mountains I sprayed copious quantities of mosquito repellent all over me, but this only served to provide a degree of psychological comfort.

The forest in summer was verdant and lush. The fragrance of green pine infused the entire forest. Wherever I looked, my eyes were met with a profusion of shades of green. All kinds of small wildflowers sparkled in various colors. If a camera was somehow able to capture the entire scene in its splendor, the viewer would be overwhelmed by beauty. However, if a city person went into the forest and spent time there, before long he or she would feel quite fed up with everything; anyhow, that was how I felt. I soon became quite tired of the forest. Although I had managed to avoid the assault from the ticks, I was not able to escape the assault from a vast array of other bugs. I waved my hands constantly in front of my face, yet no matter how hard I tried, or wherever I tried to hide, the unwavering swarm of insects still managed to find and attack me. To my amazement, the hunters were extremely relaxed. They did not madly wave their hands about to swat away insects like I did, but rather simply allowed the insects to flutter about in front of their eyes and land on their skin. The sight of this caused me to sigh, "This must be an in-born difference between the hunters and me."

It was July and August, the summer season in the Greater Khingan Range. The trees were more vibrant and the forest stirred with life. During the daytime it was rather hot. But around 4:00 P.M., when sun's golden light began to drop down off the mountains, the temperature would immediately begin to drop. Almost every day in July and August it rained in the vast forest. The ground was wet and muddy. The dark reindeer dung mixed with rainwater and became black mud.

During this period, I had made many trips to the campsites. Because of the muddy and rugged road, my new rubber shoes were ruined in less than a fortnight. The hunters wore army-style rubber-soled shoes or rubber rain boots in the mountains. Their shoes were also ruined quickly. There were a lot of gadflies around in this season, a time when the reindeer needed people to help them the most. Every day, the hunters burned smudge fires, which in the Ewenki language are called *sami*,[8] for the reindeer. During the day, the reindeer rested surrounded by the *sami*, and at night when the temperature dropped and the insects were less active they would graze on lichen.

The summer in the Greater Khingan Range was brief. By the end of August into early September the weather was so chilly and accurately described as cold. By now the reindeer had started mating, and mushrooms were also growing. Both the hunters and reindeer ate wild mushrooms. The hunters praised their reindeer and always noted with satisfaction that they were extremely intelligent animals. The reindeer's intelligence was demonstrated by their ability to tell which mushrooms were poisonous and avoid them. The hunters learned which mushrooms were edible by watching the reindeer. Now that it was becoming cold, the reindeer no longer needed the smudge fires. Throughout the daylight hours they would roam widely. This was because the reindeer loved the mushrooms that grew all throughout the mountains and so would rove throughout the region in search of this tasty food. During this season, the hunters' main work involved hiking over the mountainous terrain and wading across rivers in search of their reindeer herds. The work was very demanding, and normally done by male hunters. The hunters explained: "In recent years, people from the outside set up many leg-hold traps. The reindeer can be caught easily when they do not pay attention and will starve to death if they are unable to escape, or they might be injured by the trap and die from their wounds. So we regularly need to go to find them and keep an eye on them."

My narrative follows the order of the four seasons to provide a general description of the Ewenki hunters' activities. However, the Ewenki hunters explained to me that in the past they did not employ any clear and definite division of the seasons. To this day they continue to say: "It is time to get ready for the reindeer births"; "it is time to hunt roe deer"; or "it is time to hunt hazel grouse." Their division of the seasons still followed the yearly cycle of hunting activities. Several of the male hunters said to me: "Can you understand my feeling? Now hunting is forbidden, but my hands and soul itch for the hunt. The terrible dread and longing in my heart—words cannot possibly describe this feeling!"

Life at the Hunters' Campsites

My First Stay at the Alongshan Campsite

Despite the fact that I often visited all of the hunters' campsites in the mountain forests, in the beginning I did not live at the sites. There were two major reasons: first, the living space in the tents was quite limited; second, it was possible to make a round trip by car from the Ao Township to nearby mountain campsites in one day, and thus it was possible for me to return to the Ao Township at night. Later during my stay in the region, I wanted to live at the campsites for a lengthy period and learn more about what it felt like to truly become a hunter. So I picked a good season, packed up my belongings and went to the largest hunters' campsite—the Alongshan hunters' campsite (also known as the Maruia Suo campsite[9]). Comparing this campsite with several other campsites, it was the largest camp in terms of physical size and number of Ewenki hunters living there, and had the best-preserved traditional customs and practices. The Ewenki language was used almost exclusively at this camp, with Mandarin Chinese only spoken occasionally. The camp was known for Maruia Suo's high moral and behavioral standards and everyone at the campsite greatly respected the elder matriarch. Between late July and early September, on two separate occasions, I lived at the campsite that the hunters termed "the big campsite" (Pinyin: *da dian er*).

The trip to the campsite for my first stay did not proceed smoothly. On that trip, I boarded the train to the Mangui Township with two young male hunters and several college student travelers and we stayed at a small hotel in Mangui for the night. The next morning, we bought some food—raw meats, vegetables, and fruits—for our campsite hosts, and then hired a pickup truck to transport us across muddy and rocky gravel roads to the camp. Halfway through the trip we were forced to stop because repeated downpours had washed away the wooden bridge, which provided the only way to the campsite. The two young hunters quickly hopped off the truck and walked into the high hills and thick woods along the road in search of suitable logs and poles. They carried the wood over and made temporary repairs to the bridge. Shaking and heaving, our truck was finally able to pass over the creaky bridge and we soon arrived at the Maruia Suo Campsite.

Unlike other hunters' campsites where the tents were erected along the roadside, the tents in the Maruia Suo Campsite were set up in the depths of the thick woods. After getting off the truck, everywhere I looked my gaze was met by the emerald-green of the verdant forest. The trees were so high that it felt like they blocked the skies and the sun, and shrouded the area with a sense of mystery. Drifting in from afar was the sound of dogs barking, and soon two large hunting dogs appeared, chasing each other. Following the dogs were several young male hunters. The two hunters on the truck had already begun unloading. I scurried along, following the hunters and brushing aside grass and shrubs along the way. After following a narrow muddy zigzag trail that had been stamped out by countless feet, I was able to see in the distance several tents with smoke wafting skyward from the smoke-hole at the top. There were three tents at this site; each was located 50 meters away from the next. The tents were set up in one single line that led deep into the forest. After arriving in the forest I lost all sense of direction. Several young Ewenki women stepped out from the tents and greeted us with broad smiles. I thus started my life at the campsite.

I lived at the campsite for just over one week during my first stay. Since it was July it was mercilessly hot in the lowland regions, and I had packed only two changes of regular clothing for my trip up to the Alongshan campsite. I had no thought that it would be necessary to bring any extra clothing. To my dismay, due to many days of consecutive rain, it was much colder up in the mountains than I had been expecting. After several days I could no longer tolerate the cold and returned to the township in a vehicle that had come to pick up antlers. To be honest, however, my inability to endure the cold was just an excuse. All the women at the campsite had extra clothing to offer me. The main problem was that I did not enjoy living at the campsite. I was overwhelmed by the dirtiness of the tough lifestyle and felt that each day was nearly beyond my endurance. I suspected I had become fed up with fieldwork because I no longer had the same willingness to endure hardship that I had at the beginning of my fieldwork. In the beginning, I had only made day trips to the campsites and so had no clear idea of what living in the forest would actually be like. When I finally made the decision to live in the campsites, it was my strong curiosity that enabled me to endure the harsh conditions for the first few days.

At the Alongshan campsite, life seemed impossibly hard for me. Most difficult to endure was the lack of quiet and tranquil toilet use—a situation caused by the reindeer. The reindeer liked to graze for food around the tents. They need and enjoy salt, but the salt provided to them daily by the hunters was not enough and so the animals were always looking for salty food around the tents. Their search for salt also caused them to follow everyone to the toilet where they ate excrement, apparently because of its salty taste. This caused my distress, though it does seem humorous now. Other things also wore down my ability to adapt. For example, the hunters were excited and in very high spirits after they shot a roe deer. From the deer meat they made meat buns, which they were very pleased to offer me; however, to me, the gamey taste and smell of the meat was unbearable. At night I lay staring into the dark on the hard wood bed, feeling a dull ache through my stiff bones. All night I had to endure not only the endless squeaking of the mountain mice, but also their pulling on my hair. Up in the mountains, I suffered from a poor appetite and sleep loss. During the day I was the only person strolling around without any physical work to do. The men were busy cutting antlers and sorting wood while the young women milked the reindeer and prepared meals. Maruia Suo was busy rubbing reindeer tendon into thread, sewing leather, or making yeast dough for *lieba*.[10] In the evening when there was liquor available, the men gathered and drank by candlelight. When the liquor had run out, the men would ask the young women and me to join them to play poker. There were usually around ten people at the campsite. In the mountains the number of daylight hours was short. It was a hard time during the evening without any light except for the stove firelight in the tent. After several days I felt considerable anxiety, slightly ill, and longed for the vehicle from the township to arrive sooner than the arranged date and take me back. Thanks to this short stay at the campsite, I had lost weight and had to draw in my belt by more than two buckle holes.

Old Hunters' Forest Complex

Having experienced life at the hunter's campsite, I had not only lost all my desire to experience life in the forest, but also after returning to the Ao Township, decided that I would have no more of this living up in the mountains business. But this left me even more intensely puzzled than before. Why was it that this place where I was so reluctant to live was the same place that the old Ewenki hunters longed for with all their hearts? I was even more astounded and puzzled when I learned that two sisters who were over a hundred years old living in a nursing home had returned to stay at the hunters' campsite. One of the sisters, a woman by the name of Marian Bu, was the oldest person in the Ao Township. Her daughter Dimeiya brought her to her new campsite—Dimeiya Campsite at Jinlin forest farm. Everyone told me that Marian Bu had been living at the campsite for over a fortnight. My curiosity arose again and I planned to visit her at the campsite. One day, Serezha and his wife gave me a ride to the Jinlin campsite. Serezha was an Ewenki hunter and the last head of the Ao Township before the ecological migration; after the ecological migration he was transferred to the United Front Work Department of Genhe. His wife would come to the forest campsite to pick *dushi* (wild blueberries); one time they picked up their young teenage son, who had been living at the Dimeiya Campsite for over a week for the summer vacation.

Rough terrain in the region made it difficult to access the Jinlin campsite, which was located on a steep hillside not far from the road. The other side of the road was also a steep slope. Among the green ocean of trees stood two light green tents, only occasionally visible when sunlight glittered through the clouds. Patches of lichen grew here and there and seemed to be more abundant than at other sites they had previously occupied since the ecological migration. However, Dimeiya was still not happy about this site, saying, "Although the reindeer more or less have enough to eat here, there are too many traps around. These traps have injured several of our reindeer. This place is not as good as the Alongshan region. I want to move back. Seeing the reindeer killed in traps—the pain of it pierces my heart!"

Marian Bu was well advanced in age. Her vision was blurred, but she could still think clearly. She sat quietly inside the tent, and when the weather was good she would sit at the entrance of the tent. She did not understand Mandarin. I asked her why she moved up to the mountains, and she replied, "It is so good up in the mountains. There are reindeer around." But I was puzzled by her answer, because most of the time there were not any reindeer in sight. Was it not nice staying at the cozy nursing home? From what I saw—from the eyes of modern civilization—the conditions at the nursing home were far better than those of the tent.

Marian Bu's sister Hasha was just one year younger than her. Hasha had never married. In the summer, Hasha was brought to the hunters' campsite on Jingguan road by her nephew Dageli. Both the elderly women said the campsites were better than the nursing home. Though they could do nothing at the campsite, they still loved staying there. These two elders would rather give up the comfort of the nursing home to live in rustic and simple conditions at the campsite. Although I felt surprised by this, I was able to understand it. I could see that they returned to the hunters' sites out of their profound love for the forests, just as they themselves said: "We have lived in the forest all our lives; we are used to everything there. We do not feel living here is hard; everything feels good here." What really surprised me was that there was such a tremendous difference between each person's assessments of what exactly constituted good or poor conditions.

I reflected on my ten days that I had spent living in the mountains. Why did I not possess a passion for the forests like that held by the hunters? Was the time I spent in the forest too short? Later it occurred to me. The answer was simple. I was not a hunter. During the days I lived there I did not view the living world from the perspective of the hunters. I was an outsider; I had been evaluating the hunters' life and world using outsider values. That was why I did not understand the hunters' joy. Having thought about this, and pondering it for some time, I decided that I should return to the mountains; go up there and enjoy life as a hunter.

Second Stay at Alongshan Campsite

In mid August, the elder, Maruia Suo, returned to the Ao Township from a Tungus language research conference in Hailar. She was anxious to go back to her Alongshan campsite. Helped by her son-in-law Ahai, who was the former head of the Hunting Service Center, Maruia Suo, a male hunter Maoxia and I rode in a jeep lent by the township and driven by Ahai. Together we set off on the trip to the Alongshan. This jeep had been loaned to the Ao Township from the Genhe County government and although a glance at its odometer revealed it had only 10,000 km on it, the vehicle was already in poor shape. Even when we were driving on the smooth roads in the county, the jeep was bumpy and shaky, not to mention the bone-shaking ride we were treated to while driving on the gravel roads to the Alongshan campsite. With the jeep bumping and rocking along the way, several times the white cabbage piled behind the back seat jumped onto Maruia Suo and me, which caused her to break out giggling. Finally, after suffering a seven-hour ride we arrived at the hunters' campsite when it was almost five o'clock in the afternoon.

With the sun slipping down below the mountains, it was already dim at the campsite. It was drizzling. A blast from the jeep's horn brought out male hunters, who unloaded various supplies from the vehicle. I hurried to keep up with Maruia Suo; she was close to eighty years of age but her steps were stable and light, and before long I was lagging behind. I picked up my speed to keep up, and after some time we finally made it to the tent. The drizzling rain suddenly turned into a downpour. I felt lucky that I had managed to increase my pace otherwise I would have become a "drowned rat." Thus I began my second stay at the campsite.

This time there were three more elementary school students at the site. There were two girls; one was Maruia Suo's granddaughter, and the other was her grandniece. The little boy Xiaodong was Maruia Suo's youngest grandson, Ahai's son. They all came to have fun here during the summer break. In addition to them, there were also seven male hunters and two female hunters—all of whom were related by blood. Two of them were Maruia Suo's grandsons, both in their twenties. They had lost their parents during their teenage years and since then they had been living with Maruia Suo. I had heard from the hunters that the main reason that Maruia Suo was so highly respected was because she had brought up more than ten orphans. Axing was Maruia Suo's youngest son at around 35 years old, and although he had an official job in the city, he had not been to work for a long while after the relocation, and instead had been staying with his mother on the mountain. Yuying was Maruia Suo's second daughter-in-law (28 years old) and was the mother of one of the young girls staying at the campsite. Her husband Agang had been a well-known skilled hunter, tall and handsome, but sadly, several years ago, he accidentally drowned in a river. Ningdao, who was able to craft traditional hunters' tools, was Maoxia's father. Ningdao was around sixty years old, younger than Maruia Suo, but according to the clan genealogy, he was a generation older than Maruia Suo. Keqian and Jiali were sister and brother. Their mother was Halijie, a woman who also accommodated me when I lived in the new Aoluguya after the relocation.

Halijie was one of several old hunters who had an official job at the Ao Township. She was once the representative of the People's Council of Genhe County. When I was staying at her new residence at Aoluguya, she promised to take me up to the Alongshan campsite when the weather turned warm. But an unfortunate turn of events transpired. One day in July, Halijie decided to take her three grandchildren, who attended school in other cities and had come back for their summer vacation, to the campsite. The four of them caught a ride with one of the government vehicles that was going in the same direction. The driver, who was the chauffeur for one of the leaders of the Genhe County government, was unfamiliar with the Mangui roads, and on the road near the Mangui Township he hit a violently bumpy section of the road. The severity of the jolt was too much for the elderly Halijie's spine, which fractured under the stress. She was quickly driven to the hospital in Mangui, and was later transferred to the hospital in Genhe. Before I set off to Alongshan for my second stay, I went to visit her in the hospital. She mentioned that I could live in her tent at the Alongshan campsite.

But during my first night back at the Alongshan campsite, I did not stay at the tent of Halijie's family. Since we had just arrived and had brought a considerable quantity of liquor, the male hunters and Keqian all got drunk. Maruia Suo felt uneasy about putting me in the tents, sharing with these drunken people, so asked me to stay in her tent. Entering Maruia Suo's tent, on the left side there was Yuying's bed; on the right side was Maruia Suo's; in the middle there was an iron stove. Behind the stove were two beds pushed together. These were not really beds, but rather several wood planks that had been laid on top of logs. At nightfall, Yuying and I slept together under one quilt; Maruia Suo snuggled with her granddaughter and grandniece; Ahai and Xiaodong respectively slept on the beds behind the stove.

During the night the woods were very quiet, though I was able to hear many sounds that went unnoticed during the day: the sound of rushing water in far-off valley creeks, the breathing of the reindeer outside the tents, the crackling noise of the firewood in the stove. Around midnight when I was fast asleep, a cacophony of yelling and cursing pierced the quiet stillness and startled me awake. Yuying woke up and she called out to her brother-in-law Ahai. Ahai put on a coat and went outside. I remained wrapped inside the quilt and listened. The fighting and cursing sounds were coming from Ningdao's tent located some 50 meters away. Someone came out of the tent, and the cursing was louder than before. Their shouts echoed through the forest. Shortly after, I heard Ahai's loud scolding to break up the fight and calm things down.

The next day Ahai would drive back to the Ao Township and take the children with him. Maruia Suo's oldest grandson, Manglie (27 years old), would also return with them. In the morning, just prior to his departure, Manglie was still drinking liquor from an enamel cup he was grasping. His long bangs dangled down his forehead and covered half of his face. Some of his hair was matted with blood and his face smeared with a red stain. He patted his uncle Axing's shoulder merrily, and then turned to me in a smile, "Did you hear our fight last night?" Before I could answer, he laughed and walked away. Ahai drove all of them down the mountain back toward the Ao Township. I remained at the campsite.

Axing's eyes were swollen and on his head there was a still-bloody cut. He must have been exhausted and was suffering from a hangover. He soon crashed onto the bed in Ningdao's tent and fell asleep. Maoxia and Ningdao were also sleeping. They slept the entire day, and none of them got up for any food. On the third day Axing got up. He came over to Maruia Suo's tent asking for reindeer tendon thread. He wanted to use the thread to mend his glasses that had been broken by one of Manglie's punches. Axing asked me not to talk or ask about the fight two days ago. Now there were only nine people remaining at the mountain campsite and we returned to our routine lives.

On the third night I moved to Halijie's family tent. In Maruia Suo's tent it was taboo for adult women to set foot in the area at the back because this was a sacred place for the Malu god. Although there were two empty beds in that area, because of the taboo, we could not use them and this forced Yuying and me to share a bed. I was unable to sleep well because of this arrangement, and Yuying must have suffered as well. The two of us shared one small quilt, and during the night both of us frequently woke up because of the cold. Maruia Suo worried about my move. She had Yuying ask me if I feared Jiali. Jiali was a single male hunter, very talented at painting. He was forty years old, but he still looked like a big child. Maruia Suo felt Jiali was kind-hearted but he did have a volatile temper, so she was worried that he would scare me. But I had talked with Jiali several times at the new Ao Township residences. I knew that he loved reading, possessed a broad knowledge of many things, and had even

Figure 1.7 A painting of the mountain camps by Jiali

attended college in Beijing. This left me convinced that we would have a lot to talk about and I decided to move over to Halijie's family tent.

About 100 meters between Maruia Suo's tent and Halijie's tent was Ningdao's tent. Inside Halijie's tent there were four beds in an arrangement very similar to that of Maruia Suo's tent. The siblings Keqian and Jiali, as well as Manglie's younger brother, Ashuai, lived in the tent. Keqian and Jiali had no objection to my moving into their tent. Keqian set up the bed for me and took out a clean quilt especially for me to use. During the first night in Halijie's tent, I became aware that Ashuai was roughly prodding my quilt with something. I had no idea what was going on and was too scared to make any sound. The next morning I learned that Ashuai had killed two mountain mice with a tree branch just at the foot of my bed.

The wooden planks that I slept on were short and bumpy. At night the clothing I used as a pillow often fell to the ground, so my sleep quality suffered. However, the hunters at the campsite all treated me kindly. Jiali made a special trip to some faraway meadow to gather mushrooms so that I might be able to enjoy the special and fresh flavor. He was very creative and carved reindeer antlers into beautiful artistic shapes that he then painted, and then presented them to me as a gift. Other male hunters also made all sorts of reindeer antler decorations for me as Jiali did. Over

Figure 1.8 The bed in the tent in the Alongshan campsite

time I felt our relationship more dear and close. It really felt like we had become one family.

Up in the mountains this time, I gradually gained a thorough experience of what it meant to be a hunter. Every day I made lengthy journal entries on my observations and feelings. In general the days in the Alongshan campsite changed very little. In the morning I would follow Yuying and Keqian to the pen to milk the reindeer. They first tied the bridle to the reindeer, fastened it to the horizontal top log of the pen, and then they both milked the reindeer skillfully, collecting the milk in white enamel cups. Every day, Yuying would collect a big full cup of milk, which had a capacity of roughly two liters. Then she filtered the milk with gauze to remove reindeer hair, and poured the milk into a plastic bucket, which she then covered with a lid. The bucket was put in a traditional storage place next to the tents, and, later, cheese would be made out of the milk. At noon and during the evenings I would help to cook lunch and dinner.

When there was no other pressing activity to attend to, I would tan reindeer hides and sew leather with Maruia Suo. There was a *cuoluozi* not far from hers and in it hanging everywhere were many hairy animal leathers, mainly from roe deer and reindeer. During my first stay at this campsite I witnessed a reindeer die from an overdose of anesthetic in preparation for antler cutting. The old hunter Ningdao skinned it perfectly in one large piece. Later, the skin was stretched and fixed to several wooden poles outside the tent for drying. Once it was dry it was put back in this *cuoluozi*.

On days when the weather was clear and bright I followed the hunters to the riverside to fetch water, or we walked long distances through the mountain paths to pick wild fruits. Living with the hunters and taking part in their daily lives, the days passed quickly and I gradually got used to the life at the campsite. Though the flies still came in swarms, the hunters explained, "In the forests the flies are clean and healthy; you will not have diarrhea or fall ill, even if you eat food that the flies have landed on." They were right.

The most exciting thing to these people living so deep in the forests was hunting. And, for me, the most exciting thing was to go hunting with them. Once, the five of us went to pick *dushi* and *yageda* (wild red berries), which were indigenous types of wild fruits up in the mountains. The three men carried hunting rifles; Yuying and I had large enamel cups in our hands and carried iron kettles on our backs. Half way to our destination we ran into a big pheasant, but unfortunately Yuying and I were too deep

Figure 1.9 Maruia Suo's tent

Figure 1.10 Tanning and drying reindeer hides and meat

in our conversation to notice it. The pheasant, startled by our voices, ran away.

I followed the hunters along the paths that weaved in and around trees and shrubs. Their steps were light and agile, while mine were visibly clumsy and rigid. I was always in need of their help and they often had to wait for me to catch up. When we were picking *dushi* and *yageda*, I stumbled twice and fell flat on my face. This made us laugh out loud. The paths through the forests were in some places easily passable, but in other places hard to traverse. I trudged clumsily along while the four of them hiked so swiftly that it seemed to me that they were flying. We walked for a total of over 20 km there and back that day. Upon returning to the tent, my legs ached for three days. However, this was a trip full of joy, and we savored it long afterward.

On another occasion I went hunting with Jiali. Despite my best efforts I could not keep up with him. Eventually he had me wait for him at a clearing in the woods. Waiting proved too unendurable to me: it was frightening to wait alone in the silent and dense verdant forest. When after one hour Jiali returned with his catch, words could not express how happy and excited I was to see him. Thinking back on this time, I realized that when I stopped holding the attitude of an outsider and learned to heartily enjoy the lifestyle of the hunters, I became content and relaxed. By learning to view the forests through the hunters' eyes, and experience the forests with the hunters' senses, everything became peaceful and was merged in a symphonic harmony. In the remote and isolated forests we enjoyed a simple and leisurely life without disturbance. Everything was so quiet, content, relaxing, and free, like the life of a bird.

During my second stay at the Alongshan campsite I was able to change my mindset and perspectives and strove toward becoming a "hunter" and feeling true appreciation of their lifestyle, which was so closely connected with the rhythms of nature. Shortly after arriving, my appetite improved greatly. After two weeks at the campsite, the green vegetables we had brought to the campsite were all gone. In the following days we lived mostly on the easy-to-stock potatoes and Chinese cabbage, of which the hunters always maintained a large stock. Perhaps because I was more engaged in everyday life and moving around more often, my appetite increased greatly and I enjoyed the food far more than during my first stay. The male hunters caught hazel grouse and pheasants and left all of the best cuts of meat for Maruia Suo and me to eat. Maruia Suo made the wild fruits we had picked into *dushi* jam and *yageda* jam. These fruits and the jam that we prepared not only looked appealing but were delicious as well. My favorite food experience was to dip the *lieba* (bread) made by Maruia Suo into the mixture of *dushi* jam and cheese made from reindeer milk. I also became accustomed to drinking the strong red tea brewed with reindeer milk, and going about for days at a time without a shower or bath. I even got used to the reindeer following me and circling around me when I had to go to the toilet in the open woods. After twelve days or so, Maruia Suo watched me skillfully tanning a reindeer hide and cheerfully said, "Yimanna is now an Ewenki."

Over a fortnight had passed since I had arrived at the Alongshan campsite. During this time, the Ao Township had not sent any vehicles to the campsite, and our supplies of rice and flour were almost gone. We had run out of Chinese cabbage and only a few potatoes were left. Meal after meal consisted of only boiled noodles with some vegetable leaves, salted with soy sauce. In these deep and remote forests, cell phones received no signal at all. To get in touch with the outside world, one had to walk to a patrol station 25 km away to use their landline telephone. When only a three-day supply of foodstuffs remained, Jiali was given the task to set off on this honorable mission to secure us more food. He needed to walk on foot for 25 km; if he was lucky he might encounter a passing timber-cutting truck that could give him a ride.

Maruia Suo was upset that no vehicles had come up from the Ao Township. In their free time, Yuying and Keqian would play poker, using the game as a fun way to predict whether or not a vehicle would

Figure 1.11 *Cuoluozi* and the stove used for baking *lieba*

Figure 1.12 Maruia Suo scraping a hide

Figure 1.13 Rolling reindeer tendon thread

arrive from the Ao Township that day. They had been greatly looking forward to people coming to bring food and news. Maruia Suo said to me, "The Ao Township has not sent a vehicle for so long. Are they afraid there might be some accident? We have a PhD student here, are they not worried that you might have trouble adjusting? What if you got sick up here?" I could sense a hint of anger in the melancholy tone of her voice.

Loss and Confusion

During my time at the Alongshan campsite, every day I observed, listened, sensed, and engaged in reflexive contemplation. I discovered that the hunter's life I had experienced here differed greatly from the descriptions I had read about the hunters' primitive living conditions. I also noticed the change that the hunters themselves had not realized—a change in the way they saw the world; or perhaps to explain more clearly, there was a gap between older local people's traditional worldview and a younger, more current worldview.

The forests were home to the old Ewenki hunters but not to the young hunters. The classic representative of the old hunters, Maruia Suo, never considered the house down in the Ao Township as her "home." When she said "I want to go home," the "home" always meant the rustic tent up in the mountains. All of her belongings were in the mountains. She said she had never become used to living down in the township where she felt unhealthy and suffered from constipation. But up in the mountains, she felt completely at ease. Old Ewenki hunters had a passionate love for the forests. It was a love that stemmed from the depth of their hearts. They loved every blade of grass and every tree, every hill and river, every bird and animal. Old hunters loved reindeer and treated reindeer passionately. They would assign funny and interesting names to the reindeer, like "superstar," "pale nose," and "blue jeans"; they regarded the reindeer as members of their family.

In the eyes of the older generation of hunters, the grand forests where they lived, labored and reproduced comprised their entire world. Quite a few old hunters said to me: "Back when I was young, how shocking it was when we saw people from outside. We thought, 'Wow, there truly are people living outside the mountain regions! There indeed are people who are not like us!'" In a way it can be said that, during the period prior to the large-scale development by the nation in the 1950s, the Ewenki hunters lived a rather free life that was quite isolated from the rest of the world. Several hundred people lived in a region consisting of tens of thousands of square acres of forest. They had access to a great diversity of resources in the forests whenever they wanted, and they were able to take as much as they needed without ever exhausting the forests' ability to provide. They were not even particularly aware that there was another world outside the forest that was different from theirs.

In the isolated forest environment, the primary dangers faced by Ewenki hunters were in the form of natural disasters, accidents, and attacks by wild animals. Since the grand forests were full of danger and hardships, how could the Ewenki people have survived continuously for over three hundred years and create their own language and culture? The fact that the Ewenki hunters' culture has endured to this day demonstrates the people's adept capacity for creating technologies and cultural practices that enable them to survive and live meaningful and satisfying lives. During my time in the mountains, I gradually discovered many small details that illustrated the Ewenki hunters' cultural adaptations to life in the forests. Ewenki hunters use a small square table that at first glance appears to be quite common; but a closer examination reveals that because it has four pointed legs that can pierce into the ground, the table can more easily be leveled and provide a stable surface when used on bumpy, unsmooth ground. The birch-bark container that they use to store salt, cigarettes and various small items is made without any nails or thread, and is also quite unbreakable, moist-proof, light and easy to carry, and thus is very practical. The variety of moist lichen used for making the *sami* smudge fires will not burn with a flame but rather only smolder and create a great deal of smoke. The hunters often chew *yimixina* (chewing tobacco) in their mouths because it provides the stimulating benefit of cigarettes, and because there is no need to ignite it—it does not present any possibility of igniting forest fires like regular cigarettes. Countless other examples of indigenous wisdom and local knowledge like this could be found. Experienced hunters are able to determine which places have suffered from "lightning fire"—a natural fire disaster caused by lightning—just by listening to the chirping of birds. From the moving clouds they are able to forecast the weather for the next several days. By observing the reindeer excrement they can ascertain what type of disease the reindeer has, and by scrutinizing an animal's footprints they can conclude the size of the animal. All these various skills were extremely mysterious to me—never in my life would I have been able to decipher these clues in nature and understand what they might mean. However, to the old hunters these things are simply natural and common knowledge. The old hunters are not only adept at living in the forests; they also never stop pursuing the beauty embodied in such a lifestyle. The birch-bark tools and reindeer bridles they make are unique and highly practical technologies, yet they exude a simple beauty of which the maker is quite aware.

Figure 1.14 Smudge fire for protecting reindeer from insects

What pains and puzzles the old hunters most is how the Ewenki hunters' group came to this point today—a stage at which "the population decreases and people live increasingly worse lives," in their own words. Forty years ago—even twenty years ago—they still enjoyed lives characterized by dignity and pride, and were a kind of people who felt confident about their identity and their future. But today the situation has changed greatly. While changes have taken place, it cannot be said that the ecological migration has changed the hunters' lives to the degree that their lives are completely different from before. Rather it is more accurate to say that the process of change has been slow and gradual. The hunters were not able to pinpoint a definite point at which their lives changed significantly. Rather what they could sense is that after this relocation, conditions became much worse. They did not understand exactly why and therefore placed most of the blame on the ecological migration. Elder hunters see things like this: in the past all hunters were diligent and skillful, and there was always work to be done in the mountains. Everyone respected the hard-working men and women, especially those who were skilled at hunting. Diligence and skill were virtues that hunters valued and pursued. However, "The young hunters nowadays want to do nothing, they could not be lazier," Halijie, a wise old hunter, explained. "The young people drink themselves to death like this, and all of this is because they have nothing to do. The government arranged for them to clean the streets but they do not want to do it; neither do they want to work at the hunters' campsites. All they want is to wait for the meat pies to drop from the sky!" Halijie continued:

> I know there is not any profit from reindeer antlers nowadays. Anyways Jiali and I have salary income every month that is enough to cover our living expenses. I make Jiali and Keqian herd reindeer at the hunters' campsite, mainly to let them have fun, and give them something to do. Otherwise they would have already drunk themselves to death down in the new Ao Township. However, we also need to diligently herd the reindeer. If the reindeer were to disappear, our tribe would no longer exist. Now the government forbids hunting, so if the hunters had no reindeer to herd, what else could we do? The only thing left to do would be to drink ourselves to death.

What Halijie said indeed reflected much of the behavioral phenomena in the Ao Township. The degree to which young hunters were addicted to alcohol surely caused many elder hunters' frustration and anger. In fact, the young hunters did not lack dreams and visions of a better future. In the Ao Township, the person most admired by young hunters was Maruia Suo's oldest son Keliqi, who worked as the legal assistant in the

Ao Township but was not confined to an office all day. His monthly salary was four times higher than the quarterly benefits the other hunters received. In addition, he was allowed to possess guns, so could go up into the mountains to hunt. The other young hunters hoped for such a life with a high salary, no requirement of office work, and the privilege of being able to go hunting.

Young people already knew the comfort that came with modern living, so most of them were unwilling to go up to the hunters' campsites to live in the simple conditions and face hard work. However, they did like occasional hunting in the mountains, because it was still a much-loved hobby among the hunters. It was not only the young people who did not want to engage in hard work at the campsites. Even Jimina, a 51-year-old female hunter, was unwilling to return to the hunters' campsite and live there. Once, I went to visit the hunters' campsite where Jimina stayed. Only Jimina and another young man were there. Jimina, trying to drown her sorrows with alcohol, was drunk and murmuring to herself: "Who wants to live here? The reindeer cannot survive down there, so now they ask us to live back here in the mountains. It is awful here! It is awful! . . ." She was so outraged that she did not know what to do. She was striking the ground with her fingers, and the skin underneath her fingernails was bleeding. She then picked up one of the empty liquor bottles and raised it, angrily positioning herself to smash it. The man was trying to calm her and eventually she put the bottle down. Jimina was unwilling to live up in the mountains but she was also unable to say exactly who had told her she must come back to the mountain campsite to live. When she went down to the Ao Township she often went to her elder sister Halijie's home. She blamed Halijie, "It is all the fault of such representatives of the People's Council as you. Why did you move us to Genhe? What for? The reindeer cannot survive and the people cannot survive! Only your reindeer are happily living at Alongshan."

Halijie was a representative of the Genhe County People's Council. In the beginning, the county invited several hunter representatives to a meeting to decide upon the new location for the ecological migration, and Halijie was among them. Originally Halijie had considered the inconvenience of the long distance between the new Ao Township community and the Alongshan hunters' campsite and had planned to move her reindeer from the Alongshan to a site near Genhe County. But later when she saw that the reindeer did not adapt well—that many died, and that many of the other reindeer herders had moved back to the mountains—she cancelled her original plan.

I had asked the hunters about the type of lives they dreamed of having. The elder hunters replied, "Living up in the mountains, with no outsiders to come to disturb our normal lives." The young hunters replied, "A life like Keliqi's." Elder hunters explained that, nowadays, the outsiders' attitude toward the Ewenki Reindeer-Using Tribe had changed: before, the outsiders' attitude toward the Ewenki was respectful, and everywhere Ewenki Hunters went they felt a pride; now, "Outsiders look at us as if we are very strange. Our self-esteem is often hurt." However, they were unable to articulate any specific reason behind the change of attitude.

An Ewenki woman who was working at Hailar Political Consultative Council said, "An ethnic group living off state welfare has no hope!" The leaders at the Ao Township said, "Would any of us dare not provide a living to the hunters now? They are used to our providing for them. It is not an issue for us to choose. The issue is that the hunters force us to pro-vide for them, and then we simply have to do it!" The words of the former reflect the self-reliant spirit of the older generation of hunters, while the words of the latter reflect the habitual dependency of the current Ao Township hunters. How did the active spirit of the people engaged in traditions get lost? This question demands more thorough and deeper reflection.

Notes

1. Sipsongpanna is known in Chinese Pinyin as Xishuangbanna, a region in Yunnan famous for its natural beauty and minority cultures.
2. A local expression, especially when the ecological migration move was completed. Aoluguya refers to the site of residence prior to the ecological migration. The new site they called Sanchejian. Later, the local government wanted to develop the tourist brand in the name of Aoluguya, so Aoluguya was used as the new site's name after the relocation in 2003.
3. Another opinion about the Tungus tribe in China is that nowadays there are still some Tungus people living in the Chenbaerhu Banner of China.
4. When I attended the Fourth World Reindeer Herders' Congress in Norway in 2009, I found in the English materials distributed by the Conference that both Russian and Chinese reindeer herders were translated to Evenki, with parenthesis respectively to show the country as Russia or China.
5. The name Sanchejian in Chinese literally means Forestry Department's Third Production Warehouse. The site was so named by the Han people in the 1950s.
6. "White disaster" is when the ice and snow are too thick on top of the lichen, which prevents the reindeer from gaining access to their food, leaving them facing potential starvation.
7. The reindeer pen is built in open meadow and is completely enclosed by a wooden fence constructed of five or six stripped logs laid horizontal and fixed onto vertical

fence posts. There is a movable gate consisting of several poles that can be removed to allow entrance into the pen.

8. The *sami* smudge fires are created by placing several rotten logs end to end and then covering them with a type of wet grass. Once ignited, the logs and grass smolder, driving insects away.
9. Currently every hunters' campsite is named after the most authoritative person at the campsite.
10. *Lieba* is a type of Russian bread.

Chapter 2

The Culture of Reindeer Ewenki and Historical Settlements

≥•≤

Kinship among the Ewenki Hunters

Shortly after I arrived in the Ao Township, I learned of the hunter group's tangled kinship relationships. I soon found that one way or another they were all related by blood. Even in Genhe County, a friend had told me that because Genhe was tiny it was definitely a bad idea to talk casually about others because there was a good chance that the person you were speaking about was related to the person you were talking with. Because the Ao Township was even smaller, news traveled faster yet. No matter what happened in the Ao Township, in less than three days everyone there would know about it.

It has been reported that the Ewenki hunters originally had twelve clans, but later those who moved to old Aoluguya only had four major clans; within each clan there were several branches. There were four main surnames respectively—Suoluogong, Bulituotian, Kaertakun, and Gudelin[1] (Lü 1983). In the 1960s, after the nomadic Reindeer-Using Tribe was resettled at the old Aoluguya, they found themselves increasingly under the influence of the Han Chinese. Gradually their last names were changed from the multiple syllables to the single syllable: Bulituotian was shortened to Bu; Suoluogong was shortened to Suo; Kaertakun was shortened to Ge or He; and Gudelin was shortened to Gu. Additionally, due to the fact that historically this tribe often roamed the borders of China and Russia, they had many connections with Russia, and they intermarried with Russian descendants living in China. As a result, there were many Russian names among them. For example, some men were named Grishka (Russian: *Гришка*); and some women were named Maria (Russian: *Мария*) or Marusya (Russian: *Маруся*). In the past, a brother and sister held the position of Ao Township head consecutively. These siblings had Russian names, Serezha (Russian: *Сережа*) and Jenya (Russian: *Женя*). Since the 1959 relocation, the children of this first generation of the resettled Ewenki Reindeer-Using Tribe had both Ewenki names (including Russian names) and Han names. For example, Serezha, the former head of the Ao Township, also had the Han name GU Xinjun, and his sister Jenya had the Han name GU Xianglian. The surname GU represents the Gudelin clan. After settling at the old Aoluguya, the first and second generations, who only had Ewenki names, used their names in the Western order (first name-last name), for example, as: Malia Bu, Malia Suo, Bater Gu, Damala Gu, Damala Suo, Anta Bu, Nihao Gu, Jimide Suo, Balajieyi Ge. The surname Kaertakun (which was shortened to He) in the second-generation descendants and all surnames in the third generation, in general, were all simplified to single-character surnames and given a Han first name. For example, HE Lin, HE Xie, HE Yinggang, HE Ping, SUO Re, SUO Qiang, SUO Wei, SUO Yulan, GU Gejun, GU Liying, BU Lina, BU Neli. Due to the tremendous increase in intermarriage with other ethnic groups after resettlement, nowadays in the Ao Township there are many more Ewenki who are using surnames of other ethnic origins (mainly Han surnames).

The Reindeer-Using Tribe originally practiced exogenous marriage— i.e., marriage outside the clans. However, because of their dwindling population, later the Ewenki changed their rules—permitting marriage within the same clan but not within the same branch of the same clan. After the second resettlement in 1965 there were only four clans left in the Reindeer-Using Tribe, and with their low population it became more and more difficult for marriages between different branches. Meanwhile, they experienced increasing levels of culture contact with other groups, which led to far more cross-cultural intermarriages, especially with the Han group. When I sorted through the Ewenki genealogies in Aoluguya, to my surprise I discovered that in 2004 among the Ewenki Hunters who were under eighteen years old there was only one pure Reindeer-Using Tribe descendant, but he did not even have an Ewenki name. Regarding the current mixed-blood population of the Ao Township, the hunters had a vivid description: "Nowadays, there are more and more *erchuanzi*."[2] Erchuanzi is a slightly derogatory and humorous term, meaning "mixture." Almost every one of the Ao Township hunters shared the same belief that intermarriage with other cultural groups was one of the main reasons behind the rapid loss of their cultural traditions. This realization caused them a great deal of unspoken sadness and apprehension. They often worried that in another twenty to thirty years, when the older hunters are gone, their ethnic group will no longer exist.

When the Ao Township hunters address each other they do not use their last names. Normally, among people of the same generation, they use the first names directly. Even when talking about persons with the same first name the Ewenki will not use the last names, but instead they add prefixes like "big", "middle" or "little" before the first names to distinguish one person from the next. For example, there were three separate women with the same first name Nihao; there was Big Nihao, Middle Nihao, and Little Nihao. When only Middle Nihao was still alive they continued to call her Middle Nihao, as people had got used to this name.

Complicated relationships among relatives had arisen among the four clans of the Ao Township Reindeer-Using Tribe. The earliest tribe leader that could be remembered by Ao Township elders was Kundeyiwan, who belonged to the Suoluogong clan. The Suoluogong clan was the largest clan in the Reindeer-Using Tribe and consisted of two branches. According to the Ao Township records, Kundeyiwan was born in 1925 and died in 1965 of heart disease and hepatitis. From February 1950 to July 1953, Kundeyiwan held the position of the head of Ust-Urov[3] village; he was the first groomed national official among the hunting tribe since the founding of the People's Republic of China. He represented the Reindeer-Using Tribe by attending the People's Representatives Conference of Inner Mongolia Autonomous Region in 1957. He also provided significant advice regarding the standardization of his tribal group's official name. When the Qiqian Ewenki Township was established in 1957, Kundeyiwan served as the first township head. Even today the old hunters hold a near-mythic impression of him and talk about him with reverence and respect.

Currently the only person in the Ao Township who descends directly from Kundeyiwan is Kundeyiwan's grandson, less than thirty years old in 2003. Several years ago, during wintertime, he got drunk and fell asleep in the snow. Unfortunately, his right foot was severely frost bitten and the surgical amputation of his toes was necessary. During the ecological migration, the Ao Township assigned him a new Hunters' house, but he refused it, saying that because he was a single disabled person with no family there was no need to have such a house and that he preferred to live in the nursing home with the most senior elder. While living at the nursing home, when the weather was good, he would come out and stand against the wall outside, or squat beside the roadside to have a look around. As the only grandson of Kundeyiwan, he was well taken care of by the Ao Township people.

When Kundeyiwan was the head of the township, there were two assistant heads; one by the name of Jimide, and another by the name of Nigelai. Jimide also belonged to the Suoluogong clan, but he was from a different branch to that of Kundeyiwan. Jimide's younger sister, Dajiyana, was Kundeyiwan's wife. Nigelai belonged to the Gudelin clan, and his wife was Dajiyana's older sister. Nigelai was also Kundeyiwan's uncle by blood. In another word, Kundeyiwan and Nigelai were connected through a brothers-in-law relationship and uncle-nephew relationship, whilst Jimide was a brother-in-law to both men.

Still widely remembered to this day, this group of long-since deceased Ewenki who once served as officials included HE Lin, who served as the head of the Ao Township for twelve years, and assistant head Guoshike, whose eloquence was highly praised by the hunters. The hunters said that during the time these two men served as officials, the lives of the hunters were, for the most part, happy and satisfying. In the 1970s, both HE Lin and Guoshike were selected by the government to attend college. They later returned to old Aoluguya to become officials. HE Lin's wife was Guoshike's older sister, a woman by the name of SUO Jihong (her Ewenki name was Yuela). Like the two men, she too had been selected to attend college, and later became a teacher at the Ao Township school. Later, she became the assistant head of the township party committee. SUO Jihong and Guoshike were Jimide's cousins (his uncle's children). Jimide's wife, Balajieyi, belonged to the Kaertakun clan. Balajieyi's mother was the last shamaness, Niula, in the Ao Township.

Maruia Suo, the most highly respected elder in the Ao Township, was Kundeyiwan's younger sister by blood. Her husband, Lajimi, belonged to the Kaertakun clan and was one of the best hunters in the Reindeer-Using Tribe. In 1984, his family became the first household of Aoluguya to have a yearly household income over 10,000 RMB. Lajimi was shamaness Niula's cousin (aunt's son). The assistant head, Guoshike, was Maruia Suo's oldest son-in-law. Maruia Suo's youngest uncle was named Andao. Andao's wife was named Aobao and belonged to the Bulituotian clan. Aobao's cousin (her elder uncle's daughter) was the elderly woman Marian Bu. When asked how old she was, she answered, "Over a hundred years old," and when I asked how many children she had given birth to, she replied she had had over ten children, but she could not remember the exact number. Now only three of her daughters were still living; Middle Nihao, Damala, and Little Mani. Their father belonged to the Gudelin clan, and so they have the surname Gu.

Marian Bu was the grandmother of the head of the Ao Township at the time of the ecological migration in 2003. That is to say, the head of the township at that time had three aunts by blood. The township head's younger sister, Zuoye, was HE Xie's wife. HE Xie was Maruia Suo's son. In other words, Maruia Suo's son married Marian Bu's granddaughter. Marian Bu had over ten brothers and sisters, some of whom had children. Thus, people from the lineage of Marian Bu were all closely related to the Ao Township head.

To sum up the above, the four great clans of the Reindeer-Using Tribe are all connected with each other through kinship relations. Overall, even today, the kinship relations are extremely complex and involve all types of interconnections between people, for example Balajieyi's younger sister's son married Damala's daughter, etc. After the 1957–1959 relocation, the Ewenki hunters experienced far more intermarriage with other ethnic groups, but this did not weaken the kinship relationships among the various families. For example, three brothers of the Han group married Ewenki female hunters in the Ao Township. Because the three brothers lived among the Ewenki, their marriage to these three unrelated women had the effect of drawing the women into a strong family relationship. In light of these woven networks of kinship, the various officials working in the Ao Township all agreed that their work was not so easy to do because so many of the people were closely related. Understanding this complicated network of kinship relations provides a helpful backdrop for understanding the existing problems in Aoluguya.

Historical Characteristics of the Ewenki Reindeer-Using Tribe

Population and Living Environment

Population

According to historical records, since the eighteenth century the ancestors of the Aoluguya Ewenki hunters have been living in the primeval forests to the east of the Argun River and northwest of the Greater Khingan Range. Looking at a map, the areas between 51 and 53.5 degrees north latitude and 120 to 123 degrees east longitude comprised the extent of the hunting region for the roaming Ewenki hunters. The area of the broad primeval forests was around 20,000 square kilometers, while the Ewenki hunters' population always hovered around several hundred. Elderly hunters said their population reached over 700 people during the Qing dynasty under Emperor Kangxi's reign. However, by the early nineteenth century, as Russia's power expanded toward Siberia, their peaceful lives were disturbed and the population began to fall.

Later, the Ewenki experienced a dramatic population loss under the rule of the forces of the Japanese Imperial Army's secret service. The Japanese fascists set up the Eastern Mongolian Trading Company and the Manchu Stock Production Company to conduct a monopoly over trade and confiscate furs and game in the region, which created cruel economic deprivation among the Ewenki hunters. The Japanese army also established the Kwantung Army Woods Training Camp into which they drafted all male adult Ewenki hunters to undergo strict military training with the intention of using the Ewenki hunters to fight against the Russian Red Army and the Anti-Japanese United Forces. Furthermore, the Japanese invaders worked to foment trouble among Ewenki hunters and other ethnic groups, and forced Ewenki to undergo slave obedience education. Recalling these events, the elderly hunters' brows always furrowed, their eyes narrowed into thin slits, and the position of their jaw and disposition revealed the pain and suffering endured by their people. After World War II, the population of the Ewenki hunters dramatically dropped to 34 households with 170 people (Qiu 1980 [1962]: 6).

Natural Environment

The broad and dense Greater Khingan Range forests provided a treasure trove of natural resources for Ewenki hunters to use. The mountains, rivers, forests, wild animals and mineral deposits were rich resources that satisfied all the needs of several hundred Ewenki people. In the region where the Ewenki hunters roamed and hunted, there are many branches of the Greater Khingan Range. Zigzagged among the mountains are the ever-flowing rivers. All the rivers eventually merge into the Argun River. It was the Ewenki hunters who originally named these mountains and rivers. Every one of the older Ewenki hunters could serve as a "living map" of the Khingan Range and had been guides for government exploration teams that came to survey the Greater Khingan Range. They provided every manner of assistance to surveyors, geological research teams, forests research groups, land and irrigation survey organizations, railway line planning institutes, railway builder crews, and border patrol armies. They have guided these strangers into and through the primeval forests where they had lived for generations. However, when the old Ewenki hunters looked at the Greater Khingan Range later, the tone of their voice fell heavy and they noted with sadness, "The forests are fewer and smaller, there are more and more outsiders, and many wild animals have not be spotted for many years." To reconstruct an image of the region as it once appeared, we can only rely on the old men's vivid and passionate descriptions interspersed with helpless sighs, and try to imagine what it must have been like.

Fortunately, several anthropologists, such as Pu Qiu, were eyewitnesses to the exploration of the Greater Khingan Range in the years shortly following the establishment of the People's Republic of China. Pu Qiu's account provides a detailed description of the region and the natural environment in which the hunters lived.

> Overlaying the Greater Khingan Range are the endless primeval forests. The forests are comprised of varieties of pine trees, black birch, white birch, poplar, willow, oak . . . Meadows are home to countless wild flowers and exotic grasses. Forest dwellers can pick *dushi* . . . wild berries, wild onions and mushrooms. Each time you walk into the grand forests, it feels like entering another world. The sunshine is blotted out by a canopy of branches, and no roads or paths are visible. In every direction, there are thick and massive tree trunks, luxuriant vegetation and dense leaves that block one's line of sight. Everywhere the forest is filled with birds chirping and flowers blossoming; the freshness of the air and fragrance of the mossy forest floor instills an incomparable sense of relaxation in the mind and body.
>
> In the primeval forests of the Greater Khingan Range, there live a wide range of wild animals, including deer, moose, bears, wild hogs, roe deer, roebucks, otters, wolves, lynxes . . .There are also many species of birds . . . The rivers that crisscross this mountainous area are home to various species of fish . . . The Ewenki people are drawn to everything beautiful existing in nature. (Qiu 1980 [1962]: 2–3)

The beautiful Khingan Range is not only attractive to the Ewenki people but also to those people who long for forests; who long for a verdant environment of beauty, and long for good health.

However, the weather conditions here are indeed harsh. Throughout the year there are only eighty frost-free days. Seven months experience temperatures below zero degrees centigrade. During the coldest periods in winter, the temperature can reach as low as minus 50 degrees Celsius. Some areas are covered by snow and ice all year long, with snow as thick as one meter. This harsh natural environment, besides a lack of medical necessities, might contribute to the low levels of population growth among the forest-living Ewenki hunters.

Traditional Lifestyles

Historically, Ewenki hunters herded reindeer in the vast forests and lived their lives as hunter-gatherers. They wore clothes made from animal hide and fur, and so relied on wild game. They lived in the *cuoluozi*. The *cuoluozi* is easy to build and set up—extremely compatible to the hunting lives led by the Ewenki hunters, who were constantly on the move. When they moved to a new campsite, they never dismantled the wooden pole structure of the *cuoluozi*, but left it standing for future use should they return to camp in the area again. In daily life, men were primarily responsible for hunting, while women were in charge of gathering berries and herding reindeer. Reindeer are commonly found in the Arctic Circle. The global population of reindeer currently stands at about five million and the largest herds are found in Russia. In China, reindeer are only found on the northwest slope of the Greater Khingan Range. The Ewenki hunters are the only reindeer herders in China.

The Ewenki hunters frequently changed the location of their campsites to ensure a steady supply of food for their reindeer herds. Reindeer feed primarily on lichen, which grows at a very slow rate; it takes five to ten years for lichen to grow several centimeters—just long enough for the reindeer to eat. To ensure an area is not overgrazed and to allow the lichen in the grazed region to recover, during the summer months the Ewenki will move every couple of weeks; in winter they will move the campsite every couple of days. They tend to move more frequently in the winter because animal tracks left in the snow make it easier to hunt game. When moving campsites, the reindeer are used as their primary tool of transportation and are used to carry the elderly and young children. The reindeer are indispensable to the Ewenki, and the Ewenki see them as good companions. Because the reindeer are physically well adapted to travel in forests, they serve as good helpers to the Ewenki when they go out on hunting expeditions. Ewenki hunters care deeply about their reindeer and protect them carefully. The women, who are in charge of raising and herding reindeer, show an especially deep compassion toward the animals.

In the past, the Ewenki hunters used simple handmade tools for hunting and gathering wild berries. Because of the low productivity and a tough natural environment, Ewenki hunters lived communally, organized by clan. When the People's Republic of China was established in 1949, the Ewenki hunters lived in patriarch social systems, organized in the form of family-based communal campsites known as *urilen* (Qiu 1980 [1962]:59–62). Over time, the *urilen* campsites in which all members were related by blood changed by the early 1980s to hunters' campsite in which members were not necessarily related by blood, but were based on practical and profit-based considerations.[4] The older term *urilen* fell out of use and was gradually replaced by the term hunters' campsite. In the early 1960s, when Pu Qiu and other ethnologists went to study the Ewenki hunters, five *urilen* were still extant, each one led by a *shinmamalen*—a camp leader who was in charge of general affairs. During my fieldwork period (from September 2003 to October 2004), there were five hunters' campsites (Pinyin: *lie min dian*) in the Ao Township with each site led by a campsite head (Pinyin: *dian er zhang*), who served the same role as the *shinmamalen* in the past.

Living traditional lifestyles as nomadic herders in the mountains, there naturally arose a set of behavioral norms and rules that the Ewenki hunters refer to as *aojiaoer*, a term that means "the customs or rules passed down by ancestors or ancient traditions." Because the aojiaoer customs represent the best interests of all members of society, everyone feels a sense of responsibility to follow and obey them. The aojiaoer tenets cover broad aspects of social life ranging from hunting to daily life, to religious beliefs. For example, after Ewenki hunters kill a deer or roebuck they have to clean up the bloodstain on the ground, and to do otherwise would be regarded as unmoral behavior. The reason is simple—if the bloodstain is not cleaned up other wild animals will smell it and stay away, which would make it difficult for others to have success in hunting. Other examples include: when hunting, people are forbidden to say things like "let us go hunting"; when a dead deer or roebuck is being carried back to the campsite on the back of a reindeer, the dead animal's head must not drop to the ground; when fishing, one should not step over fishing nets; when preparing fish, the chest area must not be cut open. The Ewenki hunters believed that the violation of these taboos would enrage the gods and harm hunting and fishing activities. The hunters practiced a system of evenly allocating game among households. For each specific intake of game, they had corresponding methods for allocation. This is known as the aojiaoer for allocation (Qiu, 1980[1962]:68–69).

Ethnic Characteristics

Ewenki hunters' lifestyle has given them a thorough indigenous knowledge of their hunting areas and the surrounding natural world. They were familiar with every mountain peak, every hill, and every creek. Every location had a name brimming with vivid meaning that fully described the site and its characteristics. Whenever they went hunting or moved the campsite they usually did not describe places with regard to compass directions; instead, they indicated their location by the name of a nearby mountain, or vis-à-vis a particular headwater, mid river, or downstream area of a river.

Though the Ewenki people have their own language, they do not have a system of writing. A language that lacks a system of writing can easily fade into extinction, especially when it faces considerable external language pressure from another dominant cultural group. The fast disappearance of the Ewenki language in Aoluguya was appalling. Speaking Mandarin, the language of the majority, seemed to make more sense, and thus they had little sense of the Ewenki language as an important part of their self-identity. The result has been that most young Ewenki Hunters do not even understand the Ewenki language. An Aoluguya Ewenki girl who competed in the Ewenki public ambassador pageant was criticized by other candidates for not being able to speak the Ewenki language, but nevertheless she still won the pageant. In recent years, more researchers have been paying attention to the Aoluguya Ewenki hunters (Siqinfu 1999, 2000; Heyne 2007; Fraser 2010; Xie 2010; Kolås 2011; Beach 2012); among them, linguists wished to learn the Ewenki language. This made the Ewenki hunters feel both proud and surprised. From the outsider interest in their language, Ewenki people became aware that their language itself embodied local knowledge and helped to define them as a people. With this new awareness, Ewenki hunters began to revalue their language and took measures to ensure it would continue to be used. Those women who were able to speak Ewenki were employed at the local elementary school to teach school children. It was the attention from the outside world that prompted the Ewenki hunters to develop a stronger cultural self-identity.

Religious Beliefs

Like many early tribes, the Ewenki hunters were engaged in the animistic worship of the power of nature. They believed that one particular god dominated each natural phenomenon. They paid special homage to the mountain god and fire god. It was their belief that all wild animals were raised by the mountain god. Hunters could hunt and catch prey only because of the divine blessing of the mountain god. Through the worship of the fire god, Ewenki hunters created many taboos, such as forbidding women to step over fire. When moving to a new campsite, they dared not extinguish the campfires, or fight the most damaging mountain fires, because they believed that such fires were an act of the fire god to drive out demons (Qiu 1980[1962]:85–91). In later times, when a range of exploratory survey teams were sent to the Greater Khingan Range, many young Ewenki hunters joined forest-patrol and fire-fighting units organized by the government. In spite of this, the Ewenki still maintained a reverence toward fire. At the hunters' campsite, on every occasion that liquor is consumed, the Ewenki will first always take their cup and pour a small amount of liquor over the burning stove as an offering and to show their respect to the gods. To this day they still bear in their bones a deep reverence toward the tremendous power of nature, an attitude very much unlike many "modern" people, who hold a belief in the necessity of taming, overcoming and conquering nature.

The Ewenki people not only believed that people had souls, but also believed that wild animals had souls too. They believed that every animal's soul dwelt in the heart, lungs, liver, and brain. For this reason, after killing a bear, the animal's head, esophagus, lungs and liver were not eaten but were given a "wind-erosion burial"; these body parts were not buried in the ground, but left on a tree exposed to the elements of nature, which would see to their decomposition and return them to the sky and earth. Similar beliefs existed about the treatment of other animals as well. The head and heart of moose, deer, roebuck and other animals were only eaten after they had hung on trees for several days (Qiu 1980[1962]: 96–97).

Having lived as a clan-based society for centuries, Ewenki religious beliefs also included worship of a clan-god. They called the clan-god Shewoke, which in the Ewenki language means "the god is represented by the shaman." Ewenki people placed an icon of the Shewoke god in a leather bag together with icons of eleven other gods, which were known collectively as the Malu god. Normally, the Malu god was enshrined at the clan shaman's tent. Later, when patrilineal families split off from their main clan, if the new independent family did not have a shaman among the members to take care of the Shewoke god, the head of the patrilineal family took responsibility for this. The gods were placed in the corner of the *cuoluozi* that was furthest away from the entrance. Female adults were strictly forbidden to go close to the Malu god, and they were not allowed to cross in front of the Malu god shrine to get to the other side of the *cuoluozi* (Qiu 1980[1962]: 98–99). The above descriptions about beliefs are those of the past. Religious belief and practice have undergone considerable change, although some belief in taboos still goes on. Nowadays in the hunting campsites, almost all of the tents place nothing in the Malu god shrine except two tents: in one hangs a portrait of Chairman Mao; in the other hangs a portrait of Saint Mary and her baby Jesus. In some tents, the ancient taboos are strictly followed; while in other tents, the women can walk around freely without any taboo restrictions. These changes in practice indicate that many Ewenki hunters no longer hold the same religious beliefs of their ancestors.

Shamanism is a relative common religious practice among the minorities of northern China. Ewenki hunters also believed in shamanism. They considered the shaman as a medium between the world of deities and the world of humans, and as possessing the magical power to drive demons out of those stricken with disease. Shamans could also request the deities

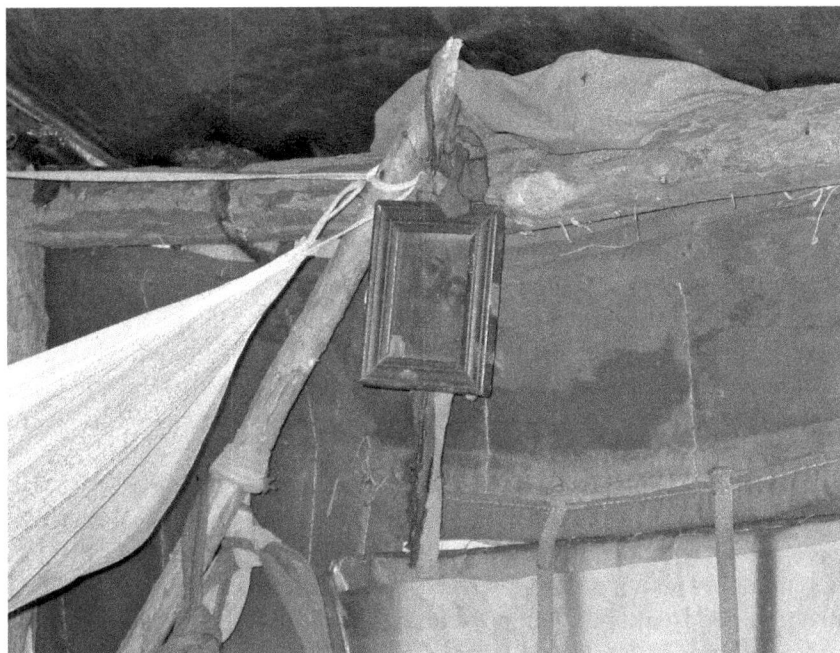

Figure 2.1 In Maruia Suo's tent

to bless and protect the hunters. The shaman enjoyed a high reputation among the Ewenki hunters. In his or her religious rituals, the shaman often sacrificed white reindeer as an offering to the gods. Shamans never request payment for making inquiries to the gods, or for treating the sick.

Although Orthodox Christianity had a certain influence on the Ewenki hunters' beliefs, the Ewenki did not accept its doctrines, but adopted some rituals. Thus, religious activities among the Ewenki hunters were still largely characterized by shamanism (Qiu, 1980[1962]: 98–100). However, the shamanism belief system of the Ewenki hunters has been in a state of flux. The last shamaness, Niula, died in 1997. She left no inheritors to her practices, and no other shaman has arisen among the group to maintain this religious tradition. The shamans' costume and drums used by local Ewenki shamans are now displayed in the Ao Township museum.

Views on Life and Death

I was quite astonished after discussing with Ewenki hunters their views about death. They regarded death quite lightly and regarded the ending of a life to be natural and common. They explained, "All creatures will die. We can eat the animals; the animals can also eat us." Observing three Ewenki funerals, I was struck by the simplicity in comparison to the elaborate funerals of Han Chinese. It might even be said that there was almost no ritual. When a person died, the body was dressed in a set of clean clothes that were not new or specially made funerary clothing and then wrapped in a blanket. The township government would send a vehicle to pick up the body for cremation. Family and other members of Aoluguya did not cry or express grief, but rather looked calm and seemed to have an indifferent attitude toward death. These practices suggested that they hold a specific attitude toward death—simple and easy. Perhaps in living a traditional lifestyle in close contact with the natural environment, death was a frequent affair and thus people came to see it as a natural occurrence—not as a terrible event, or as an event of much suffering.

For these Evenki hunters, individual death brings émotional loss to some, but is not as painful as most people find it. The plausible explanation lies in shared community life. The Ewenki hunters had lived in communal clans for so long with several families living together. Their material goods and property are evenly distributed, the same for the risk of loss of some individuals. Living in a harsh natural environment with a low production level, an individual will find it hard to survive unless they adopt a communal clan-based lifestyle based on mutual support and aid. When parents lost a child, other people's children would come to tend to them kindly. If a child's parents died, other adults in the community would raise the child as their own. This was best illustrated by the following example of a seventy-year-old woman named Nihao. About fifteen years ago, a young Ewenki hunter killed Nihao's second son. That young man served his term in prison and was then released. When he came back he lived at the same campsite with Nihao. He had no reindeer, and almost no food or clothing. It was Nihao that provided him with all forms of help and shared food with him until he died naturally in his fifties many years later.

Another fact stunned me more: several years ago, an Ewenki hunter got drunk and after attempting to rape two women in his drunken stupor fell asleep in the snow. Then he was arrested, but because his hands and feet had been severely frost bitten, he was sent to the hospital to be amputated. Later, because his crime was not thought to be particularly serious, the police intended to release him. However, his mother refused, saying to the police, "Do not let him come back. He can do nothing without hands and feet. We have no one to care for him. Please execute him." There was unwritten immunity in criminal law in China that precluded Ewenki hunters from capital punishment. But finally, this hunter was executed on his mother's request. If his mother had not told me the story herself, I would never have believed it.

These two incidents are almost unthinkable to most outsiders. The hunter's mother explained, "He [the son who lost his hands and feet] would suffer if he remained living, and others would suffer too. Death is just death." The old woman Nihao explained her behavior this way, "My son is already dead; he [the young man who killed her son] came back. We see each other every day, so I treat him kindly." She shared food with him simply because they lived close to each other and saw one another now and then during life at the campsite. The old woman never thought about exacting revenge for her son. She explained, "It is quite normal for men to pick fights when they are drunk. That was so common in the past. And sometimes people get killed." If we consider the high death rate among the Ewenki hunters it becomes easier for us, as outsiders, to understand their seemingly cavalier attitudes toward death. This attitude likely did little to curb dangerous behavior, which, in turn, has led to frequent early deaths. Thus, the two factors become interlinked in a cycle—a high death rate led to a cavalier attitude, which in turn led to high-risk behavior that contributed to a high death rate.

During the course of my fieldwork, I gradually came to understand that the Ewenki male hunters' habit of drinking and fighting had to be understood in a way completely different from the way in which outsiders imagined it as viciousness. I encountered several incidents during which male hunters got drunk and started fighting. Once, a man was injured so badly that he had to have twenty stitches at the hospital. However, the next day he still joined the other men, including the man who had beaten him, to drink liquor together again as if nothing had happened the day before. In another case Aqihuang, a young hunter, stabbed Xiaoyingke, the younger brother of the township head, because of their jealous feud over a woman. The incident happened when Xiaoyingke was working as a security guard for the Ao Township government. Based upon eyewitness accounts, Xiaoyingke did not drink any liquor that day, but Aqihuang got drunk and by chance encountered Xiaoyingke on the road. Suddenly, maybe in a fit of jealous rage, Aqihuang stabbed Xiaoyingke in the belly. Xiaoyingke's intestines spilled out of his body, and he almost died from this grievous wound. The strange thing about the whole event was that four months prior to this incident, Aqihuang, despairing over his love affair with a woman, had attempted to commit suicide by cutting open his own belly. Xiaoyingke, who had just got off his night shift, found him in a puddle of blood on the roadside. Xiaoyingke quickly took Aqihuang to the hospital and thus saved his life. So when several months later Aqihuang stabbed Xiaoyingke, many people found this to be rep-rehensible and felt that Aqihuang was wicked and "had no conscience." But when asked about this Xiaoyingke said, "He [Aqihuang] just drank too much." In their defense, the Ewenki hunters believed these kinds of fights that caused loss of life were not deliberate, but accidental under the influence of alcohol. Even Xiaoyingke's older brother Serezha, the former Ao Township head and current deputy head of Genhe County United Front Work Department, went to see the Genhe County assistant judge to appeal on Aqihuang's behalf. He asked the judge, "Let it go. Release him quickly." There had been countless incidents like this. Maybe the low population under arduous living conditions demand cooperation from all members to ensure survival, which contributes to their perspectives of for-giving their behaviors; they have extraordinary tolerance between them.

After the ecological migration in 2003, many male hunters felt uneasy, and complained, "Now the regulations are too strict. When the fighting gets wild, the police arrest us and sentence us to prison. Nothing like this happened before!" In their eyes, fighting was not such an awful matter and some hunters even claimed, "Fighting shows our intimacy." Later, my friends in Genhe County happened to be talking about how the people in northeastern China tended to pick fights easily. My friends noted, "There is nothing special about it really. It's just a custom among the people in the northeast. Often they just start fighting without really saying much, but then after the fight, all is resolved. This is much better than people in other areas who appear to be nice, but then later stab you in the back." Perhaps the habit of fighting among Ewenki hunters in Aoluguya is a culturally accepted way of venting frustrations and carries little mean-ing in terms of long-term hatred, so after fighting, all returns to normal. A policeman with nine years of experience in the Ao Township police department said to me:

> In the year following the relocation to Genhe, the Ao Township had a total population of about two hundred people. There were four criminal cases, and seven public mischief cases. We did not enforce regulations too tightly; otherwise, the actual case numbers would have been much higher. Before in the old Ao Township, the regulations were enforced even less strictly. Fighting was quite common and there was no way to catch every case. Now that the hunters have moved close to the county downtown, the upper levels of the Police Department demand tighter controls and stricter regulations. Indeed now we act to enforce the law more than before, and the actual situation has improved a lot.

Not only from the outside discourse, but also from the hunters' own words, we can see that they are impetuous and irrational. The problem is that they are not rejecting this irrationality. In another word, the emotion can always surpass the rationality without any restraint, which is not regarded as shame in their understanding.

The presumption of the modernization theory is that the subject should be rational. Thus, to modernize Ewenki people it is necessary to modernize their value system alongside the material. However, who is the ultimate judge of rationality and irrationality? We might be treated as the irrational ones in the eyes of Ewenki people. Subconsciously, we adopt values from the mainstream discourse and use them to judge Ewenki people. It may truly lead to a deep understanding of the different value systems if we can jump out of our own value system and stand in the perspective of Ewenki people.

The Evenki hunters said, "We have always been living this way. We never interfere with your lives. Why you come to interfere with our lives? What make you come to observe our lives? Why we cannot observe your lives?" These words reflect the concept of equality in their value system, but also expose the "modern" concept of self-righteousness, arrogance, and conceit. In the perspective of the hunters, I found the paranoia of the modern rationality. In other words, modern rationality requires people to accept its value judgment and try to deny the value judgments of others. In this case, the government decided to change the Evenki hunters' lifestyle and let them live like everyone else in city, but hunters have never intended to change city people's way of life so they can live like them.

Historical Settlements under New China

Before the establishment of the People's Republic of China, the Ewenki hunters suffered grave losses during the arduous War of Resistance against Japan. In August 1945, the Russian Red Army marched to the northeast of China where they defeated the Japanese Kwantung Army. Following this defeat, the Japanese imperialist forces surrendered unconditionally. During the seven years from 1938 to 1945, the number of Ewenki hunters declined sharply from 253 to 170 and the number of reindeer also dropped rapidly from 853 to 400. Among the surviving 170 people, the tuberculosis rate was as high as 70 percent (Siriguleng 1991: 21–22). By 1949, the ethnic Ewenki were on the edge of extinction.

On 1 January 1948, the Hulun Buir League (city) government was established, which combined the administrative regions of Argun Left Banner (county) and Argun Right Banner (county) into Argun Banner (county), and established its base of operations at Sanhe. In the same year, the Party and government set up a supply store especially for Ewenki hunters at Qiqian (Siriguleng 1991: 23–25).

"Settling Down without Occupancy" at Qiqian

Qiqian used to be called Wuqiluofu (Ust-Urov is the Russian name). White Russians who fled from the Russian October Revolution first inhabited it. Most of them worked in agriculture and livestock and brought with them technologies from Russia. Out of the need to trade with the Ewenki hunters to obtain animal hides, many Russian and Han merchants gathered in Qiqian on the banks of the Argun River where they traded hides, furs, and mountain products. Intermarriages between Han and Russians were quite common in this region, and this gave rise to a unique Chinese-Russian descent group.

Over the course of many years trading together, the Ewenki hunters and Russian and Han merchants and their mixed-blood descendants developed strong economic relationships. The Chinese-Russian descendants spoke both Mandarin and Russian and followed customs of both cultures. The degree to which the Ewenki hunters had become "Russianized" was even more obvious. Their commonalities enabled the two groups to easily find common ground in their social and business dealings. Over time, the culture of the Chinese-Russian descent group in Qiqian became more influential in the lives of the Ewenki hunters. With regard to their social lives and communications with outsiders, the Ewenki hunters became increasingly influenced by the Han culture and the emphasis on fixed agricultural settlement.

After the founding of the People's Republic of China in 1949, the Party and government became concerned about the situation and began extending various forms of assistance to help a small group of just over a hundred Ewenki hunters that still remained. In the early 1950s, based upon the economic and cultural ties between the Ewenki hunters and the mixed descendants of Russian and Han people in Qiqian, the Party and government established guidelines to end the Ewenki people's nomadic lifestyle and encouraged them to live in permanent settlements in Qiqian. The government gradually built the cultural and economic infrastructure in Qiqian, including a supply and sales store, an elementary school, a tuberculosis prevention clinic, a club and an animal feeding place in order to provide the cultural and economic support that would enable the Ewenki hunters to leave their camps in the forested mountains. The establishment of these facilities enabled the Ewenki hunters' hunting products to be integrated into the nation's generalized pricing system. Ewenki economic production increased significantly. Children of Ewenki hunters were admitted to the elementary school that was exclusively built for minority children, where they received free board and education. Sick people were cared for with free medical services. Through the Party and government's assistance, a number of hunters were employed in the Qiqian Township government and resided in the town, while other hunters became workers at a reindeer and animal feedlot. The establishment of forest exploration and preservation programs enabled all adult males in the community to have jobs as forest patrol workers. In February 1957, according to the Party's ethnic regions self-governance policies, the Second People's Representatives Conference in the Hulun Buir League decided to set up the Ewenki Ethnic Township in Qiqian. For the first time in history the Ewenki hunters had their own political authority (Hao 1994). The average hunter's income grew from 93 RMB in 1952 to 220 RMB in 1958, and the population also grew from 136 in the early 1950s to 146 in 1960 (Guobuku and Manduertu 1960).

In 1959, the country allocated a special fund of 48,000 RMB for the construction of 30 Mukeleng[5] houses in Qiqian. Their purpose was to provide the material conditions necessary for the Ewenki hunters to give up their nomadic lifestyle and live in a permanent settlement. An investigation conducted at that time showed that in addition to the 8 families who already resided at Qiqian there were another 18 hunter families, out of a total of 31 families, who had requested to settle down (Guobuku and Manduertu 1960). In 1962, another 13 families moved to this residence. However, except for the township head and the head of the supply and sales store, who resided in town most of the year, all other hunters spent long periods of time in the mountains hunting and herding, and only spent short periods of time living at the settlement. As most of the population spent much of the year in the mountain camps, the government's desire to see the Ewenki hunters living in fixed settlements was never completely realized. This was because living in fixed settlements was not conducive to either hunting or reindeer herding, both of which required a nomadic lifestyle in the forest. In addition, elderly Ewenki were unable to adapt to the non-nomadic lifestyle of fixed residence in lowland regions. For these reasons, although they had fixed residences in Qiqian, they did not really live there (Kong 1994: 36).

I interviewed the hunters who were over sixty years of age. When asked what their childhood was like, their faces lit up with excitement. One hunter began talking in an animated tone:

> When we were young, Ami [dad] and Eni [mom] both hunted and herded reindeer in the mountains. Before starting school we all stayed in the mountains. It was so much fun up there. In the summer, wild flowers and

berries covered the entire hillside—it was so beautiful! At a young age, we had already learned how to ride on reindeer to play. We knew our own reindeer. At that time, all households evenly shared the game that we shot. Of course it was not absolutely equally divided—that was impossible to do. But the division was largely equal. There were special rules as to how to divide the game. Back then, there was a great amount of game to hunt. It was fairly easy to get them. There were too many for the reindeer to carry, and during each hunting trip much game was thrown away. Each time Ami came back from hunting, he brought with him lots of game. Then, we all danced and sang in one circle. Drinking liquor, dancing . . . everyone was happy!

When we went to school and lived in the school dorms, food and boarding did not cost anything. The country even gave us money. Each class was taught by three teachers together. Firstly the Mandarin-speaking teacher presented the materials once; then the Russian-speaking teacher repeated once; lastly the Ewenki-speaking teacher went over once. It was so interesting! Many old hunters could speak several languages.

I asked, "Well, you basically did not live in the houses that the government built, so why did you ask to settle down?" One hunter answered:

The government built the houses for our benefit. In the past, the officials were able to endure hardship. They always spent time with us in the mountains, saying the *cuoluozi* we lived in were too backward. They wanted to build houses for us to improve our living conditions. In that case, then why would we not live in them? Anyways, we still need to go down the mountain to buy things. They asked us to settle down and offered us houses.

Jimide Incident: Move to Old Aoluguya

After 1958, throughout China, leftist ideology was beginning to cast a greater and greater influence on every aspect of life. Its effect on ethnic groups was no exception. However, because the Ewenki Ethnic Township in Qiqian was remote and had a low population, the region was not subject to the same political extremism that followed the "Meteoric Advances" or "Running Toward Socialism"[6] movements, which in other parts of China led to the organization of production communes.

However, located just across the river from Russia, Qiqian did suffer from the relationship deterioration between China and the USSR. After the relationship between China and the USSR turned sour, the situation at the border became tense. Qiqian became the front line battlefield of anti-revisionism. Ewenki hunters, who, historically, were visibly Russianized, and who shared blood ties to the Russian Ewenki people with whom they still maintained regular exchange and contact, were under close scrutiny and subjected to much attention because of the domestic leftist ideology and the hostile relationship between the two countries. During that time, as the forests were exploited, hunting and reindeer herding areas were restricted. This prompted the local government to develop a new hunting area for the hunters in the region of Alongshan. Right at that time, in 1964, an incident occurred in the Ewenki Township of Qiqian, which was referred to as the so-called Surrender-to-Revisionism-Treason Incident. This incident strongly contributed to the decision to move Ewenki hunters to a more inland region around Aoluguya. The move was intended to serve the needs of "anti-revisionism and guard-against-revisionism" (Hao 1994: 10). In the publically available documents, I only found the name of the event—the Surrender-to-Revisionism-Treason Incident—but was unable to locate a detailed description of what it was about. But when I asked the hunters over the age of fifty about this incident, every single one of them knew about it. One of the elderly hunters recalled the event:

That Surrender-to-Revisionism-Treason Incident was also called the 'Jimide incident.' Jimide was one of the great leaders among the Ewenki hunters. That year [1964] the weather was quite frigid. One of the hunter's children suddenly fell sick, and the situation was very urgent and serious. No treatment was available locally. At that time, Jimide was the township deputy head [Qiqian Ewenki Ethnic Township], and was also the deputy head of the township police station. He went to his superior, the head of the township police station, to request a helicopter to airlift the sick child to an out-of-town hospital. Well then, why did he make such request? It was because right before this incident, one of the People's Liberation Army soldiers from the border troops fell sick and he was airlifted by helicopter out of the region for treatment. Therefore, Jimide made a similar request. The head of the township police station—he was a "bogeda" [Han ethnicity]—disagreed. He insisted that using a helicopter was impossible, saying it belonged to the People's Liberation Army and that we could not use it. Consequently, they started quarreling. Jimide said that we must then cross the Argun River to USSR to save the child. Then a fight broke out between them. They said that, in the end, Jimide attempted to grab the head of police's gun, but instead was shot dead by the head of police at the scene. At that time, he was labeled as an anti-revolutionary who had surrendered to revisionism and treason. He was not yet forty years old when he died. This incident had a very strong effect on the hunters. They felt this was a case of the strong Han group bullying the weak minority group. During those days following the incident, the atmosphere was very tense. All of us felt something was going to happen. Additionally, the relationship between China and USSR had soured during that period. The government was afraid that the hunters would flee to USSR and so, soon enough, we were moved further inland to [old] Aoluguya.

In 1964, after the "Jimide incident," the upper-level authorities allocated special funds for the hunters and built a reception center, a dining hall, a clinic and other service facilities in the community of the Alongshan Township. The construction of these facilities was to provide convenient services to encourage the Ewenki to move from their remote hunting areas near the China-USSR border to the Alongshan areas further south. On 25 May 1965, the Qiqian Ewenki Ethnic Township government based in Qiqian, Argun Right Banner (currently Argun County), moved to the Mangui Township seat, which was officially renamed Mangui Ewenki Ethnic Township. In September 1965, Ewenki hunters were moved from the old Mukeleng houses in Qiqian to (old) Aoluguya in the Argun Left Banner (currently Genhe County) where the government provided them with thirty-three new Mukeleng houses. The distance between the original site in Qiqian and the new site in (old) Aoluguya was about 200 km. Additionally, in Mangui, where the township government was located, 17.5 km away from the old Aoluguya community, service facilities like a medical clinic and food store were set up. The Ewenki hunters had just begun their second settlement journey.

In regard to the relocation to old Aoluguya, Mr Fanzhi Kong, as a witness, in his book *The Ewenki of Aoluguya* wrote the following:

> The day of 23 September 1965 was of great significance in the history of the Ewenki hunters. Under the loving care of the Party and government, illuminated by the radiance of the Party's ethnic policies, the Ewenki hunters have fully achieved settlement. Their long-term desire for settled residence was finally realized. This is an unforgettable day. In the same year on 28 October the settlement celebration was held. On the bank of the Jiliu River, the country built spacious Mukeleng houses for the hunters. All 33 hunter households settled and made home there. The Aoluguya hunters' new village stands at the mighty country's north borders where it decorates the beautiful Greater Khingan Range. Settlement and residence, a social transformation of historical significance, enabled the Ewenki hunters, in the short course of twenty-odd years since the founding of the People's Republic of China, to leap beyond their long history of several hundred years. From now on, the Ewenki hunters have ended the unsettled roaming and hunting lives they have led since ancient times. Their extremely backward production and living styles have undergone a revolutionary transformation. This lays a solid foundation for the Ewenki hunters to develop a diversified livelihood and achieve wealth and prosperity. (Kong 1994: 36)

From the above passage, we can detect a powerful sense of passion, and feel a jubilant air regarding the settled residence at that time. Undoubtedly, for both the Ewenki hunters and the newly founded government of the People's Republic of China, the settlement of the Ewenki was a highly significant event. If we take in this account, we will be left with a strong sense that the Ewenki hunters finally achieved settled residence and finally bid farewell to the itinerant lives of nomadic herding and hunting in 1965, and that by doing so they left behind the barbarism and backwardness. However, when I interviewed the old educated Ewenki hunters, hunter Sword said:

'Jimide incident' was the direct cause for us to be moved further inland. Back then, the China-USSR relationship deteriorated, and the government was worrying that we were influenced by it and would flee to USSR. At that time, the Hulun Buir League formed the Hunting Area Work Team that they came to re-educate the hunters about socialism, and work to suppress the repercussion of 'Jimide incident.' They did some work to appease us. One of the jobs they did was to help the hunters develop new hunting areas. Some of the old hunters at that time felt that there was more game in the Alongshan region, so were willing to move further inland.

After the move to Alongshan, some officials began to persuade the hunters to live in fixed settlements. They reasoned that our production and living styles were too backward, and that we had remained in the phase of late primitive society. The Ewenki people in other places had experienced feudal society but we never had, and thus we were the most backward. The government intended to help us leap in one jump from primitive society into socialism. It was for our benefit. We were primitive and backward, and of course it was a good thing to enter advanced, civilized socialism! They said that a nomadic hunting lifestyle was primitive, barbaric, and backward. Only settled residence was civilized. So they built houses for us to have us settle down. We felt it was a good thing to have houses down the mountain. When we went down, we would have place to live in. At that time, the officials and leaders were very capable. They were sincere and were genuinely concerned for us hunters, and we also supported them.

When talking about the government's efforts to select a new place and the move to Aoluguya, the old hunters all expressed satisfaction with the relocation at that time. Hunter Butler said:

At that time, the country built brand new Mukeleng houses for us. The houses were tall and spacious and were of good quality. The site was well chosen too. The officials back then were very nice. They lived and ate with us in the mountains. They knew that we, hunters, are hunting for living. That move essentially helped us to open up new hunting areas. During the move to [old] Aoluguya, the government's policies were very beneficial to us. Back then, food coupons were in use. Each month we could receive

25 kg rice and white flour. The flour we received was refined wheat flour, whereas the forestry workers only got coarse grain flour. Additionally, each month we received more bean oil than they did. Many hunter families purchased cameras, bicycles, and several wristwatches. At that time, we all bought thick wool coats. Actually, wool coats in the forest easily got caught on things, but because the township leaders all wore wool coats, we did the same. When we had money, we also purchased floor rugs. Although they were not as warm as bear hides, it was an indicator of our wealth. We enjoyed excellent welfare then. Schooling and health clinic visits did not cost money. The students all received living allowances. Each of us male Ewenki hunters was a Forest Patrol worker and every month we were entitled to a Forest Patrol salary of 18 RMB. Later, it increased to 36 RMB. Women from outside all wanted to marry hunter men. Men from outside were also willing to marry hunter women.

From the above interview records, we can see that, although the hunters relocated to Aoluguya and owned Mukeleng houses, they did not give up their hunting lifestyle. In other words, during the time they lived at Aoluguya, they did not give up hunting. Other than the township officials, workers, and students, there were still many people who remained in the mountains living a traditional lifestyle of hunting and herding. However, as time went by, fewer and fewer people remained in the mountains to live a traditional lifestyle. Right before the ecological migration in 2003 there were about forty people still living in the mountains for most of the year.

Living in settled residence in old Aoluguya had a tremendous influence on the lives of the Ewenki hunters. One way they were affected was through the facilities and infrastructure that the government built. The infrastructure needed management and staff, so the government brought in workers, who increased the population in old Aoluguya. Another way the Ewenki were affected was through the good living conditions in old Aoluguya, which in turn attracted many outsiders, and this greatly expanded the scope of potential marriage partners who the Ewenki hunters could intermarry with. It also strengthened their ties with the outside world. In particular, the obligatory nine-year boarding school education provided by the government enabled all of the Ewenki hunters' school-age children to study for free. This practice separated Ewenki hunters' children from their traditional family environment, and gradually drew them away from traditional lifestyles.

Government Policy Transition at Old Aoluguya

"Hunting at the Forefront"

In 1967, during the heat of the Cultural Revolution, Aoluguya was organized into a commune. The Oriental Red Hunting Brigade was formed with its official policy to implement "Hunting at the Forefront: Protecting, Herding and Hunting Simultaneously."[7] All Ewenki hunters joined the commune by registering their assets. In 1968, in consideration of the fact that the Ewenki hunters had just emerged from the condition of "late primitive society," the government decided that they should help the Ewenki catch up with the socialist revolution. To accomplish this, the government divided them into categories based on social class status. This led to the creation of class enemies and enemies of the state, such as "high level reactionaries," "Russian revisionist spies," and "Japanese spies." When I asked the people who were denounced during the Cultural Revolution to tell me about the situation at the time, some of them were twisted with distress, and others did not want to recall that period of time at all, saying that it was simply too miserable and bitter.

Because the term "Ewenki Ethnic (Group)" was perceived as being a term that split society along lines of ethnic distinction, the words Ewenki Ethnic (Group) were removed from the official name of the Mangui Ewenki Ethnic Township. In 1969, under the influence of leftist guidelines, the Inner Mongolia governing region was dismantled, and the Eastern Three Leagues and Western Three Banners were put under the governance of neighboring provinces. Hulun Buir League, where the (old) Aoluguya Township was located, was put under the auspices of Heilongjiang Province. In 1973, under the leadership of Chairman Mao, ethnic policies started being implemented again and the ethnic self-governing areas that had been eliminated also gradually reverted to their original names. In June of 1973, the administrative system in the Aoluguya Ewenki Ethnic Township was reinstated with the approval of the Heilongjiang Province party committee. At the same time, the Argun Left Banner Revolutionary Committee made the decision that Mangui was to become a township and that the Ewenki Ethnic Township government would move to the settlement in (old) Aoluguya; its full name would be changed to The Aoluguya Ewenki Ethnic Township.[8]

In 1975, the Aoluguya Ewenki Ethnic Township celebrated its tenth anniversary of settled residence. At that time, the number of hunters residing in the township had increased to 186. A total of fifteen people worked as officials, teachers, business clerks and medical personnel in town. A total of six young hunters, both male and female, received education at second-level professional training institutions or received college education. Regarding economic production, over the previous ten years, the township had produced and turned in over 3,150 kg of dry reindeer antlers, 163 kg of red deer antlers, 53,872 fur hides, as well as many precious medical materials, like reindeer penises, reindeer placenta, bear gallbladders, and musk. The headcount of reindeer had also increased to 1,123, which was a 54 percent increase compared to ten years earlier. All sorts of service facilities like a tuberculosis prevention clinic, a school and a store were enhanced gradually. These created good conditions for the Ewenki people's health, education, and living convenience. At that time, the population of the entire (old) Ao Township reached a high of 375. During the ten years since the establishment of the (old) Ao Township, 215 people had moved in from outside. Of the Ewenki hunters, 26 people studied, worked or resided outside of the township.[9]

"Herding Reindeer at the Forefront"

In 1979, the Argun Left Banner sent a work team to the (old) Ao Township to conduct a comprehensive investigation in order to fully carry out the Party's ethnic policies and improve the development of the Ewenki hunters' group. At that time, the entire population of the (old) Ao Township had reached 470 people. Of them, 167 were Ewenki hunters (the total was 191 if it included those who worked and resided outside of the Ao Township), and 303 people were from outside the region. This revealed an increase of 88 people from the 1975 population of 215. The number of outsiders settling in the Ao Township continued to grow daily. These outsiders were generally migrant workers without fixed job, and were often referred to by the derogatory term *"mangliu."* The expanding exploration and exploitation of the Greater Khingan Range and the continual influx of the "mangliu," incurred disruption and damage to natural ecosystems and the concomitant decrease in the number of wild animals, which meant that the Ewenki hunting lifestyle could no longer be sustained. It was no longer possible to follow the government's economic development guidelines of "Hunting at the Forefront: Protecting, Herding and Hunting Simultaneously."

According to an investigation conducted in 1979, owing to logging, deforestation, and wildfires, Ewenki hunting production quickly declined and accounted for only 13 percent of the Oriental Red Hunting Brigade's annual income.[10] Conversely, income from reindeer antlers had reached a high of around 40 percent of the Hunting Brigade's annual income. The hunters' production activities began to change from a primary reliance on hunting to mainly herding and managing reindeer. Acknowledging the actual situation, the local government developed the guideline of "Herding Reindeer at the Forefront: Protecting, Herding and Hunting Simultaneously and Active Development of Diversified Modes of Production and Livelihood," which aimed to apply scientific knowledge and methods to reform the careless and primitive traditional management styles. The goal was to transform the Ewenki hunters' lives from what the government saw as an itinerant, almost vagrant lifestyle of "hunters-chasing-the-reindeer-around-the-forests" to a proper, civilized lifestyle in fixed residence.

However, at that time (in 1979), out of the 21 households who lived by herding reindeer, 13 households lived in the mountains most of the year to stay close to the reindeer, while another 8 households spent two thirds of their time each year in the mountains. In other words, of the 41 hunters' households in town, 51 percent of them were not able to reside in the township. As these changes were taking place, the Mukeleng houses built by the government in 1965 were by now in poor condition due to a lack of maintenance. In the hunter community, the number of widowers, widows, loners, invalids and disabled people had increased. As many as 11 households, or nearly 27 percent of the total number of households, were living in poverty. After the Cultural Revolution, the debt owed by hunters to the Production Unit for out-of-town medical services was over 8,000 RMB, yet the hunters' average income had declined to 284 RMB by 1978. In general, their quality of life had fallen significantly. This was reflected in the higher levels of alcoholism and an increase in the number of abnormal deaths. Social instability was affecting the children and the school enrollment was unstable.[11]

Aware of this situation, local and higher levels of government took measures to assist with the development of the (old) Ao Township and improve the Ewenki hunting people's economic and living conditions. In 1980, in order to improve hunting production levels, the government provided for the hunters a total of 72 semi-automatic rifles and 100,000 bullets. Tens of thousands of RMB was invested to rebuild the Mukeleng houses into more substantial structures of brick and tile. Power lines were laid from Mangui to the Ao Township; schools and dormitories were expanded, and a nursing home was opened. The (old) Ao Township was given permission to fell 1,000 cubic meters of timber each year, and with this new economic stimulus the Integrated Forest Product Mill was renovated. Tents, movable plank houses, generators and winter clothing were provided for the Ewenki campsites in the mountains. Experimental reindeer pens were built, and a contract production system for raising reindeer was adopted in 1983. In an effort to boost production and improve herds, scientific research on reindeer production was undertaken as well. At the same time, the local government responded quickly to organize rescue work after natural disasters occurred. For example, in June 1982 the region was hit by a rare and unusually heavy snowstorm that continued for three consecutive days and blanketed the hunters' camps and herding areas. It created a "white disaster" when the reindeer were unable to dig through the thick snow for food. The Hulun Buir League government immediately organized a rescue effort. Large quantities of fodder grass, bean-feed pellets, and other processed feeding materials were promptly transported to the disaster area to help the reindeer safely get through the "white disaster." In 1985, the reindeer faced another serious "white disaster." The League and Banner governments quickly provided funds of 55,000 RMB to help with rescue and relief efforts and once again the reindeer were able to safely get through this dangerous period. On 10 June 1985, at the invitation of the Argun Left Banner government, national experts and scholars congregated in Genhe and Aoluguya to conduct research on the scientific management of reindeer, including breeding selection and matching, improved breeding and rejuvenation, and domestication and herding methods. They also discussed the steps that should be taken to further improve and enhance the Economic Contract Responsibility System[12] (Hao 1994: 14).

On 1 September 1985, the hunters in the (old) Ao Township cele-brated the twentieth anniversary of settled residence. In order to improve the Ewenki hunters' living conditions in the mountains, the government set up twelve movable plank houses that provided a total living area of 280 square meters. Inside the houses were installed iron beds and iron furnaces. Portable electricity generators were installed at three hunters' sites. During the period of economic reform, through various forms of government assistance, the (old) Ao Township received a complete makeover and had a new, fresh appearance. In the brand new hunters' res-idences, the Ewenki could watch TV, a change that was indicative of how their previously isolated traditional lives in the forest were now making a transition to modernity. In 1995, before the thirtieth anniversary of settled residence celebration, to help enrich the Ewenki hunters' cultural lives in the mountains, the government equipped each campsite with a camping vehicle on top of which was mounted a TV satellite receiver. In the following years, the government continued to expend money on the Ao Township and its Ewenki Reindeer-Using Tribe.[13] Although the Ao Township was a small community of only several hundred people living in a forested area, it slowly became a community that was furnished with all manner of services and facilities.

"Forestry Processing as Supplementary"

In 1978, the Integrated Forest Product Mill (also known as the Second Light Industry Factory), a factory for the processing of timber, was established in the Ao Township. Having been granted a quota to cut 1,000 cubic meters of timber each year, this considerable source of income for the Ao Township grew annually because of the constantly rising price of timber. In 1988, production sales from the Mill amounted to 580,000 RMB, with a total profit of 220,000 RMB. In 1994, the Mill's production sales reached 960,000 RMB, with a total profit of 364,000 RMB. This factory cared about the Ewenki hunters and each year donated 40,000 RMB to support the hunting activities of the Ewenki and bolster their reindeer development and traditional lifestyle. As a result, this factory became the main economic resource of the (old) Ao Township (Kong 2002: 37). Because of the work opportunity that the Mill provided, many hunters and their families gave up hunting to work for the factory. From the statistical data, since 1979, although the hunters' population has always hovered around 160–170 people, the number of people living and hunting in the mountains has dropped significantly.

The profits from the Integrated Forest Product Mill were high and it provided free services to help the Ewenki hunters with things like transportation, antler cutting, and processing relating to reindeer production. As a result, despite the fact that the number of game obtained from hunting had become less and less since the 1990s, and the overall income from hunting had been continually dropping, the income from reindeer antlers had remained at a relatively high level. For the (old) Ao Township as a whole, the people's standard of living was among the highest in the entire Hulun Buir League area.

Notes

1. Here these surnames are converted from Mandarin counterparts. Suoluogong also spelled as Sologon; Bulituotian also spelled as Bulitotin; Kaertakun also spelled as Kaltakun; and Gudelin also spelled as Kudrin in other research books.
2. *Erchuanzi* is a term that refers to the children resulting from ethnically mixed marriages, specifically the children from the marriage of Ewenki Reindeer-Using Tribe members with another non-Ewenki.
3. Ust-Urov is the Russian name of the Qiqian area, sometimes in Chinese Pinyin: *Wu qi luo fu.*
4. Prior to the 1980s, the Ewenki people traditionally referred to the campsite as *urilen.* Later, however, the terminology changed and local people began to refer to the sites

as hunters' campsites (Pinyin: *lie min dian*). The transformation from "*urilen*" that were comprised of members related by blood to "Hunters' campsites" that were comprised of various family members united by practical and profit-based considerations appears to be connected with the implementation of the nationwide economic reform policy that emphasized the role of the market economy.

5. Mukeleng houses are constructed entirely out of wood and are built in a traditional Russian architectural style common throughout the forested border regions between Russian and northeast China.

6. These slogans "Meteoric Advances" (Pinyin: *yi bu deng tian*) or "Running Toward Socialism (Pinyin: *Pao bu jin ru she hui zhu yi*) were leftist, radical slogans of the people's communalization movement that began in 1958. But this communalization movement did not affect the Ewenki living in the Qiqian region. The Ewenki were only organized into people's communes (Pinyin: *Ren ming gong she*) after they moved to the old Aoluguya region in 1965.

7. This slogan encouraged the Ewenki to rely on hunting as their primary mode of production, while simultaneously working to preserve their environment and reindeer, and encourage herding, all for the purpose of furthering the socialist revolution.

8. Refer to: The notice about setting up the Mangui Township and the relocation of Ewenki to Aoluguya, issued by the Argun Left Banner, #58, 1973, Argun Left Banner Archives 1–26.

9. The data comes from the archives: The glorious victory of Chairman Mao's revolutionary course, presented by Jushan Bu at the tenth anniversary of the Ewenki relocation, 1 August 1975, Argun Left Banner Archives 1–26.

10. Prior to 1979, the Oriental Red Hunting Brigade's total income was derived from the following sources: 70 percent from hunting, 20 percent from the sale of timber, and 10 percent from the sale of reindeer antlers. Note: percentages are all approximations.

11. The data comes from the archives: The report about Aoluguya Ewenki Township, issued by the Argun Left Banner, #203, 1979; Aoluguya Township Revolutionary Committee Archives 1–26.

12. The Economic Contract Responsibility System was similar to the Household Responsibility System (Pinyin: *Jia ting lian chan cheng bao ze ren zhi*) that began to be implemented in agricultural areas throughout rural China in 1981.

13. Because wood plank houses were not conducive to disassembly and transportation through the forest, it was not long before the hunters abandoned them. The camping vehicle equipped with satellite TV also soon fell into disuse because there were few roads in the forest and the satellite signal reception was very poor. The government's investment in the plank houses and equipment was only useful for demonstrating the government's sincerity and concern about the Ewenki. But in terms of providing practical and useful aid, these expenditures were a waste of money.

Chapter 3

Ecological Migration Path

"Out of the Woods toward a Well-off Society"

⇒•⇐

Reasons Behind the Proposal for Ecological Migration

In order to address the problem of unbalanced development between the eastern and the midwestern regions of China, in the 1990s, the central government proposed the Grand Western Development Plan. Development planning in the western region has to take geographic and environmental conditions, such as the region's expansive mountainous terrain with relatively few types of grassland, into consideration. The region's extremely fragile ecological environment currently faces serious desertification. Most parts of the northwestern region suffer from drought and low forest and vegetation coverage. For example, forest coverage in Ningxia Province is only 1.54 percent, and is 4.33 percent in Gansu Province. Deforestation, conversion of fragile land to farmland and over-grazing have expedited the loss of forests and grasslands, which in turn have led to increased rates of desertification. According to recent statistics, 46 percent of the total area of Qinghai Province is facing serious soil erosion. In Shaanxi Province, the condition is even worse with 75 percent of the entire province facing soil erosion (Liu 2002). The poor ecological environment in the western region also constricts attempts to improve the lives of the population, among which live large groups of minorities. Most of them live in poverty and harsh environmental conditions.

The government believes that, to fundamentally change this situation and improve ecological conditions in the western region, it is necessary to change the production mode and lifestyle of these pastoralists and herders living in this area. The improvement of the ecological environment and the minimization of human damage to the environment can only be achieved by moving people and livestock out of the region and by implementing reforestation programs. With these considerations in mind, the government developed a policy of ecological migration to move highly dispersed populations out of fragile environments and relocate them to new villages and towns that are more ecologically sound (Meng and Bao 2004). The entire process of relocating migrants from their original places to new residences is a massive project requiring careful planning and engineering.

We can get to know the ecological migration policy in terms of its reasons and goals. The reason for implementing ecological migration is that the natural environment has suffered serious deterioration caused by human population beyond the carrying capacity of the ecosystem. The goal of ecological migration is to protect and improve environmental conditions and help the ecological migrants increase their overall productivity and standard of living. By implementing ecological migration, the maximum goal of the government is to achieve "ecological restoration, production improvement, and enhanced living standards; the perfect unification of ecological, economic and social profits." If not fully realized, at least the minimum goal should be achieved: "the gradual diminishment of ecological damage and gradual ecological restoration; the preservation of production and livelihood and gradual improvement."

The Aoluguya Ewenki ecological migration was carried out under such a historical background. However, Jianxiong Ge, the author of *History of Chinese Migrants* and professor at the History and Geography Research Center of Fudan University, argues that these Ewenki hunters living in the deep mountain forests cannot be classed as ecological migrants.

> If their hunting activities do not bring environmental pollution or cause only minimal damage, they should not be moved out in the excuse of the ecological protection. The government should provide only assistance and guide, even though their survival is very tough, or their production is very backward. Even if they are willing to relocate, they should belong to survival immigrants, instead of ecological immigrants. (Yidi 2003)

The important difference between survival migration and ecological migration lies in whether the population being relocated has caused serious damage to the original ecological environment or not. Survival migration refers to the migration where people are forced or voluntarily leave either because of a harsh environment or because they seek better economic development. Ecological migration refers to the migration where people are forced to relocate due to the severe ecological damage caused by the population.

In news reports, as well as local government reports and documents about the Aoluguya hunters' relocation, the phrase "ecological migration" was used extensively. Although the use of this phrase has been criticized and rejected by migration-research specialists and questioned by Aoluguya Ewenki hunters, in order to maintain consistency in terminology I will continue to use this phrase to describe the entire operation planned by the government. I caution readers to note that the meaning of the term used in this work has gone beyond the academic concept of ecological migration. I will use the term "(ecological migration) relocation," as it is used in the popular media in China to describe the event that occurred on 10 August 2003 when the government moved the Ewenki Hunters from old Aoluguya to new Aoluguya.

Until the eve of the relocation in 2003, the old Aoluguya had accommodated the Ewenki hunters for thirty-eight years. According to the 1965 census, the entire population of the Ao Township was comprised of Ewenki hunters; a total of 34 households and 126 people. In 1966, the government arranged for the Ewenki hunters to register as non-agricultural residents. In 1966, the total number of households in the Ao Township grew to 54, and the total population increased to 248, among which 171 were of Ewenki ethnicity (Kong 1994: 220). This shows that in the first year when the Ao Township was established, it drew a large number of outsiders to come and settle in the area, among which were government employees dispatched to assist the buildup of the Ao Township. According to the Ao Township census, on the eve of the 2003 relocation, there were a total of 179 households, with a total population of 498, among whom 232 were Ewenki.

According to the information I gathered, the ecological migration project was first proposed and documented by the local government, and was later carried out after being authorized by higher officials. As reported by the news media, the local government's goal regarding the ecological migration plan was to improve the Ewenki hunters' lives, change their lifestyle, protect forests and wildlife, and implement sustainable development. Simply put, the aim of relocation was twofold: first to improve the hunters' lives; second to protect nature. The relocation was undertaken because the community infrastructure at the original Ao Township residential site had severely deteriorated, and the Ewenki hunting lifestyle had caused serious damage to the natural and ecological environment. Based on the reason for relocation provided by the government—the deteriorating residential infrastructure and the goal to protect the natural environment—we can then consider relocation as both "ecological migration" and "survival migration." If this is the case, then why did the local government choose to use the term "ecological migration" rather than "survival migration?" What were the specific underlying causes for using the term "ecological migration?"

In order to gain access to the official documents, I first sought out the director of the Genhe County Ethnic Affairs Bureau. He provided a copy of the document that elucidated the significance of "ecological migration." The document was entitled "Changing modes of production; following a route for the settlement of the population; and raising reindeer in pens: The fundamental methods for improving the lives of Ewenki and bringing improved levels of wealth." He told me that the document was penned by the County People's Council deputy director, Mr Kong, and other officials had only made minor changes to it. Later, I obtained the original document, dated 18 March 2003, from Mr Kong. This was obviously not the report originally submitted as the application for undertaking "ecological migration," because the funding for the ecological migration was approved in March 2001. When I requested the original document, the director of the Ethnic Affairs Bureau regretted that the original copy no longer existed. At that time, they only submitted a simple report asking for funds to start the ecological migration. He said:

> This ecological migration project was of a grand scale. The central govern-
> ment provided 5.1 million RMB [5.7 million RMB if counting the nursing
> home and health clinic]. However, even that was not enough and the local
> government had to pay a portion of the costs. Genhe County had a tight
> financial budget and was forced to borrow a considerable sum to keep the
> construction going. Altogether the project cost over 11 million RMB.

After reviewing the document, he explained to me the significance of this ecological migration. I recorded the interview and later found his explanation to be quite consistent with the content of the document.

The following section outlines the content of the document and clearly lays out the government's perspective.

> Over the past fifty years, the Ewenki hunters have gone through enor-
> mous changes in all aspects of their lives ranging from production and
> living, to ideology and religious belief. They have achieved outstanding
> accomplishments. Their accomplishments serve as an example of the
> soundness of the Party's ethnic policies.
>   However, we should face the fact that to this day, there has been no fun-
> damental change in regard to the Ewenki hunters' lifestyles and reindeer

herding in the mountains. They still continue their traditional ways of roaming in the forests and allowing the reindeer to find food in the forests.

The document mentioned that in 2000, thirty reindeer were killed by wolves at one of the hunters' campsites in the mountains. Also, it provided yearly data of reindeer deaths due to trap hazards, getting lost, predation, disease, and other natural hazards. Moreover, the document described the living conditions at the hunters' sites:

> It is still as primitive as before. The rough, poor and backward situation has not changed. If any change at all, tents have replaced *cuoluozi*; also, sometimes there are vehicles to transport the Ewenki up and down the mountains. However, the situation is worse with regard to food. In the past, when there were more wild animals around, people could enjoy animal meats. Now there are fewer and fewer wild animals, many of which are protected from hunting. Therefore, even animal meat is rare. The regular meals at the hunters' camp are rice mixed with soy sauce. *Lieba* [a kind of Russian bread] coupled with pickles has become a common staple. According to the statistics, in 2002, net average income per person was 658 RMB, which is below the poverty line. It is truly the time to change the Ewenki hunters' production and lifestyles.

In regard to the application for an ecological migration fund, the material stated:

> In light of the government policies for ethnic groups with populations less than 100,000 to permanently get rid of poverty, and the Grand Western Development Plan, the Genhe County party committee and government decided to implement 'ecological migration' and relocate the entire group of Ewenki hunters out of the [old] Aoluguya region. The goal of migration is to improve their incomes and bring about improvements in the overall well-being of all of the Ewenki hunters, by changing their nomadic herding mode of production and lifestyle thoroughly, settling them down completely along the banks of the Xiwuqiya River and establishing the reindeer farming in fenced-in pens.
>
> According to social development theory, human societies develop from low levels to high levels. It is not possible for one ethnic group to stay forever at one social level. An ethnic group's culture is preserved and also enriched during development. An ethnic group cannot live forever at one social formation for the sake of preserving its traditional culture. Only when a people's livelihood and standard of living are improved can culture be passed down. When life is threatened, nobody would choose to preserve culture, instead everyone would choose to preserve life over culture. Normally speaking, underdeveloped ethnic groups have preserved more traditional cultures; whilst advanced ethnic groups

tend to have vibrant modern cultures. It is inevitable for the ethnic groups to develop; underdeveloped ethnic groups desperately need expedited development.

Therefore, the Genhe County party committee and government have decided to carry out entire group resettlements of the Ewenki hunters living in the [old] Aoluguya Township. This will be of important significance in thoroughly changing the reindeer herding mode of production in the mountains and enhancing the reindeer herders' production and living environment, increasing self-development skills, and developing the economy and productivity in the ethnic region. This represents the fundamental interests of general Ewenki hunters and exemplifies the essence of the 'Three Represents.'[1]

In 2001, the Ao Township ecological migration project began to select a new site. Out of respect for the opinions of the hunters, and after thorough investigation, research, and data gathering, the decision was made on June 30, 2002 to locate the new site at Sanchejian, the western suburban region of Genhe County. What impressed me most were several strong affirmative phrases in the document:

> Is it acceptable not to change the Ewenki mode of production? In short, the answer is NO.
> 1) Without changing the production method, it is impossible to speak of settlement.
> 2) Without changing the production method, it will be nearly impossible to diversify the economy.
> 3) The current backward production method hinders development in the population.
> 4) By changing the production method to reindeer farming in fenced-in pens, the economy of this ethnic region will develop more quickly.

The material clearly expresses the following views:

> Only through ecological migration can the production method be thoroughly changed.
> 1) Only through ecological migration can the Ewenki hunters completely give up living in the mountains and realize permanent settlement.
> 2) When reindeer are fenced in, their loss will be minimized, and this will allow the ethnic economy to develop.
> 3) Only through ecological migration to urban areas or close by, and living directly under the influences of urban economies, will the Ewenki hunters be able to quickly diversify their economic activities, and ethnic industries can be developed.
> 4) When the hunters leave the woods and put down their hunting rifles, wild animals and the natural environment will be protected.

As shown in the document excerpt below, the Genhe County government considered the need to preserve and develop traditional ethnic culture after the relocation.

> After the Ewenki hunters leave the forests we need to attach high value to the preservation and development of ethnic group cultures. We want to recognize ethnic cultures within the perspective of overall social development. As the society progresses and the times change, ethnic cultures gradually become refined and enriched; some unsuitable culture phenomena will slowly disappear. It is this way today as it was in the past.

The document continues by pointing out that traditional Ewenki leather clothing is no longer in use today. Traditional costumes are only worn for important festival days or performances. Tents replaced traditional *cuoluozi* at the hunters' sites. Buckets and bowls made from birch bark are seldom seen. Hunting tools like spears, sleds and shotguns are no longer needed. The traditional scene of reindeer pulling sleighs can now only be seen in paintings. Fewer and fewer Ewenki hunters can speak their ethnic language. The last shamaness has passed away, and none of the remaining Ewenki can perform the shaman dances or shaman songs. By listing the disappearance of these cultural phenomena, the document continues:

> The camps in the forests are not utopian places disconnected from this world; camps in the forests are not ideal places for preserving ethnic culture. Ewenki hunters continuously benefit from all manner of conveniences from modernization, and the Ewenki ethnic culture develops continuously.
>
> It is our belief that the faster the Ewenki hunters leave behind the forests camps and accept modernization, the faster its ethnic culture will develop.

As to how to preserve ethnic culture, the Genhe County government proposed building museums, an "Ethnic Group Customs Tour Village," and hunting parks. The government document also revealed some of their concerns about the shift in the Ewenki lifestyle from nomadic reindeer herding on the mountainside to raising reindeer in fenced-in pens in the new township site.

> Reindeer herding is the main economic resource for Ewenki hunters. In the transition from nomadic reindeer herding to raising reindeer in fenced-in pens, the hunters will need to adjust to changes in their mode of production and living style. To expedite the hunters' adjustment to these changes, we need to go through necessary rearrangements and changes in areas like policymaking, ownership of reindeer, the setting up of organizations,

and the supply of necessary services. Even more so, the Ewenki hunters will face major changes in the way they think; their ideology, modes of production, and the way they live. In the past, they herded reindeer in the forests camps, and finding feed grass for the reindeer was never a problem. Now, after immigrating to urban areas, the reindeer cannot go without daily feedings, which raises questions: where will they find a source of grass? Even with the provision of grass, will reindeer be able to adjust quickly? Are the reindeer accustomed to being fenced in? How will insects be driven away in the summer? Can the old contract system that operated within the collective ownership system adapt to the changes to the fenced-in pen method of raising reindeer? Can the new contract system adapt to the new feeding methods? Will the management and production methods and tools used in the mountains still be useable in the new environment? Will the people be able to get used to the new management and production methods and tools?

In regard to the change of production style, the Genhe County government developed a plan to raise reindeer in fenced-in pens. It specifically pointed out:

The changes in the hunters' mode of production and lifestyle mark the end of the ethnic group's roaming and hunting era, and the beginning of a new era. Old thinking and views cannot change overnight but will develop gradually to form a new life ideology. This requires us to undertake work by implementing new ideologies, to help the hunters improve their views, liberate their thinking, refresh opinions, and help them to progress with time. For example, this will be done by: forming ecological migration work groups, integrating with the hunters; eating, living and laboring together, understanding their thoughts, and working in the right direction, until the Ewenki hunters can completely adjust to the new production and living style. If we ignore these key points, there will be a backlash and we will face more challenges. The consequence will be the failure of goodwill, a loss of trust, and the hunters will be drawn further away from improving their economic status and overall well-being.

The Genhe County government also envisioned plans to raise reindeer in fenced-in pens:

Once reindeer are kept in pens, scientifically herding reindeer will no longer be an empty phrase. Back when reindeer were allowed to freely roam throughout the forests to seek food, they could find food on and off, but only enough for survival. Once reindeer are raised in pens, they will be divided into groups according to gender, age, and the goals of herding. They will be fed by fixed amounts at fixed times. The feeding time and quantity will be strictly regulated and the food will be a scientific mixture offering balanced nutrition. It will be necessary to take into consideration the gradual change in the reindeer diet. Unique reindeer, male reindeer during mating time, pregnant reindeer and baby reindeer are all fed differently according to strict management methods. Protection and treatment of reindeer diseases will be required for herders. The hunters have accumulated folk methods and experience with regard to common diseases that reindeer might be stricken with when living in the forests. After fencing in, we will discover some diseases that have not yet been identified. To prevent such diseases, herders will need to take precautions and apply treatments in daily feeding. Even some of the common diseases when reindeer were raised in the forest may require new forms of treatment under the new conditions. If the hunters cannot learn the scientific ways of feeding reindeer, then it will be difficult to accomplish significant increases in the reindeer population.

About the hunters' future employment, the Genhe County government also mentioned:

Ewenki hunters walk out of the forests into the broad world outside. Their employment opportunities will be greatly increased in comparison to their lives in forests. Specifically, hunters with unique talents can take advantage of their gifts, to create traditional crafts, leather clothing, and paintings. They could also perform singing; work in transportation; prepare ethnic foods; engage in making handicrafts like carving and statue-making, and undertake diversified economic activities. There will no longer be a singular focus on a reindeer-herding livelihood. Hunters who are more ambitious will have the chance to exhibit their skills.

Last, the document pointed out the difficulty of reforming the Ewenki hunters' mode of production, but expressed optimism:

The change of production style sometimes is more difficult to realize than the change in social systems. For an ethnic group, this is a question of life or death. Throughout history there have been countless ethnic groups flourishing and prospering during changes in their production styles, and countless groups have persevered and survived amid changes in production styles. Nevertheless, there have also been countless ethnic groups that have disappeared into oblivion during the changes of production style. Today, because of the ecological migration process, the Ewenki hunters are faced with changes in their production styles, and must adapt to new levels of social development. They will eventually overcome the difficulties presented in this progress, and they will develop with time. They will definitely flourish and prosper, and realize an improved well-off life for the group as a whole.

From this document, it can be seen that according to the perspective of the local government, feeding reindeer was a critical issue and was directly connected to the success or failure in changing the hunters' mode of production. This aspect reflects that the government took notice of hunters' primary concerns—"We cannot live without reindeer; otherwise the Reindeer-Using Tribe Ewenki will not exist." Interestingly, some people felt that the lack of development among the Ewenki hunters was directly caused by the reindeer and implied that the Ewenki must abandon reindeer herding if they are to progress. However, no matter what the reasons are, at present, the reality is that both the local government and the Ewenki hunters are not willing to abandon reindeer herding.

For me, this document was not enough at all. It mainly discussed the significance of the ecological migration. However, in order to understand the entire process, I needed to learn more about how the plan was actually implemented. Later, I learned that the document was standard material, commonly provided to reporters and the media. The "significance" of ecological migration is only one aspect of the government's defense of such migration. As we know the significance of changing the Ewenki lifestyle, why did the government choose this moment? Also, why not change the lifestyle at old Aoluguya? Can the relocation really change the lifestyle? This document could not answer my questions.

After a lengthy stay at the Ao Township, I had made several friends in Genhe as well. One friend was the head of the department supervising this relocation. He shared with me other reasons behind the county government's application for ecological migration:

> The old Ao Township government building has cracked walls, is no longer safe, and needs reconstruction; the electrical grid is outdated and needs reconstruction as well; the dam has not been properly maintained for a long time, so presents a possible flood risk to the old Ao Township, which needs repair—all of these things need funds. However, Genhe is a forestry county-level city without other industries. Over the past couple of years, a Natural Forest Preservation Project has been implemented, which has led to a sharp decrease in the amount of forest that can be logged. Many forestry workers have been laid off and those who still have jobs are paid quite low, with monthly income between 300 to 400 RMB. Genhe County has a total population of 170,000, but in 2004 the county's financial income stood at only 71,910,000 RMB, which is even less than the yearly profit earned by the Hulun Buir college's school-run enterprise. Apparently, Genhe is a poor county and has no funds to support the old Ao Township. Thus, Genhe government applied for the 'ecological migration' fund in the National Grand Western Development Plan. In fact, it is not about the hunters, but about Genhe County's financial difficulties. The fund can only

be awarded in the name of the hunters. The Ewenki hunters are indeed the only hunting tribe remaining in all of China. With such a unique ethnic group in Genhe, the county government had to take advantage of it.

Hulun Buir College donated several computers to the Ao Township government for the celebration of the ecological migration. When the computers could be connected to the Internet, my friends who worked for the Ao Township government welcomed me to use a computer to go online sometimes. One day, as I used a computer in the township office to send emails, I could not help but notice a file on the desktop entitled "Ecological migration situation summary." With the permission from the township head, I got the document.

This document provided "the reasons behind the Ao Township ecological migration" from the government's perspective. I have included a section of the document below.

The reason behind the implementation of the ecological migration in Ao Township is based upon five aspects:

The first aspect is about production and livelihood. For many years, the hunters lived in a state in which they raised the reindeer naturally in a way of extensive management. Because of inbreeding among the reindeer, as well as losses caused by wolves and trapping, the reindeer quality degenerated and the population decreased. The total headcount hovered at around 800 for many years. Meanwhile, due to the decreasing forest coverage every year and damages to the ecological environment, the number of wild animals also dropped sharply. The old Ao Township is located in a nature preservation district within which, according to the governmental regulations, the animal and plant resources are strictly protected. Genhe County also began to apply protection policies that banned hunting. The traditional hunting mode of production could no longer be maintained and the hunters faced deteriorating conditions. In 2003, the average hunter's annual income was less than 1,000 RMB.

The second aspect is about the geographical environment. The old Ao Township is located at the junction of the Jiliu River and the Aoluguya River. In recent years, the ecological environment has deteriorated and the rivers often change their course, resulting in severe riverbank erosion. This has led to frequent floods every year during the flood season, and has presented a serious threat to the security of hunters' lives and assets. For many years, hunters have been accustomed to living in loose household units in the mountains. Their living conditions are simple and shabby; 80 percent of the hunters suffer from rheumatism. Also, there is a high incidence of tuberculosis among humans and animals in the area.

The third aspect is about weakened public service facilities. Located far away from urban areas, the Ewenki hunters live in rough conditions with a very low population. The financial services, postal services, commerce and other public services facilities that were established during the planned economy period have been impacted to certain degrees by the market economy system. After the financial organizations turned into commercial banks, they all moved away from the Ao Township. In order to get cash or deposit money, people have to travel dozens of kilometers to Mangui. Daily living needs and goods also have to purchase from Mangui. Postal services have shrunk, communication infrastructures now lag behind—even to this day mobile phones have no signal there.

The fourth aspect is about basic infrastructure. The Ao Township dam has been lacking repairs for years. It can no longer ward off the pressures of the Jiliu River and Aoluguya River; it is in urgent need of rebuilding. The power lines are outdated and are waiting to be replaced. The township government building has suffered severe frost damage; windows and doors are deformed; it is considered a dangerous structure. The school, museum, culture center and health clinic are all in need of repairs. The conservative estimate of funds needed for the above facilities is 20 million RMB.

The fifth aspect is about the Ewenki ethnic group's development as a whole. There are now only 248 Ao Township hunters. Due to living habits, economic conditions and other reasons, they have difficulty getting married. If no actions are taken in a timely manner, in a short time the Ewenki Reindeer-Using Tribe will face the danger of extinction.

In summary, without ecological migration it will be impossible to lift the Ao Township hunters out of poverty and improve their income and living conditions; it will be impossible to resolve these historic problems effectively and it will be impossible to improve the entire Ewenki ethnic group quality, not even to mention the realization of building an all-round well-off society. Thus, ecological migration must be implemented.

In order to transform the backward conditions in the Ao Township, protect the environment, advance the ethnic development in economy and culture, and realize the goal of common wealth and well-being, under the guidelines of the National Western Development Policy and the policy regarding ethnic minorities with populations of less than 100,000 people, the Genhe County party committee and government have decided to carry out ecological migration for all Ewenki hunters.

Later, when I attended a dinner party with the Ao Township leaders and talked about this document, they told me that the five reasons mentioned in the document were real. The Ao Township government presented these problems to the Genhe County government, but had no idea what type of solutions the county might provide. The county leaders proposed relocating the hunters as a solution to the problems because they would be able to take advantage of the large amount of funds that were being poured into the Grand Western Development Plan. The county leaders suggested that, by stating the cause of relocating the Ewenki hunters as "ecological migration" in order to protect the environment, the county would have a good chance of obtaining the funding they needed. Moreover, according to the document outlining the five reasons, the ecological migration did not even really qualify as "ecological migration," but could only be regarded as "survival migration." Furthermore, not all Ewenki migrants were voluntary migrants in this relocation.

The Steps Taken by Government for Ecological Migration

The Decision Process of the Relocation

Several hunters who worked in the Ao Township told me that the relocation organized by the county was essentially a "fait accompli." I could not understand its meaning. They explained to me: "The county had already secured money for the ecological migration, and then notified the township. The township government had to persuade the hunters to relocate, and then began to do a little inquiry and questionnaire. Before that, no one in the township knew this migration plan."

The township head had said that the county had previously called to inquire about the number of hunter households in the Ao Township. At that time, the township leaders did not realize that the county was soliciting this information for relocation; even they had no idea at all that they had been targeted for "ecological migration." Therefore, they reported to the county the number of Ewenki hunters recorded in 1960 by the State Ethnic Affair Commission—31 hunter households. This later caused serious trouble when housing was assigned to hunter families—there were not enough houses.

After the township government learned about the relocation plan, the county asked it to undertake a specific investigation about the hunters. The investigation was carried out using surveys that covered four questions in addition to interviewees' basic information. The questions were: 1) With regard to the current situation in the Ao Township, do you agree with entire-group ecological migration? 2) To which area of Genhe County do you think the entire group should relocate in order to offer a better future for the development of the Ao Township? 3) At the site you choose, what commercial business would be of benefit to the economic advancement of the Ao Township? 4) After the entire group has been relocated, how do you think reindeer should be herded and managed?

In the actual survey process, each interviewer and interviewee signed the questionnaire sheet and talked face to face. The township government required residents who were illiterate to impress their fingerprints onto the questionnaire sheet to avoid any potential errors. Interviewees were over eighteen years old with legal status as adults. To conduct the study, the township formed seven workgroups that undertook the survey at four hunters' sites and three residential committees. They paid three visits to each hunters' site. When I asked about the survey results and the original questionnaires for the township leaders, I was told, "The questionnaires were taken by the county. I cannot recall any specific results of the survey, but the majority of the hunters agreed to relocate."

Eventually, with the help of Mr Kong, I obtained the sample and partial survey results. In 2002 when the survey was conducted, there were 498 regular residents in the Ao Township, including people who lived outside the Ao Township but were still registered as residents. Among them, 238 were Ewenki people, of which 169 were Ewenki hunters and 69 were Solon Ewenki. The subject of this survey was meant for the whole township of 498 people, including the Ewenki hunters and other ethnic people living in Aoluguya. However, the actual number of people who participated was 244, and 243 people agreed to ecological migration and hoped the new site would be located close to Genhe County. Of the total 169 Ewenki hunters, 106 of them met the survey criteria of being aged eighteen and above, but only 67 hunters participated in the survey, which accounted for 39.6 percent of the total population of 169 Ewenki hunters and 27.5 percent of the 244 people surveyed, and 63.2 percent of the 106 Ewenki who met the survey criteria. Of those who were eighteen years or older but did not participate in the survey, the reasons given for their non-participation were: farming in other areas, sick, working in other areas, living in other areas, schooling in other areas, out hunting, in military services, being arrested, in prison, and retired.

The original questionnaires with answers to other questions could not be found, so I asked the hunters, letting them recall the answers and the survey as accurately as possible. A talkative male hunter who was a high school graduate warmly shared with me his memories:

> At that time, we had just learned the government would relocate the hunters and everyone was excited. This was because in the 1950s and 1960s when the government relocated the hunters, we moved to better hunting areas and the hunters were happy in both instances. So we thought this time would be so too. Later, the township came to do the survey; they told us that the nation was working on 'ecological migration,' and the hunters would be moved out of the hunters' sites in the forests and begin to herd reindeer in fenced-in pens. Upon hearing this, some of the old hunters were not willing to move. One reason was that they were used to their hunting lives in the forests and wanted no changes; another reason was they did not

believe that fencing-in the reindeer would be successful. This was because the government tried fencing-in before, but the results were not good.

When the township conducted the one-on-one survey, the officials did a lot of persuading, mainly to encourage the hunters to leave the hunters' sites. They promised that raising reindeer in fenced-in pens would be good for increasing reindeer herds. They also emphasized that hunters no longer had to live a tough life in the mountains. At that time, the first topic in the survey was asking if we agreed with the entire Ao Township ecological migration. I remember this topic clearly. Some hunters answered, 'I disagree, and so there is no need to finish the rest of the questionnaire'; but the township interviewer said, 'If you disagree with ecological migration for entire group migration, it means you agree that only the hunters should emigrate. But if you agree with ecological migration for the entire group, then it means you agree that all of the residents of the [old] Ao Township should emigrate. So no matter how you reply, you still need to answer the rest of the questions.' This showed the relocation was a sure thing. The only uncertain part was who would be moved, and where to move. As to where to relocate, the county also provided several choices. One was to move to Mangui Township, which was close to old Aoluguya; another one was to move near Genhe County. Being close to an urban area was the goal—to become urbanized and modernized.

The township employees were all willing to move closer to Genhe County because their homes were almost in Genhe, and so they wanted to be close to Genhe and live more conveniently. However, some of the old hunters did not want to move near Genhe [urban area] because they had once roamed to Genhe and found very little lichen there, and so the reindeer did not like to stay there. But both the county and the township painted a good future. They promised that after moving close to Genhe the reindeer would be raised inside fenced pens, and there would be special hands hired to feed the reindeer. All the hunters needed to do was to hold their liquor bottles and watch the reindeer happily. Furthermore, at the new site, we would be provided with spacious housing as large as 70–80 square meters, and the houses would have central-heating systems. The lifestyle would be like urban lives. The promise was tempting, and the conditions offered were very attractive, so the young hunters were all willing to move to Genhe. Old hunters, like Maruia Suo, who resolutely refused to move were very few. Some old hunters were just followers; they had heard other people say good things about moving to Genhe and so they agreed to move along. Later, the people no longer dwelt on whether to move or not; all they thought about was where to move to. They wanted to pick a great location.

In the beginning, the county's workgroup called together the residents for a discussion meeting where they offered to move us to the place four-and-half kilometers from Mangui. That place used to be a cemetery— it did not feel good from our superstitious point of view. So the hunters turned that down. Because of this, several hunters got together and skipped the authority of the township and the county and went directly to complain in Hailar [where the higher municipal government lies]. They demanded that either the hunters should be relocated to a nice place or no relocation at all. Later in Hailar, the Hulun Buir City government had a meeting and decided to respect the hunters' choice and allowed us to choose a site. After coming back to the township, some of the people who worked as township employees lobbied for moving near Genhe—they wanted to live in Genhe downtown. Actually, some old hunters were not willing to move, but nobody listened to them. Thinking back, all of those salaried people wanted to move to Genhe. Everything became convenient for them, but inconvenient to the real hunters.

The hunter's narrative provided a good overview of the situation from the hunters' perspective. Every hunter I interviewed voiced the same opinion. During the relocation, the salaried Ewenki hunters were in an awkward situation. On one side they had inseverable blood ties with the other hunters, so after relocation when their relatives were not happy at all with the relocation they felt upset and disturbed by this. On the other hand they also felt that their lives in the Genhe County seat were much improved because they could afford to have a house in downtown Genhe, and they were satisfied with the increased level of convenience compared to their previous lives in old Aoluguya. Due to such a conflicting and complicated quandary, they all regretted the relocation afterward. They said, "We never expected that the reindeer-herding hunters would suffer so much after moving down. Had we known beforehand, we would not have agreed to move."

In the eyes of the Ao Township government, the salaried Ewenki people were the main focus of persuasion during the questionnaire survey. This was because the salaried Ewenki had a pretty clear idea about the benefits they would gain from the relocation, so the government's targeted persuasion was effective. Once the salaried workers were convinced, they were then asked to persuade the other hunters. Since all Aoluguya Ewenki are relatives far or near, it was much easier for those salaried workers to discuss issues with the other hunters than for the government officials. After the relocation, jobless Ewenki hunters denied the "hunter identity" of the Ewenki hunters who had jobs. One reason for this was that the jobless Ewenki hunters felt the employed Ewenki hunters did not belong to the same interest group as they did. The jobless Ewenki hunters felt they had been tricked; they believed that the people with salaried jobs benefited from this relocation, including the salaried Ewenki hunters. Although before relocation the salaried Ewenki people and other Ewenki hunters mutually acknowledged each other's identity as "hunters," things changed after the ecological migration.

Not all of the reindeer-herding hunters had been persuaded; some of them doubted the feasibility of raising reindeer in enclosed stockade pens and were hesitant about moving. But in the end, through the government's repeated persuasion, and generous offers, they also agreed to move. However, there was one old woman who refused to answer the question on "whether you agree or disagree with the entire group's ecological migration" during the questionnaire survey. This was Maruia Suo—she resolutely rejected the relocation. She said, "Raising reindeer in fenced-in pens cannot work. Did the government not try this before? They took away our reindeer and that caused the reindeer's death. We did not even get the dead bodies in the end. If fencing-in the reindeer could work, then why would we have waited until now?" At last, when the ecological migration was carried out, all other hunters left and moved down; only the campsite led by Maruia Suo remained behind.

The Actual Installation of the Migration Project

Establishing the project

Relocating an entire community is an immensely complex and multifaceted project, regardless of where it is undertaken. From conception to completion of the plan, the Ao Township ecological migration project took three years. The leader of the Ao Township described to me the entire process in detail:

> Due to the poor infrastructure and material conditions of the old Aoluguya site, in 2001 the Ao Township government applied to the county government for funds for repairs. Genhe has always been a county-level district with forestry as the main industry. In recent years, due to the "Natural Forest Preservation Project" rolled out by the nation, many forestry workers in Genhe were laid off. Genhe's financial status was in poor shape and the funds needed for the Ao Township's maintenance and repairs were far beyond what Genhe's financial budget could afford. Right at that time the nation initiated the Grand Western Development Plan, a fund that included the provisions for ecological migration. Therefore, the county's heads thought that instead of fixing the old Aoluguya site, it would be better to have the entire Ao Township "ecologically emigrated." This solution would provide resources to cover the massive expenses, and thus solve the whole problem. As a result, the county applied to the Inner Mongolia Autonomous Region to establish the project.
>
> With much effort through various parties, the Autonomous Region's Planning Committee approved the project, and issued the formal document (No. 1080, 2001) "Approval of Implementation Plan for Genhe County

2001 Ecological Migration and Location Change Poverty-Alleviation Migration Pilot Project," and the document (No. 1246, 2002) "Approval of the Modified Implementation Plan for Genhe County 2001 Ecological Migration and Location Change Poverty-Alleviation Migration Pilot Project." The final approval of project investment was 9.8 million RMB, consisting of 5.1 million one-time national funding and 4.7 million raised by the county. The designated relocation site is Sanchejian—the suburb in Genhe County.

Site Selection

According to the requirement of the superior, the Genhe County party committee held many regular committee meetings to discuss the Ao Township migration issue. After many debates, presentation of evidence and data, repeated consultation with the hunters, and on-the-spot inspection of hunter representatives, the location for the new site was decided. The township head said:

> Before the relocation was approved, we had solicited advice from the hunters. At that time we conducted a survey. Hunters who agreed to relocate all signed up and those who could not write all left an imprint of their fingerprint as their signature. The majority of the hunters all agreed to relocate.
>
> The county paid high attention to the site selection. Regarding the selection of a new site, we went through three major changes between 2000 to May 2003. Eventually the site Sanchejian in the western suburb of Genhe County was selected. Our initial choice was at a site west of the Mangui Township, but this was dropped because of frost problems. The second choice was a site 4.5 km away from Mangui, on the way to the old Ao Township; but that site was dropped because the hunters were against it. During this period suggestions were made for sites at Niuerhe, Haolipu, Sanchejian, and several other places. On March 19, 2003, the hunter representatives inspected Sanchejian with the company of the head of the County United Front Work Department, the Vice Chairman of the County Political Consultative Committee, and the head of County Ethnic Group Affairs. The hunters felt that as the government officials had said Sanchejian offered a large open area with the mountains on three sides and near the crystal-clear Xiwuqiya River, and convenient transportation to the downtown area, schools and hospitals, finally, the hunter representatives agreed on Sanchejian as the new Ao Township site.
>
> The county leaders thought that the new Ao Township site near Genhe County and the No. 301 provincial road, would not only have enough space to build reindeer living and feeding areas with the convenient transportation and thus contribute to the growth of reindeer herds; but also, the proper distance from the county would help to maintain the

ethnic characteristics of the township. As such, the county submitted its report to the superior; eventually, the plan was approved to build the new Ao Township at Sanchejian.

Project Construction and Ideology Mobilization

After receiving approval from the Inner Mongolia Autonomous Region Planning Committee, Genhe County first moved out some of the original residents of Sanchejian, demolished many old houses, and leveled the ground. The next step involved soliciting bids for the project and starting construction. The Ao Township government provided me with data showing that construction of housing and infrastructure for the Ao Township ecological migration project began in July 2002 and was completed in July 2003. The total investment was 16 million RMB, of which the central government contributed 5.1 million with the rest provided by the county government. The main construction site, occupying an area of 360,000 square meters, included 31 residential buildings that would provide housing for 62 households. Each household was 50 square meters, with an indoor washroom, central heating, and running water. There were a total of 48 reindeer pens, each pen having an area of 350 square meters. Other construction included one 800 square meter office building, one 1,229 square meter museum, and a 560 square meter warehouse for the processing of reindeer antlers. Transportation through the complex was facilitated by the construction of a 2,400 meter asphalt road.

When introducing the Ao Township project to outsiders, the Genhe County leaders would invariably begin by emphasizing:

> We adhered to very high standards throughout all stages of construction of the new township site. Our goal was to improve the standard of living of the people to the national standard of 'modern and well-off,' to develop ecotourism and stock-raising as the primary industries, and construct a community that was both modern and ethnic; which represented the culture of the Ewenki hunters. After long periods of planning and a flurry of construction, we completed the main sections of the project, including the Hunters' houses, the warehouse, the school, the museum, the government building, and the reindeer pens. The new site features a closely knit layout. There were a total of 62 Hunters' houses, each of which has one bedroom, one living room, one restroom, one kitchen, one storage room, and one outdoor yard. Electricity, phone, cable, water and heat were all provided.

The county and township heads were all satisfied with the new Ao Township construction. The basic construction project was an important part of the overall plan. The government officials also stressed that working to change the hunters' mindset and convince them of the value of modernity was of equal importance during the relocation process.

The township head explained that once the migration project had been approved, the township leaders split into two groups. One group, led by the head of the township party committee—the highest political authority in the township—supervised and inspected the construction progress. Another group, led by the head of the township government— the second highest political authority in the township—did the political propaganda work when inquiring about the demands and desires of the hunters who were unwilling to emigrate.

Media Propaganda

The Genhe County government placed strong emphasis on the importance of media propaganda throughout the ecological migration. The media section belonging to the county party committee propaganda department conducted many interviews and broadcasts regarding the migration relocation.[2] A special news report column was set up on the Genhe County website to report breaking news regarding the migration project, and a news feed was provided to the *Inner Mongolia Daily*. The ecological migration event received wide publicity and attracted both domestic and international news media. The media reported not only on the relocation, but also on the changing lifestyle of the Ewenki hunters. Several special nightly news programs covered this topic. Furthermore, from 8 August until 12 August, China Central Television (CCTV) produced a series of reports on how the hunters were leaving their traditional lifestyle and coming down the mountain to live in modernity. The reports were broadcast on various news channels. The most influential was the Comprehensive Channel, the International Channels and the News Channel where the coverage continued by the hour. The Culture and Art Hour program on the News Channel also broadcast two special eighteen-minute programs. The county head and township head were extremely proud of all of this media coverage because it helped to create in the public mind an awareness of Aoluguya as the home of the exotic Ewenki hunters and helped to establish Aoluguya as a "brand name" for the future development of tourism resources. The township head spoke proudly about the tremendous media attention that had been focused on the Ao Township relocation:

> Honestly speaking, this relocation was forced in such a hurry, mostly due to the media. Shortly after the completion of major projects here, all the TV stations and newspaper reporters swarmed into the town much earlier;

before we had time to paint these houses. Senior journalists from the CCTV news department were the first to arrive in the Ao Township on July 21. This forced us to expedite the next process, and it was so hastened that both officials and the residents suffered. Days before the official reloca-tion date, the leaders went up to the mountain campsites to help hunters track down their reindeer. There was heavy rain that day, and the hunters were all impressed by the fact that the leaders had come up and were work-ing in the downpour to help round up the reindeer. It rained again on the date of the relocation. To cooperate with the TV station's film schedule, the hunters waited for quite some time in the rain before they began moving into their new houses. By the end we were all exhausted. Of course we must go through the relocation anyways, but were it not for the media bombardment, we wouldn't have moved so early. We probably would have postponed it for another month or so. That way, things would have gone more smoothly, and the hunters would not have complained about the empty new houses in which nothing had been installed.

The township head asked me, "Now that you have seen the hous-ing provided for the hunters, what do you think about it?" I replied, "The houses are quite attractive and are much better than the little motel I stayed at. Both the restrooms and kitchens are quite modern. However, the houses are somewhat small." The township head replied:

> Even journalists from the capital often exclaim how beautiful the houses are here! The houses are small, but we have no other options. We had only limited funding for the project and so it was impossible to build bigger houses. There is another problem. Genhe County can only offer three years of free heating for the hunters' new houses. In this region, the winter is long and the heating period is eight months from mid September to mid May, so the costs for the heat supply are very high. If the government starts to charge heating fees in three years, the cost is going to be a burden for the hunters. If the houses were bigger, then the costs would be even higher.

Outtakes of the Migration Project

To learn more about the ecological migration project, I interviewed the retired deputy director of the County People's Council, Mr Kong. He had been involved in the project from its initial planning stage to the actual moving stage, and had retained a keen interest in the project even after retirement. He told me that the Genhe County government was seriously committed to the project and had undertaken careful con-siderations at each stage of the planning. However, several twists and turns were encountered during the course of selecting a new site. He explained:

Initially, nobody expected to move to Genhe [the current suburban site]. The search for a new site was focused on finding a suitable place near Mangui. Indeed, many hunters felt quite satisfied about the site 4.5 km from Mangui. However, around seven or eight hunters disagreed. They went to Hailar together to complain to the Hulun Buir Ethnic Affairs Commission. Then, a meeting was held at Hulun Buir City to discuss the site selection. Later, the hunters made a proposal saying, 'Is it not the goal to realize modernization? If so, then we should move closer to the city. Let us move to Genhe urban area.' Once the idea had been tossed around, people started to consider moving to the Genhe urban area.

The leaders of the Genhe County party committee and government held many meetings to discuss the site selection issue and negotiate with the hunter representatives. Genhe County leaders had to take into consideration not only the Ewenki hunters, but also the concerns of Genhe County residents. Initially, the hunters favored a place on the south side of the Genhe County seat, but the county leaders did not approve because the site they wanted was the area from which Genhe's drinking water supply comes from. If the hunters raised reindeer in that area there would be a danger of contaminating the water supply with the tuberculosis bacteria carried by the reindeer. So, they had to be relocated downstream of the urban water supply. After negotiations with the hunter representatives, Sanchejian was officially chosen as the new site. The selection of Sanchejian was not bad. To the west lay the Xiwuqiya River, and to the north were mountains. In 1962, the National Forestry Department deputy minister paid an inspection visit to Sanchejian and had highly praised it.

As soon as the location of the new site was decided, the associated departments immediately began to organize the demolition work at Sanchejian in order to prepare for the construction of the new community. Altogether, over a hundred original households in Sanchejian were expelled and the old structures were demolished. The government paid out 1.14 million RMB in compensation to the expelled residents. On 9 July 2002, the County party committee and government set up the Ao Township ecological migration project Construction Command Center that was to oversee all work involved in the migration project. On 12 July, after the bidding auction, three companies were awarded the bids for the construction project of the Ao Township. On 27 July, the groundbreaking ceremony was held.

Mr Kong had always kept a deep concern for the Ewenki hunters. He was a highly observant man who systematically recorded in his journal all manner of changes that took place in the Ao Township. From Mr Kong's journals, I learned about the overall situation in the community in the days just prior to the relocation.

In order to guarantee a smooth relocation on 10 August, the government leaders went up to the mountain camps on 5 August to check on how preparations for the relocation were proceeding. The hunters' raised their concern about difficulties that they were likely to face in the new community. In response, the government leaders suggested that each hunter family would be assigned a work unit of Genhe that could provide assistance. Their primary concern was whether the reindeer could survive if they lived in fenced-in pens. To allay their concern, county officials assured them that they could continue to herd reindeer in the mountains close to the new site and this would help them to adjust in the transition to the use of fenced-in reindeer pens. The hunters were aware that after they moved to the city the police would confiscate their hunting rifles. But what concerned them was that when they herded the reindeer back to the mountains, they would have no weapons at all and thus be unable to defend the reindeer from other wild animals. In response, county officials promised to relay Ewenki concerns to the superior and stated that a probable solution would be to allow a rifle to be kept at each mountain campsite for the protection of people and reindeer.

At the new Aoluguya, a total of 62 houses were built and assigned a number from one to sixty-two. When the county applied for funding for ecological migration, they had simply used the year 1960 census data and reported the number of hunter households as thirty-one. So when construction began, they originally only built thirty-one houses. When they found out that in fact there were far more people than houses, one of the residences was remodeled and divided into two residences. The 62 houses were designated as "Hunters' houses," designed to hold, at the most, four people each, and were paid for out of funds assigned for "ecological migration." However, the thirty-four "non-hunter" households, who also used to live at old Aoluguya, were not qualified to receive a new Hunters' house in the relocation plans. They were only entitled to receive relocation funds but had to move out of old Aoluguya. That was because the Genhe County government had already sold the old Ao Township site to a real estate company.[3] Additionally, the ecological migration project did not build houses for Ao Township employees. Faced with many worries and concerns emanating from the hunters, employees, and other residents, the Genhe County Ecological Migration Workgroup were busy explaining the situation and calming frayed nerves for days prior to the relocation.

In Mr Kong's journals I found a detail about the relocation on 10 August 2003. A total of twelve semitrailer trucks transported eleven hunter households with thirty-seven people and 260 reindeer to the new Aoluguya. The moving convoy had set off from the old Aoluguya site and traveled 200 km toward their destination when just several dozen kilometers away from their destination the dark skies unleashed a torrential downpour. In order to enable the news media to shoot footage of the Genhe County residents extending a warm greeting to the Ewenki hunters, county officials asked the convoy to wait on the road until the rain stopped. Because of the official request, the convoy of hunters and reindeer waited with empty stomachs from 8 A.M. in the morning until 5:30 P.M. in the afternoon. Though the hunters complained about this, they still fully cooperated. From this detail, the hunters' strong sense of self-esteem and willingness to make a personal sacrifice for the sake of others can be clearly perceived. Of course, if we examine this from another perspective, we can see that the government and media cared more about putting on a good performance for broadcast television than they did about the hunters or their reindeer. Despite these unexpected hitches that took place in order to cater to the news media, the first part of the relocation was completed.

Celebration Ceremony for the Ecological Migration

On 28 September 2003, the fortieth day since the relocation, the Genhe County government held a celebration ceremony for the success of the ecological migration. The sunshine was bright yet soft amidst endless crystal blue skies. The crisp, chilled air seemed to enliven the mood. Early in the morning, red carpet was rolled out in front of the township office building, and two rows of tables and chairs were set up to form a platform for the celebration. Huge red banners hung down from the brand new three-story office building. On each side they read, "Ecological emigrants on the road to happiness" and "Walk out the forest and run toward a well-off life." In the middle of the huge red banner was written in both Mongolian and Mandarin "Aoluguya Ewenki Township Ecological Migration Celebration." Dozens of Genhe County middle school students holding colorful flags in their hands surrounded the unpaved square. Dozens of policemen in navy blue uniforms stood along the edge of the square, their hands behind their backs. Standing in the middle of the square were the orderly queues of people from every Ao Township work unit, as well as several slightly jumbled queues of Ewenki hunters dressed in ethnic garb. Surrounding them was an audience of approximately one thousand people comprised of the residents from Genhe and nearby regions. Dozens of reporters from the media wove in and out of the crowd across the square with video cameras on their shoulders or cameras in their hands. The ceremony was hosted by the Genhe County party committee deputy head. When he announced the start of the ceremony, all trumpets and drums roared while fireworks blasted with helicopters hovering over, which added more jubilant flavors to the celebration.

Government officials presented several speeches. The first speaker was the Hulun Buir City deputy head, who was followed by the head of Genhe County and the head of the Ao Township. They all affirmed the tremendous importance of this ecological migration. After the ribbon-cutting ceremony, various guests visited the museum, the new residences, the clinic, the nursing home, and the reindeer pens. In the afternoon, the guests were bussed to nearby hunters' campsites for a visit. In the evening, a traditional bonfire party was held in the Ao Township Square.

In the morning, during the celebration ceremony, I wove my way in and among the lines of Ao Township schoolteachers and hunters to chat with them and take photos of the celebration ceremony. The Ao Township schoolteachers were all neatly dressed in formal suits and stood in orderly, straight lines. Presenting an interesting contrast to the teachers, the hunters wore their traditional colorful ethnic clothing and stood in a chaotic line. It was obvious that having the hunters dress in their traditional garbs was a ploy specifically for the purpose of emphasizing their status as an exotic minority. Their clothing was indeed beautiful and the silky materials draped with elegance, providing a stunning contrast against the rather drably colored clothing that everyone else was wearing. Their cuffs and collars were embroidered and inlaid with colorful strips of cloth. The long robes worn by women were of a single color and were carefully embroidered with flowers. The style of their robes were exactly same; the only difference lay in their color, with some resplendent in red, yellow, turquoise, grass green, and ocean blue. Men's traditional clothing was comprised of simple grass-green shirts, worn with a belt. Their shirt collars, which were large and flipped down, were similar to those on the women's dresses. The hunters said that in everyday life they did not wear such clothing but rather only wore it for performances on the holidays. These clothes were all made in exactly the same style; the government had paid for them in 1995 when the Ao Township celebrated its thirtieth anniversary of settlement.

The Ewenki hunters exclaimed, "How could we wear this kind of clothing up in the mountains? They cannot keep us warm, and they would get caught on things and tear very easily. In the past, all of the clothing we wore was made of leather—thorough authentic hides!" One young Ewenki hunter pointed to the township head and said to me, "Do you see her dress? That is from reindeer hides. Linda made it for Xueyina. It used six reindeer hides." I asked, "Doesn't the township head own a set of traditional leather clothing herself? Even she needs to borrow?" He replied, "Now, very few hunter women know this craft, and reindeer hide is not readily available. Nowadays, it is hard to find such traditional leather clothing like this. If there are any such clothes, they have already been placed in museums." Xueyina had shown me this set of clothing and asked me to try it on. After putting it on, I marveled at it in a mirror and we took photos. This set of leather clothes was designed by her and hand sewn by her mother. I thought it was beautiful and even hoped that I might be able to own such a lovely ethnic dress myself. But when I learned that even the township head did not own a leather dress like this, I realized that my initial wishes were unrealistic. It was apparent that the majority of Ewenki hunters already dressed in modern clothes and during their daily lives had no need of traditional ethnic garb at all. The traditional-style leather dress was, for most of the year, hung on the wall as a decoration at Linda's home. However, people's feelings of sentimental nostalgia do not quickly change. When outsiders pay increasing attention to the uniqueness of a particular ethnic group, the group's sense of identity will be strengthened and this often impels them to show and display the distinguishing customs and practices of their culture. As expected, the increased curiosity and attention on the Ewenki hunters has encouraged the hunters to restart making traditional ethnic clothing and finding occasions to wear and display their handicrafts.

Chatting with the young hunter was effortless. He spoke Mandarin with a northeastern accent. Soon, the township head began her speech. She first spoke in the Ewenki language; I understood nothing at all. When I asked the hunter standing beside me to explain the speech, he shook his head and smiled "I do not understand her either." "But you are Ewenki! At least you understand a little bit more than me" I said. He argued, "Anyone could not understand or even speak Ewenki language if he or she did not stay a very long time at the mountain campsites. Now, out of the campsites, almost no one uses Ewenki. Only the older people at the mountain campsites use it." When I told him my intention to learn the Ewenki language, he shook his head, "We grew up in the Ao Township and cannot speak it. You'd better forget it. It is hard to learn and inherit the Ewenki language without written words. Furthermore, you do not have the necessary environment for learning, unless you go up to the campsites and stay with the older women." As he finished, the township head's speech in Ewenki came to an end; she then repeated the entire speech in fluent Mandarin.

During their speeches, three leaders offered their highest compliments and congratulations for the success of the ecological migration. They also expressed strong confidence in the Ao Township's future development. The head of Genhe County presented the longest speech that covered all of the content of the other two speakers. I recorded the speech and have provided an excerpt of the key points below.

The success of the ecological migration marked the end of the Aoluguya Ewenki hunters' nomadic lifestyle. Now, they are on the road to progress toward a well-off standard of living. This is a great event of our county's political life and stands as a model of the successful application of the national ethnic policies. The smooth implementation of the Ao Township migration project will bring new life, energy and motivation to our Genhe County's development . . .

The Aoluguya Ewenki, also known as the "Reindeer-Using Tribe," is an important branch of the Ewenki group in China. The Aoluguya Ewenki played an important role in modern Chinese history and they have a glorious revolutionary history. . . For the past three hundred years, the Aoluguya Ewenki have never left the embrace of the forests . . . Prior to Liberation, the Ewenki were still living in the stage of late primitive society. After Liberation, under the caring support of every level of the party committee and government . . . the Ewenki leapt from primitive society directly to a socialist society and so underwent a highly significant transformation . . . After the Reindeer-Using Tribe established the settled community, the nation invested generous amounts of money, which led to a stride toward improvements in the Ewenki hunters' living conditions. However, owing to various external factors, the Ewenki hunters maintained their primitive and backward mode of production regarding raising reindeer . . . With the implementation of the Natural Forest Preservation Project, the area that reindeer could be herded became strictly limited. Now, with the total number of reindeer hovering at around eight hundred, the group's economic development has slipped into a predicament . . . Because of the arduous conditions in the mountains, and overall lack of medical services, the number of premature deaths of Ewenki hunters has been growing each year. The ethnic group faces a challenging battle for its very survival.

In order to fundamentally change the Ewenki hunters' poverty and eliminate the existing inequality between various ethnic groups, the Genhe County party committee and government have conducted several thorough surveys at both the Ao Township and at the hunter sites. After consulting with the hunters extensively, and entering discussion and debate with various parties, the county came to the decision to carry out the ecological migration. The ecological migration project was widely supported by the people of the Ao Township. Taking into account the wishes of the majority of hunters, the new Ao Township site was chosen to be located on the bank of the Xiwuqiya River . . .

The total investment in the ecological migration project was 11 million RMB. Since the construction began in 2002, within two years we have completed a total construction area of 221,600 square meters. The entire village uses a central-heating system. Telephones, cables and indoor water have all been installed and necessities of life are also supplied. Up to this point, a total of 62 Ewenki households comprising 162 people have moved to the new Ao Township. We have also moved over 380 reindeer. The villagers are gradually adjusting to modern lives.

The new Aoluguya, which is exquisitely designed and styled, offers breathtaking views and convenient transportation. Especially after being featured in many media reports and broadcast by CCTV and all other major media, the Ao Township has become well known. We aim to fully take advantage of this and quickly transform the new community of the Ao Township into a popular tourist spot and an attractive place to invest. . . We believe that the ecological migration has saved the Ewenki culture from extinction. Their culture will be permanently preserved as it transforms and develops. The Reindeer-Using Tribe will stand proudly among the world's ethnic groups because of its unique customs and culture.

The success of the Ao Township ecological migration will enhance the Reindeer-Using Tribe's overall quality and it will improve the level of scientific ecological environment preservation, and sustainable development of the ethnic economy. All of these are important and will have lasting historic significance because they will lift the Reindeer-Using Tribe out of poverty and help them to achieve a well-off standard of living. It is the dream and desire of county officials and the entire nation for the Reindeer Ewenki hunters to live happy lives and become part of modern society. Today, the Ao Township ecological migration has succeeded; first and foremost because of the care and dedication of every level of government, the tremendous support we received from the superior, and the diligent, hardworking and selfless people of Genhe County.

During the relocation, each county department and each government employee exhibited a spirit of self-sacrifice . . . The joint effort of all of the various groups led to the resounding success of the Ao Township relocation.

The Ewenki hunters put down their hunting guns and walked out of the mountains to blend into modern society. This is the general path of development followed by all ethnic groups. The success of the ecological migration is just the new beginning of the creation for our future. The new journey ahead of us will be long and arduous, but we will persevere and continue to implement the important ideology of the Three Represents and endeavor to fulfill the national ethnic policies. We will use the market as guidance, seek opportunities for the development of specialty niches, work to enhance and expand the reindeer preservation project, and continue our work to organize and promote ethnic culture. And we will work to bring significant improvements in the hunters' mode of production and living conditions.

We, as the victors, have presented to all the citizens of the entire county a perfect score sheet for our efforts. Today, the Ewenki hunters have walked out of the mountains; tomorrow the Aoluguya brand name will walk out of China and step into the world. We firmly believe that the Ewenki hunters will have wonderful lives and a glorious future . . .

Changes in the Social Structure

The Aoluguya Ewenki hunters were the main group involved in the ecological migration. Both the original Ao Township site, established 1965,
and the new Ao Township site, established during the 2003 migration, are
located in Genhe County, Hulun Buir City, Inner Mongolia Autonomous
Region. Genhe lies within the Greater Khingan Range in northeastern
China. On the map, the county is shown entirely in green, indicating the
county's heavy forest coverage. Strictly speaking, Genhe does not belong
to the "western" region of China that is within the auspices of the Grand
Western Development Plan.

Genhe County derives its name from the Gen River, a Mandarin
Chinese interpretation of the original Mongolian pronuncia-
tion Gegengaole, which means "crystal clear river." Genhe County,
with an elevation of 800 meters above sea level, covers an area of
19,929 square kilometers. Currently, 1.46 million hectares of forest cover
as much as 73.6 percent of the entire county, which has a forestry-based
economy. The county has a total population of 176,940, comprised of
people from fourteen distinct ethnic groups. The county is subdivided
into six townships, which are under the jurisdiction of the county government. Of these townships, the Aoluguya Ewenki Ethnic Township is
the most distinctive.

Old Aoluguya is located about 17.5 km from Mangui Township to the
north of Genhe County. The old Aoluguya Township shares an eastern
and southern border—delineated by the Jiliu River and a road—with
the Mangui Township. To the west and southwest lies Argun County.
Directly north of the old Aoluguya site lies Mohe County, Heilongjiang
Province.

On the eve of ecological migration, the entire population of
the Ao Township included 179 households, comprising 498 people. The
population was comprised of six different ethnic groups, including the
Ewenki, Daur, Mongolian, Manchu, Russian, and Han. Of the total population of 498 people, 232 were Ewenki, 241 were Han, and the remaining 25 people were Daur, Mongolian, Manchu, or Russian. The ethnic
composition of the population is shown in Chart 3.1.

The new site was located in a suburban area west of the Genhe
County town, only 5 kilometers from the downtown region. The new
Ao Township site, approximately 260 km from the old site, was origi-
nally named Sanchejian—the Third Production Warehouse of Genhe
County Forestry Department. The earliest residents in Sanchejian were
the timber production workers of the Third Production Warehouse.
When the Natural Forest Preservation Project was implemented in

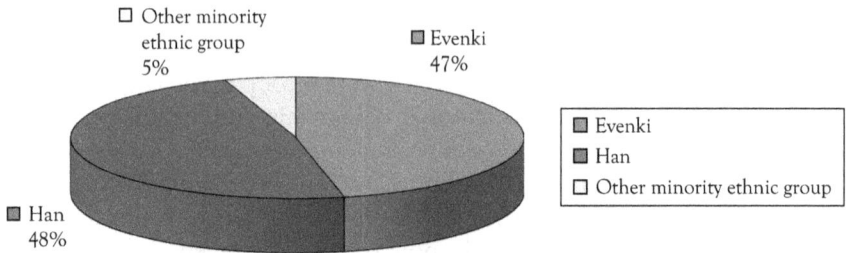

Chart 3.1 The ethnic composition of the population in the old Ao Township on the eve of the ecological migration relocation

2000, timber production in the region was sharply scaled back and the Third Production Warehouse was dissolved. However, some of the workers chose to stay in the community and they, together with a number of migrant workers and drifters, made up the entire population of Sanchejian. Most of these people worked as manual laborers and supplemented their income by growing vegetables. When the ecological migration plan required the relocation of the entire population, the Genhe County government provided compensation to these residents for the expropriation of their land and houses. Brick and tile houses were compensated at the rate of 400 RMB per square meter, while for mud and wood houses the rate of compensation was 200 to 300 RMB per square meter. To receive the money, residents were required to demolish their old homes and relocate themselves. After the old residences were demolished in Sanchejian and the original residents moved out of the region, the entire site was renamed Aoluguya. Only people who were designated as Ewenki Hunters, a total of 62 households comprising 162 people, were relocated to the new Aoluguya. The other residents of the old Ao Township site, who despite having lived there for many years, were not allowed to move to the new Aoluguya. Among them, unemployed residents received relocation compensation—a one-time payment of 4,500 RMB per person—to move away from the old Ao Township and look for somewhere else to make a living. Meanwhile, the other people, who had formal employment in government departments or in the state social service sectors in the old Ao Township, did not even receive any relocation compensation and had to find new places to live by themselves. They held out hope that the ecological migration program would undertake a second phase of construction to provide housing for them. In the meantime, because there was not enough housing in the new Ao Township site, most of them moved to the Genhe County seat where they purchased or rented accommodation. Several of them found new jobs in other places and moved away.

According to Genhe County and Aoluguya Ewenki Ethnic Township documents, the 62 residences constructed at the new Aoluguya were only for Ewenki who had official status as a Hunter. This then raises the question, who were the Hunters and how did they gain this identity? The word Hunter by its literal definition is a person who hunts wild animals to survive. However, in Aoluguya, it not only refers to a kind of identity that equals a farmer and worker but also refers to the ethnic group—one of the branches of the Ewenki minority. After the founding of the People's Republic of China, the government provided various forms of special support and assistance to this small group of Aoluguya Ewenki Hunters. The current ecological migration project that expelled over one hundred families from Sanchejian for the sake of relocating 62 Ewenki households to a new, greatly improved site is evidence of the government's attempt to provide special assistance to this ethnic group.

Right after the relocation, the Ao Township was a micro-community of 62 households comprised of 162 people. Three months later in December 2003, the Inner Mongolia Autonomous Region made a decision to incorporate the other residents and land in Sanchejian into the new Ao Township administrative area. With this change, the entire township governance area expanded to 1,767.2 square kilometers from 221.6 square kilometers, and the number of households increased to 445 households and a total population of 1,390 residents, including all the Ao Township government employees who lived in downtown Genhe. The majority of the population (75 percent) consisted of ethnic Han, while the remaining 25 percent of the population belonged to the Ewenki, Daur, Mongolian, Manchu, Hui and Russian ethnic groups. The 232 Ewenki people (including Ewenki from other branches) comprised 16.7 percent of the township's population. The Aoluguya Ewenki Hunters, numbering 162 people, took up only 12 percent of the population.

Even after the Sanchejian area was incorporated into the Ao Township, the effect on the Aoluguya Ewenki Hunters' community was minimal. Its 62 households, which were spatially separate from the rest of the town, remained tightly connected. The government building and hunters' residences were located close together within an area of about five square kilometers. Because of their close physical proximity and cultural distinctiveness, when I began fieldwork, I considered the clearly delineated 62 households to be the primary focus of my research. For the purposes of clarity, throughout the rest of my work, when I refer to the relocation of the Ao Township, I am referring only to the relocation of the 62 households of Aoluguya hunters, who were the sole official occupants of the Ao Township prior to the new governance stipulations that came into effect in December 2003. When I speak of the relocation of the Ao Township, I am not referring to the Sanchejian residents who were later incorporated into the township, because they were not fully involved in the ecological migration project. Only the 62 households of Aoluguya hunters were involved in the migration from beginning to end. Therefore, my fieldwork has focused primarily on this group and I spent most of my time living with them.

Here I find it necessary to further clarify the identities of the various groups of people who were relocated. Although the 31 buildings that housed 62 residences were officially called Hunters' houses, not all the people who lived in the houses were necessarily members of the Reindeer-Using Tribe. The Ewenki living in the Ao Township today are the second and third generation of Ewenki hunters since the founding of the People's Republic of China in 1949. Among this third generation, very few have ever lived in the forest or engaged in a traditional hunting, gathering and herding lifestyle for extended periods of time. Because of a great deal of intermarriage with other groups, for many families, only one parent is of Ewenki hunter posterity and he or she is the only one capable of speaking the Ewenki language. As a result, the language is not used within the family and most people in the community today cannot speak the Ewenki language. Having not lived in the forest, most do not know how to herd reindeer or how to hunt, or how to make traditional hunting tools such as birch bark canoes, skis, and hunting knives. Their knowledge of traditional hunting life is often inferior to that of outsiders who intermarried with the second generation hunters. However, because they are descendants of the Aoluguya Reindeer-Using Tribe bloodline they are recognized as Hunters.

Ao Township government leaders were really exhausted by the problem of how to allocate the "Hunters' houses" for the ecological migrants; that is to say, they encountered a problem when they began the task of ascertaining who should be entitled to a "Hunters' house." The township head said to me:

One day [in 2001] the county [the Genhe County party committee and government] suddenly called, and they asked us to submit the total number of Ao Township Ewenki hunter households, but did not mention what they wanted this information for—they just needed a number. Because no one dared to report any unfounded data, we submitted the number that appeared in the 1960 census conducted by the National Ethnic Affairs Commission; there were 31 families of Ewenki hunters. It was only later that the county revealed that they were planning to relocate the hunters as part of an ecological migration program and needed to know the number of hunter households for the construction of new residences. By then, we all realized that the number we had reported was too low. Despite the fact that they were still counted as being in their parents' household, many of the hunters' children now had families of their own. Also, there were many cases in which one hunter had died, but their spouse remarried with someone from another ethnic group. We originally had not counted these people as hunter households, yet they were in fact raising the children who were regarded as Hunters. We realized we could not relocate without providing them with houses. Furthermore, we had not originally counted orphans either, but they should also be given a residence.

In the end, the fund approved for the ecological migration was just for 31 households as required. However, these buildings were not enough for actual households. Thus, each building had to be divided into two residences, with a total of 31 constructed buildings. How were these residences assigned? We thought hard and came up with many options. The county also called special meetings to discuss this issue. Eventually, we assigned the Hunters' houses according to the criterion of "the unemployed Ewenki ethnicity." As long as one of the parents belonged to the Ewenki ethnicity, their children were also considered ethnic Ewenki. The unmarried Ewenki descendants who were jobless were combined and counted as one household.

In the beginning, some of the hunters proposed that the houses should not be given to descendants of other Ewenki branches. But we were concerned about this and did not want to cause rifts among the ethnic groups. Even though some of them are not hunters, they are still Ewenki people; for example, the people from Nantun, Sama Street or Arong Banner—they have lived in the Ao Township for many years. So we decided that as long as they were jobless we assigned houses to them as well. As to other jobless ethnic groups, we provided relocation funds and demanded them to move out of [old] Aoluguya. Some people moved close to Genhe County seat, some moved to the Mangui Township, while others yet moved to Hebei Province or Shandong Province.

When the township government assigned Hunters' houses according to the criterion of "the unemployed Ewenki ethnicity," the use of this criterion had also defined the identity of the Hunter. These houses had been constructed in the name of Hunters, so they had to be assigned to Hunters. In the sense of the local people, "employed" means "having an official job," i.e., government or other public service job, where the salary is guaranteed all the year round. "Unemployed" means "without an official and stable job in the government"—the local people do not take temp workers as "the employed." For instance, after the relocation, the Ao Township hired an Ewenki hunter as a typist. She had a temp job but was "unemployed." She got little wage of 300 RMB per month from the township, even though she worked hard and did overtime. Considering her "unemployed" status, she got a Hunters' house. By contrast, another Ewenki women, with a disability and with the "employed" status, got a stable salary of 900 RMB per month, even though she did simple cleaning work inside the township building; because of her "employed" status, she did not qualify for a Hunters' house.

The criterion "employed" not only referred to those who had official jobs, but also included retirees. As a matter of fact, the criterion on which a person was judged to "have an official job" was based on whether or not she or he received a stable salary from the government. Prior to the 2003 relocation, there were no private commercial businesses in the Ao Township at all. The only jobs were the positions related to government. However, this criterion caused the chaos over identity. Reindeer Ewenki were the native "hunters" and they never saw other Ewenki branches (outside Ewenki) as hunters. However, other Ewenki people who had hunting and reindeer-herding experience preferred to regard themselves as Ewenki Hunters. Some Reindeer Ewenki Hunters' identities were unquestionable because of their lineage, but since they belonged to the group of employed people who had the stable salary from the government they were embarrassed to call themselves "hunters." As to those unemployed Ewenki hunters who did not hold official jobs, they also had reservations with regard to the "hunter identity" of the Reindeer-Using Tribe Ewenki who were employed by the government. For the Reindeer Ewenki retirees, they returned to the forests and lived there for quite some years, but because of their continued pension income, many people also challenged their "hunter identity." Relatively few people had the "hunter identity" that was not questioned—those who had always been living in the forests. The headcount of these people had been hovering around 30 to 40 since the 1990s. A few other people were not Reindeer-Using Tribe Ewenki, but they were the spouses of the hunters, so they remained in the forests and lived hunting lives. In the past, they had always been considered and treated as "hunters." However, after the 2003 relocation, their "hunter identity" was void and they were not entitled to houses or eligible for hunters' welfare and other benefits. Most importantly, the Reindeer-Using Tribe Ewenki group itself had undergone subtle changes in its internal self-identity, which affected the way they perceived others as real hunters or not. In addition, the criteria by which they defined themselves changed in response to varying external circumstances.

Before and after the ecological migration, the proportions of different groups in the Ao Township varied, as shown in the following charts and graphs.

From the charts and graphs, we can clarify the complicated identity issue. Before the ecological migration, Ewenki hunters recognized Group 1 and Group 2 as "hunters," which indicates that the way they self-identified themselves was the same as their identity according to their

Table 3.1 Group identity code

Lineage	Reindeer Ewenki	Outside Ewenki	Other Ethnic Groups
Employed	1	3	5
Unemployed	2	4	6	7

Note: The Reindeer Ewenki lineage is also known as the Yakut Ewenki lineage. Outside Ewenki refers to Ewenki people who belonged to the Solon tribe. All of them are long-term residents of old Aoluguya and were included in the 2003 migration to Sanchejian.

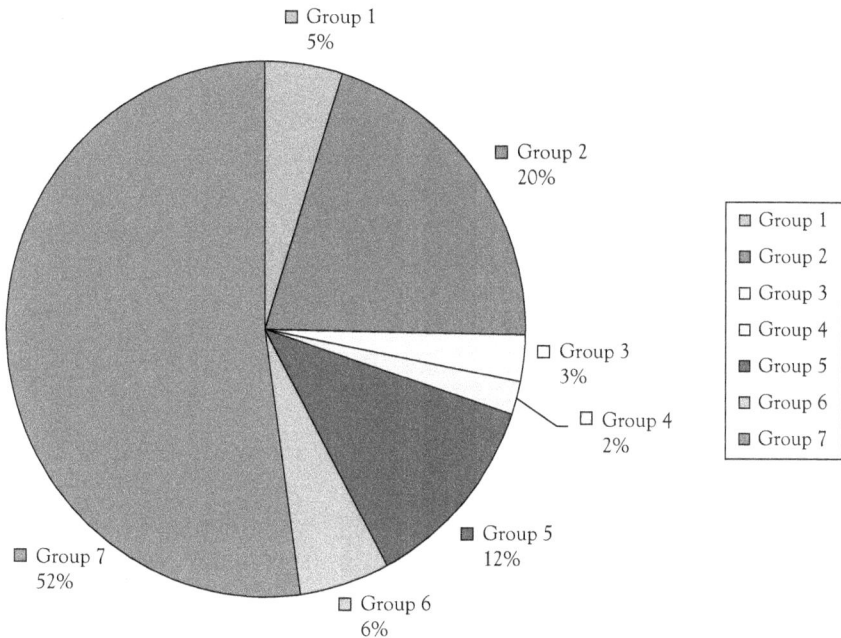

Chart 3.2 Pre-relocation Ao Township resident groups proportion chart (total 498 people)

Note: From Chart 3.2. it can be seen that Group 7 were the unemployed non-Ewenki in old Aoluguya who were provided with cash settlements and expelled. They did not move to the new site in Sanchejian. Groups 1, 2, 3, 4, 5 and 6 were relocated. Groups 1 and 2 were Reindeer Ewenki and comprised one quarter of the population of old Aoluguya.

ethnic group branch. In addition, before the ecological migration, the Ao Township government and Genhe County government also regarded both of these two groups as hunters. With regard to issues of relocation and site selection, both levels of government claimed they had consulted the hunters to listen to their ideas and suggestions. However, the government chose individuals to serve as representatives primarily from Group 1, as listed in the above chart. To summarize, before the relocation

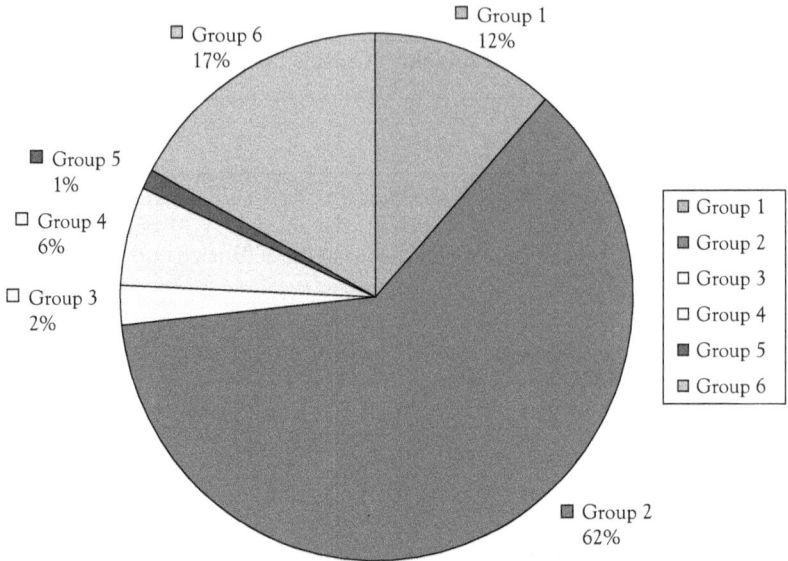

Chart 3.3 New Ao Township resident groups proportion chart (total 162 people)

Note: After relocation, most of the relocated people were the unemployed Reindeer Ewenki of Group 2.

there was no conflict between the way the hunters identified themselves and the way other people did.

However, after the new Hunters' houses were completed, and right before houses were assigned, both levels of government had selected a new criterion—they regarded Group 2 and Group 4 as the "hunters" who were entitled to receive Hunters' houses. In essence, this differed greatly from the government's criterion for the determination of hunter identity prior to the relocation. According to Genhe County plans, Groups 1, 2, 3, 4, 5 and 6 were not paid any compensation for relocation. The main difference between Group 6 and Group 7 was whether or not they were entitled to compensation for relocation. Because Group 6 was comprised of the spouses or children of Group 2 and 4, they could live in the Hunters' houses with the Hunters. The members of Group 7—primarily migrant workers, drifters, or family members of township government employees—were not related to hunters. They moved away from Aoluguya and found living quarters in other places after receiving relocation compensation funds. According to the policies the government set up, in principle, people employed by the government (Groups 1, 3 and 5) had neither relocation fees nor housing, while the people who were not employed by the government (Groups 2, 4, 6 and 7) either received relocation fees or were assigned Hunters' houses. They were entitled to either one benefit or the other, but not both.

From above it can be seen that, in principle, those who were entitled to live in the Ao Township Hunters' houses were only Group 2, Group 4, and Group 6. Members of Group 2 and Group 4 comprised the primary body of people to whom housing was assigned. A few people from Groups 1, 3 and 5 continued to live in the new Ao Township after the relocation. They were able to do so because they lived in the houses assigned to their parents, children, or siblings. There were also cases where Ewenki hunters who remained in the forests rented their houses to township employees. Among the residents who were government employees at the new Ao Township, or who worked in the school or hospital, some of them had always lived in the Genhe County seat, while others purchased or rented residences there after relocation. Some people in Group 7 were the children or other family members of Group 1, Group 3, or Group 5, and although they had registered residences in the Ao Township, they did not actually live in the Ao Township. Another portion of the people in Group 7 completely detached themselves from the Ao Township and severed all ties; after the relocation they dispersed in all directions, leaving no trace of their whereabouts.

The hunters went through subtle changes in self-recognition after the relocation. Without a doubt, Group 2 had the indisputable identity as "hunters." Meanwhile, people generally felt that the members of Group 6 were taking unfair advantage of their situation, because they were able to live in the Hunters' houses simply because they were relatives or the spouses of official Hunters. Group 1 and Group 2 also tended to believe that Group 4 took unfair advantage of their situation. When criticizing Group 4 of illegitimately benefiting from their connection with official Ewenki Hunters, Group 1 and Group 2 tended to mutually recognize each other's status as hunters. However, when talking about the issue of hunters' desires, Group 2 would deny the authenticity of Group 1's hunter identity. In such cases, Group 2 would often ask rhetorically, "Is he [person in group 1] really a hunter? How could he speak on behalf of the hunters?"

On the other side, the term Hunter no longer simply indicates an identity, but rather has many emotional connotations. When I developed pictures in a photo studio in the Genhe County seat, the clerks spotted the pictures I took of the Ao Township hunters. Astounded, he said to me, "You are very bold indeed! You blend in with the hunters!" I replied that in fact it was not a big deal, and asked if they had ever been to the hunter campsites up in the mountains. They all answered no. Although they had no firsthand knowledge of the hunters themselves, it appeared that their understanding of the hunters was based entirely on hearsay. It was obvious that, to a certain degree, they were afraid of the hunters and disliked them. Similar situations were not rare in Genhe County. I am quite perplexed why outsiders, and even local people in Genhe County, held such impressions of the "hunter identity." Additionally, the hunters themselves also harbored certain subtle and complex feelings regarding the "hunter identity." Once, I accompanied an Ewenki hunter woman downtown to go shopping. The sales clerk saw her Mongolian appearance and said, "You are Mongolian, right?" The Ewenki woman remained silent as she wrapped her scarf more tightly around her face. Another sales clerk said in a hushed voice, "She's from the Ao Township." Without purchasing anything, the Ewenki woman asked me to leave quickly with her. With anger on her face, she exclaimed, "These people always cause trouble over something or another. It's disgusting." I realized that the sales clerk's remark "She's from the Ao Township," contained a derogatory connotation associated with being a hunter, which the elder woman was very much aware of.

To the Ewenki Reindeer-Using Tribe, regardless of whether they were employed by the government or not, old or young, the "hunter identity" was a problem that haunted them and left them with complex feelings. Sometimes they were proud of this identity and considered it an asset, while at other times they were frustrated by it. There were also times when the Ewenki emphasized that the "hunter identity" was crucial to the survival of their ethnic group, yet there were also times when they felt lost and confused about the meanings and connotations embodied by this identity.

There is one point that needs to be stressed. In Groups 1, 2, 3 and 6 there were a certain number of people who lived hunting and herding lives in the forests prior to the ecological migration and who returned to the forests after the relocation. During my field research, there were a few people living primarily at the mountain campsites—no more than 40 people lived over three months each year in the mountains. During May, June and July, they were busy tending to pregnant reindeer, preparing for birthing, cutting reindeer antlers, and caring for the herd. From the perspective of truly maintaining the traditional lifestyle, they should be called Hunters. According to my data, there were 6 such people in Group 1; 26 people in Group 2; 1 person in Group 3; and 6 people in Group 6. In total there were 39 people. I have labeled each subgroup as 1', 2', 3' and 6'. Of the subgroups 1', 2', 3' and 6', the subgroup 3' and 6' were comprised of a total of 7 people, who were the spouses of people in subgroup 1' and 2'. The percentage of every subgroup is shown below:

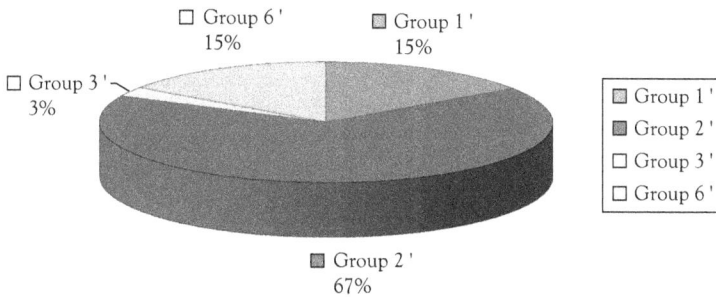

Chart 3.4 Composition of the Hunters living in mountain campsites

Note: From Chart 3.4, it can be seen that subgroup 1', a total of 15 percent (6 people), were Reindeer Ewenki with formal employment; subgroup 2', a total of 16 percent (26 people), were unemployed Reindeer Ewenki; subgroup 3', a total of 3 percent (1 person), was an outside Ewenki; subgroup 6', a total of 15 percent (6 people), were unemployed people of other ethnic origins.

Out of respect for Reindeer-Using Tribe Ewenki self-recognition as "hunters," and also because of the need of the Ao Township and Genhe County government's use of the term "hunter" to attract the interest of tourism, throughout the rest of this book, I will use the term "Ao Township Hunters," to refer, in general, to the 62 households and 162 people living at the new Ao Township site. In the eyes of outsiders, they are all "hunters." In general description, I will adopt this broad viewpoint when utilizing the term "hunter." However, when I present the viewpoints held by the government or by the members of the 62 households, the scope of what is meant by "hunter" becomes complicated as discussed above. In particular, in different circumstances, the definition and scope of identity as a "hunter" among Reindeer-Using Tribe Ewenki is even more uncertain. The seven categories shown in the above chart are based upon my own fieldwork observations and thoughts. I recommend that readers keep these categories in mind in the following chapters in order to help understand the essence and scope of the concept of "hunter" as used by each of the various parties involved. In the following chapter, we will examine various recounts and viewpoints, including those of the government and the hunters, regarding the overall situation after the relocation process was completed.

Notes

1. Three Represents, namely that the Party must always represent the development trend of China's advanced productive forces; the orientation of China's advanced culture; and the fundamental interests of the overwhelming majority of the Chinese people. This is the crystallization of the Party's collective wisdom and a guiding ideology the Party must follow for a long time to come, as Jiang Zemin said in his report in 2000.
2. Many of the reports from the media section of the county propaganda department can be viewed on the Xinhua News Agency Website.
3. The county government clandestinely sold the old Aoluguya site to a real estate development company. Ironically, the land and ecosystem "protected" through the ecological migration plan will now be used by the real estate company to open a for-profit trophy-hunting ground for rich urbanites. They will undoubtedly claim this will stimulate economic development.

Chapter 4

Post-migration Issues

"Leaving the Forest, Now Eating Chaff—
Is This the Way to a Well-off Society?"

≥•≤

The Plight of Migrants

The relocation ceremony was over. The Ao Township returned to quietness from the brief period of bustling excitement. The entire town was so quiet that it made me slightly nervous. In the daytime, few people could be found walking about on the town's clean streets. At night in particular, a moist fog shrouded the town; sporadic lights vaguely flickered in the quiet darkness. The fog and the quiet stillness reminded me of the scenes in ghost stories and it often left me feeling a sense of dread with my hair standing on end.

Another aspect of the township was revealed in the activities taking place in the office of the township head during working hours. A crowd had gathered in the twenty-odd square meter office. The township head sat in the computer chair behind her desk and the two long couches on each side were crowded with townspeople. Next to the window, occupying the small space in front of the radiator, was another small crowd. In the beginning, people were embroiled in voicing their arguments all at once, but slowly order appeared and people began taking turns to express their concerns to the township head about their situation and problems they were facing. After the ceremony commemorating the ecological migration, such scenes in the township government office were indeed daily routines.

On the third day after the official ecological migration event, some of the news media issued reports claiming that the "hunters were about to return to the forests." The governments of both Genhe County and the Ao Township were immediately alarmed. They quickly reacted through the local media, claiming that outside reporters did not fully understand the entire situation and that such reports were "total nonsense."

The reality behind the situation was that, prior to relocation, the hunters were worried about the survival of their reindeer; thus, the Genhe County government promised them they could herd reindeer in the woods around Genhe County as a makeshift measure that would help the hunters with the transition to pen-raising. Furthermore, before the Ao Township relocation, very few people had lived at the campsites in the forests. Therefore, out of the 162 people who were relocated, fewer than 40 were planning to "return to the forests." Because most people did not understand this, reading the media reports left them with the misleading impression that the entire population of the Ao Township had decided to return to the forests. Both the county and township governments felt that this sort of reporting easily misled readers, who possessed very little factual knowledge about the Ao Township and thought that the Ewenki hunters had rejected the entire "ecological migration" as a failed project. In order to counter what they saw as misleading information, the government felt it necessary to issue official statements.

It goes without saying that the government would be horrified at the suggestion that the ecological migration was a failure. However, when viewing the event from the perspective of an outsider, the media's claims did harbor an element of truth. The entire proposal for "ecological migration" had been approved and funded in the name of these forty-odd mountain-dwelling hunters. The local government's defense for the ecological migration was that the hunters' activities in the mountains were destroying the natural forest ecosystem and wildlife. Under this pretense, the hunters were relocated to the lowlands. But three days after the relocation, they did return to the nearby mountains to set up the new campsites. Thus the media's claim that the hunters had returned to the forests was, in fact, true.

At the time of the relocation in 2003 there were four hunters' campsites at the old Aoluguya in the Alongshan region. Several months after the relocation to the new Aoluguya, conflicts arose between two families at one of the campsites, which led to the camp splitting into two sites. During the period from September 2003 to October 2004, I visited all of the campsites more than once. Each campsite was not fixed all year round at any particular location, but was regularly packed up and moved to new areas in the mountains. Generally speaking, at the northern campsites around Alongshan, reindeer grew quite big and had impressively large antlers. In contrast, at the southern campsites around the Genhe area, reindeer were skinny and bony, their antlers were small and their growth was delayed. The campsites were all different sizes with some having more occupants than others. At the largest campsite there were as many as 12 to 13 people, but on average there were 8 to 9 people living in three tents and tending to over 300 reindeer. The smallest campsite had only 2 to 3 people living in one tent and tending to over 20 reindeer.

Before the relocation, there were two main daily activities at the hunters' sites: one was hunting; the other was herding reindeer. Going out hunting took up a large part of the hunters' time. However, after the government had implemented the ecological migration, the hunters' guns had been confiscated and hunting was prohibited. As a result, the main activity remaining at the hunters' campsites was herding reindeer. Since there was no possibility of earning income through hunting, the young men who used to enjoy hunting in the mountains were no longer willing to live at the campsites. Indeed, the migration only changed half of the hunters' mode of production—they were forced to give up hunting, but herding reindeer continued as before. Therefore, even after the ecological migration had taken place, the lives of the reindeer-herding Ewenki did not change much—they still lived in reindeer-herding camps and did not adopt a fixed-residence urban lifestyle. In this regard, the goal of the government—to have the Ewenki hunters live in fixed, permanent residence—was not fully achieved. Although only forty-odd hunters returned to the forests to herd reindeer, the media reports continued to focus on them.

Post-relocation Placement

One morning after the ceremony, Ewo Linda said to me quite mysteriously, "I have something I must do today." When I asked her what it was, she explained that she needed to go to the township office. I offered to go with her. I held her arm and she leaned on a thin wooden stick that served as her cane, and together we walked along the slippery snowy roads to the township government building. Later when I reflected on this incident, it occurred to me that even though I only accompanied her and had not participated in the conversation during the meeting, the very fact of my involvement had already led the township government officials to feel that I was taking sides and helping the hunters to stand up against the government.

When we arrived at the township head's office on the second floor of the government building, I found several other women elders, who Linda had often taken me to visit, already sitting on couches in the office. One of them was plump and slow moving and it made me think to myself that it must be clumsy for her to get here in such poor weather and she must have come here for some important reason. When she began to speak, I found her words to be powerful, emotional and capable of stirring people's sympathy. She complained:

> What on earth did my household get from the assistance? Nothing is shabbier than the way we were treated. What nerve of them to give us items that they themselves had thrown away as worthless rubbish! The pathetic insulated winter pants they provided for the children were so stinky and dirty that when you threw them on the ground, the pants would stand up by themselves. Who could wear such winter pants? The nerve of them to think that this would help us. It's shameful! Other people were given new TVs or new beds. The only thing we got was used stuff! This is not fair! My granddaughter is mentally handicapped. Now she is almost twelve years old, but still cannot take care of herself in any fashion. The township school refused to admit her, but it is up to the township leaders to do something to help. I am her grandma, but I cannot take care of her for her entire lifetime. She is a hunter's child! What other options do I have if the township does not allow her to go to school? I know there is a school for mentally handicapped kids in Hailar. You the government should pay the cost for her to go to school!

There were many people in the township head's office waiting to have their turn. In summary, people had come to present three main points: (1) to demand solutions; for instance, the furniture they had been promised was not in their houses (2) to demand relocation fees from the township, and (3) Hunters wanted guns or jobs. The township head was a mild-mannered woman. Facing such an array of complaints from people who were her direct relatives or distant relatives, all she could do was to listen patiently and silently. After everyone had their turn, she finally spoke, "I have listened to all of the situations that you presented. Let me discuss these issues again with the Party head (of the Ao Township), and then we will send a report to the county. We will do our best to solve the problems quickly. Now everyone, please go back home." With this, the small crowd felt it was meaningless to remain in the office, and so, one by one, they left for home.

The township head looked distressed and frustrated. Facing so many problems, she could do little to solve them. She said to me, "Every decision is made by the county. The township government has little power." I had heard people in the community say things like, "The woman township head is not very aggressive. She does not have the power to make any decisions. At any rate, the Party head is the top officer and the Township head follows the decisions of the Party head in all things. But the Party head is of

Han ethnicity. Is it really possible that he will not bully officials who are of Ewenki heritage?" Although the Ao Township is a small community, ethnic tensions are high because local people tend to attribute the causes of conflicts and social problems to differences in ethnicity. However, I feel that the key problems in the Ao Township were not related to ethnicity, but local people tended to vent their dissatisfaction with social ills by phrasing the problem in terms of ethnic conflict as a way to garner the attention of a government that is highly sensitive to issues of ethnic conflict.

Complaints from All Sorts of People

The Elder Hunters' Rage

With November drawing near, the temperature had already dropped to minus twenty degrees Celsius. One drawback of the new houses was that they had problems caused by moisture and mold. In many houses, the walls were covered with black mold. Many residents complained that the heating was not warm enough, and that it was too cold inside. The floor tiles were cold, got dirty too easily, and were too slippery, especially when people came in with snow on their shoes. This was still not the biggest problem. What mattered most was that the reindeer were not able to survive in the pens and that the hunters had to return to the mountains to live the "primitive" life like a herder did before. However, the young people liked the facilities at the new site, so they refused to return to the woods to suffer. In high mountains and deep woods, natural dangers lurked everywhere. Since the hunters no longer had guns, it was indeed a scary situation. If they did not return to the mountains, the reindeer would not be able to survive. But if they returned to the mountains, they had no way to guarantee their own safety. Stuck in this dilemma, the hunters felt tormented. The female hunter Jimina commented:

> During the relocation days, we waded in heavy rain. With no food all day long for us and for reindeer, we were all nearly starving to death. We made it here just to suffer this? And now we have to move back to forest campsites? In these new herding campsites right around Genhe County seat, the reindeer are losing weight or even dying. This is killing me. Oh hell, why we moved? We were fooled!

Hunter Wives' Complaints

After moving to the new site, except the male hunters who owned and herded reindeer in the woods near the Genhe County seat, the other people living in the township had almost nothing to do. Xiaomei, a woman of Han ethnicity married to an Ewenki man, had a good sense for business and opened a small grocery store. Her husband, a descendant of the traditional hunters, was employed at the Ao Township veterinarian clinic. The couple was not entitled to relocation fees or a house, so they rented a hunter house and set up a counter in their home selling commodities. To open their convenience store they initially invested only 300 RMB, but soon they were able to make a monthly profit of over 300 RMB—that is enough to make a living. Xiaomei complained to me:

> Nowadays, the hunters are all broke. When they do not have money to buy anything they always want to buy on credit. In the past, at the old Aoluguya, they also bought on credit but would quickly pay back whatever they owed. Back then I was not afraid to give them credit. It was perfectly fine because they would pay all of their debts. Now they cannot do that for sure. Some of them buy things on credit, and I know that they will not be able to pay me back, but still I sell them goods out of sympathy. However, I cannot afford to give too much credit. I still have to make a living myself!

She took out a journal entry and showed it to me. Those who used credit were generally the hunters who had neither jobs nor reindeer. The most purchased items on credit were liquor and instant noodles.

Young Male Hunters' Silent Protest

The Ao Township in winter was always quiet; when it was draped in a heavy blanket of white snow it was even quieter. When the weather was unbearably cold, the Ao Township officials would sneak off to one of the hunters' houses where they would play mahjong or poker to while away their working hours. Gambling small amounts of money on card games was a favorite form of entertainment in the Ao Township. However, the young male hunters did not play mahjong or gamble. All they did was drink liquor. The stuff they drank was simple—distilled rice liquor that costs 2 RMB per 500 ml and was packaged in a small plastic bag. If they used their own containers to purchase liquor sold in bulk, it was sold at the even cheaper price of 1.5 RMB per 500 ml. They simply drank the liquor straight without eating any side dishes. Occasionally, there was a side dish of peanuts, which was considered a luxury. I was present at several such scenes of three to five people drinking silently—no words spoken, no laughter. They just drank. They leaned on couches or slumped on beds, drinking one mouthful after another. It seemed that they were eager to enter a drunken state, the sooner the better. No one except themselves could enjoy what was to them so tasty and delicious about this cheap and somewhat repugnant distilled rice liquor. For their favors, I brought them a couple of bottles of better liquor; however, they did not show much interest. Instead, they exchanged the better liquor for a larger quantity of the cheap liquor sold in bulk. Did they really love the liquor and drinking so much? It is hard to believe that they did. What they really did love was the state of being drunk, which allowed them to forget their sorrows. In the brand new modern houses, there lived a group of people whose aspiration was only to get drunk to forget reality. I found this a sorrowful sight and heartbreaking.

Complaints Against Each Other

Several senior female hunters did not drink liquor. Seeing the current situation in their community, they felt pained and frustrated. They wanted to complain, but did not know to whom they should complain, so they vented some of their frustrations on me, "Do not buy liquor for them! This is all bad Han people's fault. Keep feeding them with liquor. Day after day they will drink themselves to death!" When these female hunters' rage waned, one of them started reminiscing about old times:

> The old hunters never drank like this. Back then, the men went on hunting trips for ten days or more. When they returned, every one of them was joyful and laden with prey they had shot. There was so much prey that we could not eat up. Once the men came home, we would start dancing, singing, and drinking. How joyous the drinking was at that time! We Ewenki hunters do not have any particular holidays, but rather the days when we got a lot of prey!

A male elder echoed:

> Later the transportation became more convenient. So we went down the mountain to purchase and bring back liquor. All of it was good liquor. Nobody would drink poor quality alcohol at that time. We only bought boxes of canned beers. One tin cost several RMB. Today is different; these young people have no good liquor to drink. The spirits under which drinking took place was completely different between then and now.

During the winter, the entire Ao Township was silent and dormant. People in the community hardly possessed any sense of joy, except for their memories of the past. Every resident was full of complaints. Ewenki hunters said, "The Han people take advantage of us. They follow us here and find houses to live in. Why do not they move faraway! What do they follow us for? They work to take away all the benefits the government intends to give us!" The Han people that the Ewenki were complaining about were those working for the township government. Despite the fact that some of these Han employees were relatives of the hunters, they seemed to ignore this fact when cursing the Han people. There were also hunters who said to me sadly:

> After moving here, people's hearts changed. They have turned cold. Nobody trusts one another; they dare not. We talked about everything and anything before. But it is no longer that way now. You may have noticed that very few people visit each other in this new Ao Township. But before at old Aoluguya, we gathered often at the grassland right off the Jiliu River. We drank liquor with peanuts and roe deer meat jerky. Pretty little wild flowers blossomed next to us, and we could simply just reach over and pick the *dushi* [blueberry] and *yageda* [a kind of red berry] to eat. People talked about all manner of things, and they were candid. Back then, if you visited anyone's house, they would have you stay for a meal. Every household had some wild game to cook. It is not that way now. No family has anything good to cook; nobody is comfortable to invite others for meals. Indeed we, Ewenki hunters, are most hospitable. But now we honestly dare not invite you for meals. It is so frustrating. Hunting is forbidden, what could we cook for guests? Any food has to be purchased downtown. Before, at old Aoluguya, we just needed to plant a little garden around the house, which would produce enough to eat. Every household had a lot of wild game for food. The most joyful thing was hosting guests and serving them with the very best foods. Nowadays, it is so much worse. We are about to go begging!

The outside Ewenki people felt awkward at the new Ao Township. The ethnic Han wife of one of the outside Ewenki expressed her complaints to me:

> All of this nonsense is about local Ewenki vs. other Ewenki. Are we not the same ethnic group? Why bother to draw a line? Is not this splittism? At old Aoluguya, when did we differentiate between each other like this? Why turn our guns to point at other branches of the Ewenki now? Why hate Han people now? Han people married you, raised children for you; why would you now curse the Han people? The old times were so good. The hunters' wives were treated the same as the hunters. Now look at us. Those of us who married ethnic Ewenki hunters are not even entitled to subsistence allowances! Why drive a wedge between the groups after the relocation? Only the Hunters are given jobs, but nothing is provided for us. What is the reason behind all of this?

One hunter's elderly Russian wife said:

I have been a hunter's wife all my life. In the past, we were all treated as Hunters. But after moving here, we are no longer Hunters. If no more hunting is allowed, then why even bother herding reindeer? There's no way to make any profit by selling reindeer antlers. Just stay home and receive the subsistence allowances. Anyways, the government cannot just let us starve to death!

The ethnic group's spiritual leader, Maruia Suo, had opposed the relocation. Now in the face of many predicaments, the hunters all felt that moving down the mountain was a mistake. They all admired the Ewenki elder Maruia Suo, who had refused to move down to the new township site. Her mountain campsite remained in the Alongshan region, 260 km away from Genhe County. While admiring Maruia Suo, the hunters all blamed the hunters Dimeiya and Xiren, who championed the relocation in the beginning. Many people claimed that the two of them received special treatment from the county and encouraged the others to move only because they had taken bribes. Almost all of the hunters said the same thing:

If it was not Dimeiya supporting the relocation, I would not have moved. The county had asked Dimeiya to bring a message to us—that whoever moved sooner would be given money in addition to furniture; while whoever moved down later would not receive these extra benefits. We were told this. Because she is one of us—of course we all followed her.

Dimeiya, a 56-year-old woman, was the township head's aunt by blood. She could read, knew about the outside world, and she once attended the National Minority Women's Representatives Conference. Now a widow, she had been married twice before; the last time to a man eleven years younger than herself. Because of her past and her abilities, she was highly regarded and respected among the hunters. Dimeiya was highly distressed about the situation in the Ao Township after the relocation. She felt wronged when the hunters talked poorly of her. Hurt by their words, she said softly:

The housing at Sanchejian [new site] had already been constructed. If we had not moved, it would have been a waste of the government's money! The county had said that the move was necessary. They let me be their vocal supporter, and asked me to rouse the hunters. Were the promises that the county made not good enough? Who could reject such great promises? But things turned out like this—I certainly did not expect it beforehand. If I had known, how could I have championed the move?

The curses aimed at Xiren were worse. The hunters all said that Xiren belonged to Solon (another Ewenki branch) and therefore was a "fake hunter." They said: "Who granted him the authority to represent the hunters on TV?" Later Xiren said to me:

> Now the hunters all say that the county gave me and Dimeiya 100,000 RMB—that we each have 50,000 RMB. Do you think this is possible? At the beginning, if it were not for the great promises that the county made for us, we would not have moved. Also, the choice of whether to move or not was not a new one. One year ago, the site was chosen for the construction of new houses. If we refused to move there, would not that have wasted the government's money? Back then the county promised me, 'Xiren, once you move down, your life will simply be holding a liquor bottle in hands, and smiling at the reindeer in the pens. You no longer need to chase after the reindeer; no longer need to live in danger and hardship. The county will employ helpers to feed the reindeer for all of the hunters. All you need to do is to enjoy life at home! We guarantee to build the fully modern hunters' houses with color TVs, mobile phones, and anything in need. Tap water, central heating, flush toilet—are not these conditions much better than those up in the mountains? You are a long-time Party member and must show your loyalty and ideological commitment. This is a great blessing for the Ewenki people. Although the hunters do not understand this, you must understand!' Now that I've explained it like this, can you pick out anything wrong about the government's offer? Would you not be tempted upon hearing such an offer? Of course, I led the group to move only because I thought that we would no longer have such a hard life once we had moved down to this site.

Xiren was one of the few Ewenki who had had a high school education. His father was, at one time, the Party head in the Ao Township. Xiren and Dimeiya had both received education at school and were good at expressing themselves clearly and spoke with more conscious reflection than other hunters. This was the main reason why they were selected by the government to act as intermediaries. Both Dimeiya and Xiren mentioned that they wanted to talk more about the various issues related to the relocation during the intermediary process, but government officials stopped them. Even when they did get to voice some of their concerns before the camera, the TV station did not broadcast their concerns.

Protests from the Hunters' Representatives

When the hunters talked about the way the media reported on the relocation event, they expressed their outrage. Several hunters, who were educated and served as representatives to the Ao Township People's Council, jointly wrote a report entitled "Genhe County Broadcast and Publicized False News Based upon Non-truth" to the National Ethnic Affairs Commission to express their dissatisfaction.

On 10 August 2003, in order to make a big impact and publicize the unique qualities of the county's multiple ethnic groups, the government invited the county's art troupe to perform at the Aoluguya Ewenki Township relocation ceremony. However, all of the hunters were driven out of the performing area and instead a group of actors were brought in to pose as hunters to sing and dance. The news report said that the hunters 'sang and danced joyfully' to celebrate the relocation; however, even comrade Dimeiya, hunter and current Hulun Buir County People's Council Representative, was driven from the location by security guards. Not only were the hunters not part of the celebration, they were not even present in the audience. This kind of behavior not only deceived the country, but also deceived all of the broadcast media, and severely hurt the Ewenki hunter ethnic group's self-respect. The hunters' enthusiasm was dampened, the ethnic groups' unity was damaged, and the news report lost its truthfulness.

In the ongoing news report in Genhe County, it was claimed, 'The hunters now live a settled, harmonious and wealthy life.' However, the reality is just the opposite. It became so awful that the real Ewenki hunters no longer wanted to watch the similar news reports, and are afraid to watch the Genhe News. In certain interviews, some non-hunter Ewenki people were interviewed to conduct false publicity statements, and make claims that 'we have improved reindeer stock-raising and what a happy life now we have.' This statement conceals the truth of reality, and deviates from the purpose of truthful news reporting.

The situation mentioned above hurts the Ewenki hunters and saddens them. If it is left unattended, the hunters will lose their trust in the government, and lose their trust in the country.

The authors of this report, the representatives of the Ao Township People's Council, said sadly:

> How pathetic the hunters' lives are these days! Is this a well-off life? We are close to living on chaff! The county still makes things up; they let other people come in and pose as us, as if we are having a happy life! In March 2004 at the Genhe County People's Council Conference, we, three hunters' representatives, submitted three proposals that demanded relocation fees, hunting guns, and employment solutions for the hunters. But the county never responded. The township has no authority at all. Everything is up to the county to make decisions. We, as people's council representatives, could not play much of a role. The county completely ignored our proposals.

Complaints from the "Leading Goose"

Because of the tremendous gap between the reality and the ideals originally aimed for, a strong sense of discontent has permeated the

Ao Township for the time being. Some hunters suggested "returning to the old Aoluguya." However, moving back to old Aoluguya is impossible because the county government sold the site to a real estate company. The site was closely guarded and could not be entered. However, at the new Ao Township, raising the reindeer in fenced-in pens has proved to be impractical. Therefore, with the government's permission, hunters' campsites were re-established in the sparse mountain forests near the Genhe County seat. However, lichen did not grow well in the region; the reindeer were unable to obtain enough food, let alone thrive. Additionally, since the reindeer were unfamiliar with the terrain at the new site, many of them went missing or were killed by traps set by wildlife poachers. For these reasons, the Ewenki hunters began to consider moving their campsites to the north where the conditions were better. Just as all of this was taking place, one particular event transpired that prompted the hunters to immediately move their campsites back to the furthest forests. The event was that the Genhe County leader invited the Ewenki hunter Maruia Suo to a restaurant.

It was a frigid day shortly after New Year's Day in 2004. The weather was terribly windy; a stinging wind that was like tiny knives cutting my face. The snow on the roof was blown into flurries, and the tiny snow crystals that madly danced about in the wind struck my face. With snow blustering about, I was unable to recognize if it was just the wind blowing snow or if the flakes were falling from the sky. I heard that the Ewenki elder Maruia Suo had caught a cold and had been brought down the mountain by her daughter Kolisha to stay at the big new house in downtown Genhe, which Kolisha had recently purchased. For quite some time, I had planned to visit Maruia Suo at her daughter's house. My opportunity arrived that day when I was invited to attend a banquet organized by the government for Maruia Suo.

Kolisha was in her fifties and looked young and stylish. Her deceased brother-in-law (her elder sister's husband) at one time was an iron-fisted township head. Many years ago, he had arranged for Kolisha to leave town to obtain a good education. After she graduated and returned home, she worked at the People's Council of the Ao Township government. Her husband had worked as a judicial assistant in the township government as well. In 1998, both of them applied for early retirement, but continued to receive a salary of over 1,000 RMB per month. They will officially retire and receive full retirement benefits in several years when they reach the formal retirement age. Kolisha and her husband were both skilled at finding opportunities to do business. Their business was firstly involved in selling the reindeer products of Aoluguya. Gradually, they expanded their business on a large scale. The couple owned the largest reindeer product shop in the Ao Township. By the time I completed my fieldwork and was about to leave, they had registered a trademark for a line of newly developed reindeer meat and jerky products. After the relocation, Kolisha purchased a large two-story 120 square meter house in the downtown region of the Genhe County seat. This house used to be owned by the top county official. It was spacious and brightly lit. When they bought it they did not redecorate, but kept its original furnishings because it was in very good condition. Something in particular caught my eye—the door to the house had an unusually high *menkan* (door threshold), which required anyone entering the house to step over it.[2] Local people interpreted that the previous owner used this symbol to deliver a profound message . . .

That evening, one of the deputy secretaries of the county party committee, whose main duty was to manage the affairs of the Ao Township, invited Maruia Suo to a banquet at the Tianliyuan Restaurant. I was also invited to attend. The officials exhorted that attending the event would help me with my research, and they wanted me to see the magnanimous and generous fashion in which the Ewenki were treated. I went to the banquet excitedly. Tianliyuan Restaurant was the most luxurious restaurant in the entire Genhe area and its most expensive banquet set was priced at 8,888 RMB. This was an expensive place for low-income Genhe residents. Normally, people would never choose a restaurant like this when having meals with their own friends. In other words, this type of restaurant catered only to government officials, who could have expense accounts for entertaining guests. That night, we were hosted by the Genhe County party committee deputy secretary. He had just recently moved to Genhe County, about two months after the relocation celebration. The main guest was the old woman Maruia Suo, and other guests included Kolisha and her family. Also present at the banquet were several chief members of the Ao Township leaders' group. Maruia Suo was close to eighty years old. She did not speak Mandarin, so her daughter sat next to her to serve as translator. The deputy secretary was sitting next to Maruia Suo and he addressed her and the other guests with earnest warmth. Maybe because he was also an Ewenki from another branch, it seemed that he exuded a sense of closeness to the Ewenki hunter guests at the banquet. He held the elderly woman's hands as he talked to her, trying to persuade her to quickly move her campsite from Alongshan down to the new Aoluguya.

All of the hunters' campsites had already moved down during the Ao Township relocation except for Maruia Suo's campsite. When the news reported on the county's ecological migration project, the reports often stated that although the first stage of the project had been completed, the completion of the entire relocation was being delayed because an old Ewenki woman had vehemently refused to move her camp down to the new community. Facing such media reports, the county government was left in an awkward position and hoped that this banquet would resolve the problem. Although the banquet resounded with the clink of glasses toasting and celebrating, the elderly Maruia Suo did not drink any alcohol at all. The only thing she drank was mango juice. She spoke very little, and when she finally did utter a few words, which were translated into Mandarin, the message was clear:

> I do not want to move. It is not that the conditions down in the new site are not good enough. The issue is that I cannot get used to conditions like that. I have lived in the mountains all my life and been used to it. Let the others move first. I will see if the reindeer do well or not. If they do well, then I will move down with the reindeer.

The deputy secretary talked about how the relocation was very important to the ethnic group's development. Maruia Suo just quietly listened to her daughter's translation without saying anything.

The fact was that the reindeer did not do well down in the lowlands at the new Aoluguya. This was one of the reasons why Maruia Suo had refused to move her campsite down. Though the township had provided her with a Hunters' house, she never lived in it. Instead, the house was occupied by her son Keliqi, who held a township government job and so had not been assigned a house. When I first arrived at the Ao Township, most of the reindeer had already been transported back to the mountains for herding. Only several reindeer were temporarily showcased in the specially built pen to show tourists on the celebration day.

The reindeer suffered serious losses in the first month after the relocation. Over 300 reindeer had been transported to the new Aoluguya during the first phase of relocation. To the dismay of the Ewenki, about ninety went missing or died after the relocation. Originally there were over one hundred reindeer at the Ao Township Enhancement Station. But after the heavy losses suffered by the herds that had been relocated, most of the Enhancement Station herd was given to the hunters to compensate their losses, and now there were only twenty-one reindeer left at the Station. This demonstrated that the reindeer preservation project, which involved the purchase of reindeer from Russia and involved an investment of over 400,000 RMB by the government in 1996, had failed. After the relocation, many reindeer starved to death for lack of abundant lichen, or were killed in poachers' traps. The surviving reindeer were skinny and bony and presented a strong contrast to the strong and robust reindeer living in the Alongshan. The old lady understood this and now was more determined than ever to stay. However, she could not let the county government "lose face" and embarrass them. When I stayed in the mountains with her, she shared with me her real thoughts. Her daughter and son-in-law's business in Genhe needed to maintain good relations with the county government in order to obtain tax deductions. That was the main reason for her to attend the banquet where she actually ate very little. It became obvious that the old woman was very wise indeed.

Just as the dinner was about to end, another party committee leader, the Political and Legal Committee secretary, arrived at the restaurant. He was a Mongolian like the deputy secretary and had also been transferred to Genhe after the completion of the ecological migration. This Political and Legal Committee secretary had a master's degree in philosophy and spoke in a contemplative and deliberate style. He had just finished another banquet next door and seemed to have already drunk too much. No sooner had he arrived than he said in a loud voice, "It is wrong to have implemented the relocation! But, we cannot say that!— Anyway, the goal is to get money!" He continued, "The hunters' guns are like the farmers' hoes—they are tools of production. Without the tools of production, there is no income, and then there is nothing to eat! The guns should not have been confiscated!" Others at the banquet cheered and clapped their hands in agreement. Soon news of his opinion and the banquet had spread wide and reached the ears of the hunters in the Ao Township.

Among the people who heard about how the party committee deputy secretary had invited Maruia Suo to a banquet at the Tianliyuan Restaurant, Dimeiya was the most disturbed. Once hearing about this news, she checked with me, and without any mask her first reaction was to spit on the ground, and then she said, "They made us move, so we moved. Now what benefits do we get? Those who refused to move receive more respect. If I had known, then I would not have moved! I will move back, and let's see what the county will do to me!" Later, the township head heard her aunt's anger and moved quickly to calm Dimeiya down before immediately submitting a report to the county government. Upon receiving the report, the county government quickly organized several party committee and government leaders to bring needed goods to the Dimeiya campsite and other campsites around the new Aoluguya to console them.

Later, the county leaders reflected on their treatment of Dimeiya, who was relocated, versus Maruia Suo, who did not relocate. The county officials felt it was necessary to maintain social stability in the Ao Township and provide compensation to the relocated hunters so they would feel that they had been more fairly treated. Part of the county's strategy was to ignore the Maruia Suo campsite.

The county decided to give significant preferential treatment to the hunters who had relocated to the new site. They tried, in particular, to provide preferential treatment to Dimeiya, one of the community opinion leaders, to mitigate her irritation and frustration over her decision to relocate to the new houses, and convince her not to return to a more northerly remote mountain site. Because Dimeiya held considerable influence among the hunters, the township head herself came to attend to her aunt's complaints and needs. The township head allocated two of the most affluent work units to provide assistance to Dimeiya's household and her elder son's household. The assistance they provided was not only in the form of various goods, but also included monetary assistance. When tourists came to visit hunter campsites in the mountains, they usually made purchases and paid fees. So despite the fact that the Dimeiya campsite was further away, the county still arranged for the tourists to visit her campsite. This caused the other hunters to feel this was unfair and served to back up previous gossip—that Dimeiya received special treatment or bribes to convince her to support the relocation.

Even though Dimeiya received preferential treatment, she did not drop the thought of moving back to a more northerly mountain campsite. She explained that although the county appeared to attend to her concerns it still did not help her, and if she did not move back there would certainly be more grievances in the community. By talking with the county, she built her careful strategy to ensure the government would pay attention, and mentioned the reasons why she wished to move back to a more northerly remote site:

> Too many reindeer have been killed by traps at Gufengbei [the location of the Dimeiya campsite, 30 km from Genhe County seat]. During recent days, I have found over 200 traps within a 10 km area around the campsite. We will lose far more reindeer if we continue living here. And moreover, there is very little lichen around the Genhe seat area. Reindeer do not eat well and so do not grow antlers. Now hunting is prohibited, the hunters' income is solely dependent upon reindeer antlers. Because the township has been unable to offer solutions to improve the hunters' income, I have no choice but to move back. The hunters live on reindeer; we have to follow the reindeer.

Dimeiya strongly required the township to move her campsite and reindeer back north to Alongshan. However, it would not be easy to move back. The county absolutely refused to allow the hunters to move their campsites and reindeer back to the Alongshan. Indeed, when the Maruia Suo campsite did not move down, the county had already felt considerable embarrassment when speaking to the news media. Now if word were to get out that the hunters were moving back, the county would surely lose face. Township leaders and officials came to persuade Dimeiya and eventually reached a compromise. The hunters could move a certain distance to Jinlin in the north, about 60 km away from the Genhe seat. The township first arranged to have a deputy township head and a vehicle accompany Dimeiya to visit the new Jinlin site and later arranged for trucks to move her herd of more than one hundred reindeer.

Complaints from Urban Residents

Not only did the Ewenki hunters and other citizens of the township make complaints; both the township and county leaders were also complaining. The township officials felt powerless and without any real authority because they were sandwiched between the county government and the hunters. The county officials complained that previous county leaders had gained political prominence by planning the implementation, and then got transferred to higher positions, leaving the mess to their successors. They also grumbled that the hunters did not know how to tell good from bad; that they were uncivil, dependent, and hard to satisfy. Residents in the Genhe County seat were also complaining, "The county brought over a group of barbarians and certainly the safety downtown will go all to hell"; "The county always asks us to donate to the Ao Township. We not only have to feed the hunters, but we also feed their pets—the reindeer!"

However, other groups of people, including those who were forced to leave the old Aoluguya community when the relocation took place, envied the Ewenki hunters and complained about the differential-treatment policies that were implemented for the relocation. They grumbled, "The hunters are so lucky. They are entitled to new houses at no cost at all. How could we possibly afford the type of house occupied by the hunters? We are all citizens of the People's Republic of China, why we are treated so differently?"

Figure 4.1 Non-Evenki residence in Sanchejian

Contradictions and Conflicts

A Brawl Incident

The seeming quiet of the Ao Township was often shattered by events that belied the serious problems that the community faced. One day, about two months after the relocation celebration, I heard that the party committee secretary—the highest official in the Ao Township—had his nose broken by the Ewenki hunter Qinglin. The secretary had to go to Heilongjiang for plastic surgery, whilst Qinglin was arrested and detained by the police.

The incident occurred like this: the party committee secretary was driven in a government vehicle to the Maruia Suo campsite in the Alongshan to persuade the old woman to relocate. The secretary drank liquor with the hunters, and then said several things that the hunters did not want to hear. Qinglin had also drunk liquor, and without a word he punched the secretary directly in the nose. The hunters were not surprised by this incident at all, explaining that they felt they had been lied to right after moving down to the new Aoluguya. Not only were they not allowed to hunt, and thus lost their source of income, but also, everywhere they went, they felt that they were held in contempt. They were extremely disgusted by the reporters' interviews, saying that the reporters had all lied and never broadcast any of the interviews that expressed the hunters' actual opinions and concerns. They also disliked the fact that the news reporters treated them as "savages" or as "weirdoes." The hunters were depressed about their situation and there was fire burning inside them. Almost everyone was sure that sooner or later this sort of violence would occur. It happened quickly, and was resolved quickly too. After being punched, the township party committee secretary returned to the township and reported the case to the police.

Qinglin completed his military service in 1999 when he was 26 years old, and returned back to his home in Aoluguya. During the time in the military, Qinglin had joined the Party with the hope that this would lead to a good job after retiring from the army. However, by the time he was discharged and returned back to Aoluguya, the township was no longer obligated to make job arrangements for discharged servicemen, so he had to stay at the Maruia Suo campsite, herding reindeer for his second aunt Hasha. Hasha was over one hundred years of age and could no longer work on the mountain; she had been spending most of her time living at the nursing home. Qinglin's third aunt was Linda. After punching the secretary, Qinglin was arrested and detained for over twenty days before being released on bail of 1,000 RMB paid for by his aunt Linda.

The incident of Qinglin punching the secretary caused quite some shock in Genhe County. The average Genhe citizens all said that the hunters were quite barbarian and thus they even dared to beat up a government official. But some of my acquaintances that were part of the local elite of Genhe did not blame the hunter but rather ridiculed the secretary. The hunters all held a very high opinion of Qinglin because of this incident; Qinglin himself was not upset at all about being detained. When several hunters and I talked about this incident with him, he only smiled smugly. I asked, "Did you ever think about the consequences? Hitting him was a crime indeed. Are you not afraid of being convicted?" He replied, "I did not think that much. His [the party committee secretary's] words were too infuriating. You 'Bogeda' [an unfriendly expression of addressing Han people] are good at talking, but we are not very good at talking and expressing ourselves. Well, so then if we are not good at quarrelling, then can we not fight?" While speaking, he laughed out loud.

Friends in Genhe helped me understand some of the cultural practices commonly found in the northeastern regions of China. They explained:

> Although Genhe here is governed by the province of Inner Mongolia, it still belongs to the northeastern region, because in the past it was governed under the province of Heilongjiang. You need to understand our northeastern customs. We northeastern people are sincere and transparent. If anything happens, we will not beat around the bush. We do not quarrel, but just go straight into fighting. All is even after the fighting.

I was later to witness this custom many times in the Ao Township. One day, the young male hunters would have a bloody fight and that would result in someone bleeding from a head wound, but the next day they would all sit together as friends drinking liquor. If you asked the cause of fight they had no real explanation, and both parties would simply explain that they had had drunk too much. Many young male hunters of the Ao Township had been detained or imprisoned. In their eyes, being detained or imprisoned was not a shameful thing, but rather was seen as quite manly.

The furor over the punching of the secretary quickly quietened down in the Ao Township. The secretary remained in the position of secretary in the Ao Township, but most of the time he was not in his office during the day. He appeared mostly after work or on the weekends when the township held meetings. Most of the time, citizens of the township could hardly catch sight of him. When the county party committee deputy secretary invited the Ewenki elder Maruia Suo to the banquet, the township secretary, as mentioned, was also seated at the table. When the banquet was over, Maruia Suo went over to say a few words to him in private and was translated by her daughter and the township head: "Do not be upset with the Ewenki people. Young people are not mature and are too impetuous." Maruia Suo was referring to the Qinglin punch-in-the-nose incident, but she did not name anyone. From her choice of words, I felt she was relaying a message that conveyed her status as a leader of an ethnic group. She was not only issuing an apology to comfort the secretary, but was also conveying her care and desire to protect the young men for Ewenki ethnic posterity.

The Accusation from the Hunters

In February 2004, when the whole world seemed to be frozen solid and Genhe County seemed even colder, Dimeiya wrote a letter to the Hulun Buir City party committee secretary to appeal for her own niece—the township head. The main content of the letter is outlined below:

> The ecological migration has failed and the hunters are very dissatisfied. Everyone says the same thing, 'how could this be considered a well-off life? We are almost left to live on chaff!' Now at Genhe we live on subsidy and assistance. It feels just like being a beggar! In the past, without subsidy, without assistance, we lived just fine. Now on the contrary, with subsidy and assistance, we hardly have enough to eat and everyone is depressed!

The hunters believed that all of this was because the township officials, who were of Ewenki descent, were suppressed by the hegemony of the

Han and so were unable to speak up for their own ethnic group. The proof for this belief was that the township head, who was of Ewenki ethnicity, did not have nearly as much authority as the party committee secretary, who was of Han ethnicity. Therefore, writing on behalf of the hunters, Dimeiya demanded that the township head should be replaced by a more capable person. The response from the Hulun Buir government stated, "After a one-month observation period, we will decide whether or not to change the township head." But long after the observation period passed, the township head was still in her office and the petition was not brought up again.

It was impossible for the township head not to have known about this petition, but she simply pretended that she was not aware of it. When I asked her about it, her face turned red and she responded, "I do not know anything about it." However, this was an issue that everyone in the Ao Township knew about and so I was sure that she was aware of it as well. Later she had to acknowledge that she did know about the issue. Emotionally, she confided to me her grievance:

> What would you say I should do? I have no intention of gaining benefit for myself. I myself have no housing, and have to live in a room that has been temporarily lent to me at the building constructed for the Hunter Product Trading Shop. You saw the conditions there and know it is poor. Conditions are not nearly as good as at the Hunters' houses! If you were in my position, what would you do?

I could understand her situation. She was not able to control the consequences of the ecological migration. The hunters were being too critical of her actions and indeed they exaggerated her "incompetence." She truly desired to do things for the hunters that would benefit them, but she lacked the authority to do so. Even the party committee secretary of the Ao Township was not able to make many key decisions. Although the township officials' leadership capabilities were under question, in reality, the actual economic conditions in Genhe County were far more influential in determining what actually took place. The key problem was that Genhe County had very little income and a very restricted budget. In spite of the letter complaining about her leadership ability, the township head did not take offense at her aunt's actions. She fully understood how her aunt felt, and continued to take good care of her aunt just as before. When Genhe County held a competition to select outstanding local citizens for the upcoming tenth anniversary of the founding of Genhe County, the Ao Township was allowed to select one representative. The township quietly gave this award to Dimeiya. But Dimeiya did not go to claim the award and the township head accepted it on her behalf. Despite having received this honor, Dimeiya insisted, "Though she is my niece, I still have to criticize her. Putting her in that difficult position of township head is almost like a form of torture for her."

Helplessness of the County Government

After the relocation, Ewenki hunters still lived the same dual-residence lifestyle of up-in-the-mountains and down-in-the-lowlands as before. Every few months the reindeer herders on the mountains would come down and stay in their new houses in the Ao Township for several days. During that time, they would receive subsistence allowances quarterly, and then go downtown to buy liquor. They would also gather together a bunch of hunters to go to restaurants in the downtown area and have good food there. Normally, one person's three-month subsistence allowance (totaling 300 RMB) would be squandered away in one day. Some hunters would get drunk and go to lie down in the county party committee and government building. The workers in the building had no solution other than to call 110 (the emergency telephone number in China) to have the hunters sent back to the Ao Township. When they were sober, the Ao Township hunters also frequently went to sit quietly in protest before the government building. Every time, they were warmly treated by a particular department head in the county government, who, after providing much comfort and persuasion, were able to convince the Ewenki people to accept a ride in a government vehicle back to the Ao Township. After the Ao Township relocation, this had become the hunters' "required routine" every few days.

The Genhe downtown area was only 5 km away from the Ao Township. The hunters' superior hiking skills enabled them to easily walk downtown to stroll around, drink liquor, and sing songs. Some hunters went downtown and drank liquor, but when they ran out of money and could not afford a taxi home they went straight to the county party committee building and lay down on the floor. Like clockwork, someone would call 110 and the police cars would show up and drive them home. Keqian, one of the female Ewenki hunters, told me that several times she herself had had no money for a taxi and when she was not willing to walk back to the township, she would go to lie down on the floor of the county party committee building. While talking about this, she mischievously laughed out loud.

The county officials were left scratching their heads helplessly in the face of the continuous hassles that the hunters created for them. In private they expressed to me their regrets of having moved the Ao Township hunters so close to the Genhe County seat, saying that this decision caused them a great deal of trouble indeed.

Internal Contradictions

After the relocation, not only did the conflicts between the hunters and the government become more frequent and intense, but fierce disputes, different from those in the past, also broke out among the hunters themselves. During the Spring Festival in 2004, one family of hunters spent the holidays in the hospital. The hospitalized woman was Bingyuhong, who was about 28 years old and married to a man of Han ethnicity. They had a lovely preschool-aged son. Bingyuhong was Qinglin's younger sister, and Linda's niece. Bingyuhong and Qinglin had lost their parents at a young age and were raised mainly by their aunts. When their parents were still alive, the family owned reindeer, but once their parents had died quite early, the children lacked the ability to recognize their family's own reindeer. Later, Qinglin joined the military and left town, and their family's reindeer slowly merged into other families' herds. Their second aunt Hasha never married; treated with sympathy by her parents, she received most of the family reindeer as her inheritance. In the mid 1980s, the Ao Township government implemented a family-based contract system for managing the reindeer herds. Hasha became the contractor at that time, and signed the agreement with her fingerprint. After Qinglin returned from military service, he went to herd reindeer for his aunt Hasha and lived year round at the mountain campsite. Because Hasha was quite elderly, during the eight years that Qinglin was away in the military, the reindeer were mainly cared for by Linda, Hasha's younger sister. Originally, Hasha and Maruia Suo lived at the same campsite. But later, owing to personal reasons, Linda moved some of Hasha's reindeer from the Maruia Suo site and established another campsite with Xiren's family. The reindeer Hasha left behind at the Maruia Suo site were later herded by Qinglin.

Ever since Aoluguya was settled in 1965, all male hunters in the Ao Township have received salaries to work as forest patrollers. In 2004, each man's salary was 36 RMB per month. Their salary for the year, a total of 432 RMB, was provided by the township in one lump sum at the end of the year. When Qinglin was arrested after punching the township party committee secretary, his aunt Linda bailed him out with 1,000 RMB, as mentioned. So when the year-end arrived and it was time to pick up the salary payments, Linda had expected to receive Qinglin's salary as payback for her bail payment. On the day the checks were to be picked up, Qinglin was at the mountain campsite 260 km away from the Ao Township, and so sent his younger sister Bingyuhong to the township to pick up his annual forest-patrol salary of 432 RMB. However, Linda had also gone to the township to pick up Qinglin's check, but when she arrived and found that it had already been picked up by Bingyuhong, she returned home and told her children. Everyone in her family felt they should demand this money back, for if Linda had not paid the bail money, Qinglin would have still been suffering in prison. Therefore, Linda's daughter Xueyina and her younger brother Ajun went over to Bingyuhong's house to ask for the money. Bingyuhong's husband was herding reindeer at his sister-in-law's campsite and was not home. Xueyina and Ajun entered the house and flatly demanded Qinglin's forest-patrol salary. Bingyuhong refused them, saying, "Qinglin has herded reindeer for you year after year in the mountains, yet you have never given him any share of the money made from the sale of antlers. What is the big deal about the 1,000 RMB bail money? He has made much money for you all these years." The quarrel quickly escalated into violence. Ajun began to beat Bingyuhong, who was injured in the assault, and Bingyuhong kicked Xueyina, who at the time was five months' pregnant. I did not witness the scene but the course of events was pieced together later according to accounts provided by the people involved and other people's statements.

Shortly after this incident, I happened to meet Xueyina. She was still angry and shocked that Bingyuhong had treated her like this. She said they had done nothing wrong to demand Qinglin's salary. Has not Linda fed and raised Qinglin and Bingyuhong all these years? Qinglin's food and clothing were all provided by Linda and so he should at least repay the bail money. However, I also heard people argue on behalf of Bingyuhong and Qinglin saying that, "Qinglin is so poor that he does not have any money to get married. Bingyuhong lives with her husband and they herd reindeer for their sister-in-law.[3] Obviously she does not herd for Linda!" In short, after this incident, the two close relatives indeed became enemies. When Bingyuhong's husband came down from the mountains and found his wife badly injured, he was outraged and distressed and took his wife to the hospital immediately. When Xueyina's husband returned home and heard that his pregnant wife had been kicked by Bingyuhong, he was also enraged and impulsively went over to their house to pick a fight. However, because nobody was home, he smashed the windows of the house.

Bingyuhong had been injured badly and had to remain in the hospital for over a month throughout the Spring Festival. Her husband spread the word that he would file a police report. He told everyone that the cut on Bingyuhong was over 5 cm long and that Xueyina's younger brother Ajun, who had committed the crime, would likely be convicted and receive at least a three-year sentence, and would surely lose his job. Linda and her family became very upset and nervous about this whole ordeal and regretted it deeply, admitting that they had been too impulsive in their demands for the money. To try to resolve the situation, Linda asked her niece Hexini to mediate.

Hexini was 48 years old. She had formerly worked as a government employee and accepted an early retirement package according to the Genhe County policy prior to the relocation. Now, she lived in an apartment that she had purchased downtown near the Genhe County seat. She formerly served as the chairperson of the Ao Township Workers' Union. She was the daughter of Linda's older brother, and she and Xueyina were cousins. She was also a cousin of Bingyuhong. Because she was a cousin to both sides in the dispute, Hexini was in an awkward position. Entrusted by Linda to mediate in the dispute, she asked a favor of Bingyuhong. Hexini was pained that this awful dispute had taken place among her relatives. Hexini explained:

> When in the past were we Ewenki people like this? All property used to belong to the extended family, and so who would have cared about this kind of thing? How could they injure a person for only 432 RMB? Look at Linda's loss now. The cost now far exceeds the 400 and something RMB— she has to pay the hospital fees that will exceed several thousand RMB.

She continued to explain that, as far as this incident was concerned, in her heart she took the side of Bingyuhong. "We are such close relatives. There is no way they should have beaten her like that. Now that I have to mediate in this matter to speak on Bingyuhong's behalf, I have offended my aunt Linda and incurred her anger. Because I participated in this dispute, my aunt Linda's family no longer talks to me." With regard to the problems that surfaced because of the relocation, Hexini also felt upset and powerless. Because the original Township leadership team had not agreed upon this relocation, the Genhe County government made significant changes to the membership of the Ao Township leadership team during the decision process over the relocation. Several of the leaders who had disagreed were transferred or asked to retire early. She and her husband, who served as the Ao Township party committee secretary at that time, both took early retirement.

The final result of the mediation by Hexini was that Bingyuhong did not file a police report. All the medical fees were paid for by Linda's family. The broken windows were also reinstalled and paid for by Linda's family. This incident then came to an end. However, afterwards, the two households cut all ties. Even when Linda' son Ajun got married about one month later and held a large city-style wedding party with over seventy tables for banquet guests, Qinglin and Bingyuhong were not invited. Naturally, they did not send any wedding gifts either. Later, the township introduced a reform proposal, which further intensified the conflict between the two families.

When the Ao Township government introduced its new system that reformed the old family-based contract system for managing the reindeer herds, Bingyuhong had just been discharged from the hospital. Her brother-in-law[4] supported the new plan (more details will be provided later in this chapter), and was willing to take over property ownership of the reindeer under the stipulated condition that the township was allowed to take one reindeer out of every ten belonging to his herd. In the meantime, he had asked Bingyuhong to talk to the township and demand that they speak to Linda to try to get back the reindeer that used to belong to Bingyuhong and Qinglin.

The township head came to the rescue. She went to visit her grand-aunt Linda, and asked Linda to give half of the reindeer to Bingyuhong and Qinglin. Linda's family responded that they would rather die than give up their reindeer. In response to this, Bingyuhong's family increased the pressure on the township head, indicating they were willing to be the first family to let the township take 10 percent of their reindeer, but only on the condition that the township helped them get their reindeer back. The township head was stuck in a very awkward situation. Linda's family said, "On what right do you have to touch my reindeer? If you are so capable, try taking other people's reindeer!" Xueyina replied, "These reindeer were contracted to my second aunt Hasha. The reindeer belong to whomever my second aunt gave them to. Hasha did not say to give them to Qinglin, so they are not his." Bingyuhong's family said, "Linda's children are all salaried, and yet they want to keep the reindeer. Too greedy! Additionally, the young people work, so they have no time to herd reindeer up in the mountains and the old people cannot do work in the mountains either. It is Qinglin who has been herding reindeer these years. For what reason should they own the reindeer?" Each family had their own reasons and standpoint in the argument. Other hunters in the Ao Township more or less took the side of Bingyuhong. The township government wanted to play fair and requested Linda to give up half of her reindeer to Bingyuhong. Linda's family, however, refused. This matter remained unsolved.

About one month later, a new twist appeared in the story—something happened to Qinglin while he was still out on bail. One day near the end of April 2004, Halijie's daughter, Keqian, went to the police station to accuse Qinglin of rape. Qinglin was arrested and detained to await his sentence. Unlike the last time when Qinglin was arrested for the punch-in-the-nose incident and Linda's family immediately went to post bail, this time, Linda's family expressed little concern at all for Qinglin's misfortune. Keqian, age forty-two, had been a widow for many years and had maintained a relationship with the 30-year-old Qinglin for quite some time. This time, Keqian had fallen down accidentally and broken her arm. Keqian's mother, Halijie, was angry not only about the injury, but also about the campsite, which would now be without Keqian's much needed labor. Another woman who lived at the Maruia Suo campsite where this incident took place told me that Keqian's broken arm had nothing to do with Qinglin and they had seen the very place where she had accidently fallen after drinking too much. It was said that Qinglin was arrested after Halijie and Linda conspired to report him. Halijie had wanted Qinglin to pay for medical costs associated with treating Keqian's broken arm. Linda also hoped that the sentence would help to eliminate contenders demanding the reindeer property ownership.

After the police completed their investigation, Qinglin was convicted to six years in prison. He was sent off to a jail several hundred kilometers away from the Genhe County seat to serve his sentence. Later, when Keqian recovered, she returned to the Maruia Suo campsite. During the month that I lived in the same tent with her, she talked to me frankly about the details of the case. She explained that Qinglin had not broken her arm, and because they were both so drunk at the time, neither of them clearly recalled exactly what happened regarding their sexual relationship. Many hunters felt the punishment meted out to Qinglin was too harsh. Even Keqian was shocked and felt somewhat guilty when she learned of his severe sentence.

Qinglin was gone. But soon afterwards, Linda's household welcomed a new person to the family—Xueyina's daughter was born safely. The child was healthy and lovely. When the child was a month old, at the end of June 2004, Xueyina's husband and her younger brother Ajun went to the Maruia Suo campsite in Alongshan. They moved the rest of Hasha's reindeer to the Xiren campsite. With that, there was a total of over twenty reindeer in Linda's family-owned herd. This move was completely a one-side act by Linda's family. The township government knew nothing about it beforehand. Linda's family hired a truck and expended a great deal of effort to transport the reindeer over 280 km to the Xiren campsite. There was, unfortunately, one small accident. When transporting the reindeer, the truck turned over on its side and killed a baby reindeer. The township took no action regarding this incident. Bingyuhong's family then realized that there was no hope of getting back the reindeer that they felt were rightfully theirs. All they could do was angrily curse the incompetent township leaders.

I always felt uneasy about the conflicts over the reindeer and Qinglin's salary that had caused such a rift between the two families. Indeed, both families themselves also felt very uncomfortable. The orphaned siblings were originally raised by their aunt, so should be grateful to their aunt's family. Money and family affection should not be placed at the same end of the scale. However, during the conflict between the two families, what should have existed sadly disappeared, and what should not have existed appeared. When searching for the cause of such problems, we cannot simply attribute the conflict to the selfishness of human nature. This is because such an argument cannot readily explain how the previously loving relatives, all of a sudden, turned toward each other in spite and hate. I was familiar with both families. They were all rather unsophisticated people and kind in nature. However, in reality, when arguments over right and wrong cannot reach common ground, in the end the more powerful side will often gain the upper hand. In spite of everything that happened, such conflicts should never be resolved by violence. The party who first started the fight was morally in the wrong, and other people in the community tended to sympathize with the weaker, bullied party.

In fact, this fight over property ownership had everything to do with the conflict between labor and profit allocation. In the past, reindeer were only tools for hunting and were not considered an important source of income. Therefore, this kind of property was fixed and did not appreciate in value. In other words, the hunters did not derive profit from the appreciation in value of reindeer. The entire group was owned collectively and managed collectively—everyone was regarded as an owner of the reindeer. Also, according to their traditional division of labor, people had no serious conflicts over the management of reindeer. But later, when reindeer antlers and hunting for wild game both became important sources of income for the hunters, this introduced the potential for fights over property. Due to the fact that, in the past, hunting income was quite good, and income from reindeer antlers was still secondary, the conflicts did not become apparent. But by the time hunting was prohibited, the hunters regarded reindeer as their sole source of income and viewed them as their private assets. Although nominally, according to law, the reindeer were held under collective ownership—owned by the entire community of Ewenki hunters in the Ao Township—according to my observation, in reality, ownership was not shared at all. People considered the reindeer to be their private property. And both the county and township governments had no power in governing the management of reindeer; for example, in the case of the fight over reindeer between Bingyuhong and Linda, the township's stepping in did not bring any helpful result or solution.

When the property ownership changed while the division of labor and profit allocation remained unchanged, it was inevitable that problems would arise over the question of fairness. In fact, because the notion of property ownership had changed, some of the hunters who owned no reindeer realized they worked and herded for other people without much income, and consequently were no longer willing to work at the campsites. Such hunters felt that if they continued to herd reindeer for others in the mountains, then they were nothing more than free laborers. However, consciously or subconsciously, within the hunter community, adjustments took place to adapt to the new changed relationship in the mode of production. For example, at the Maruia Suo site, Ningdao and Maoxia had owned no reindeer, but they were the main herders at the site. The old woman not only provided food for them, but she also gave them several reindeer; some "property" to motivate them and keep them at the site.

Education Concerns

Much of the written material describing the Aoluguya Ewenki people mentions that this ethnic group were poor at abstract thinking but strong in concrete thinking. Wondering about this myself, I conducted several simple experiments in the Ao Township. Among hunters who were over fifty years of age, none of them were sure about his or her birthday, and none of the hunters could provide the exact number of the reindeer at their campsite. However, the old hunters had names for each reindeer and could describe each of their special characteristics.

At the Ao Township elementary school, all of the teachers told me that the Ewenki children were smart with excellent memories. Although they were weak in areas like math, physics, and chemistry, all of the children were outstanding in music, physical education, and painting. The children in the first grade could already choreograph impressively complex dances. But despite much effort from the teachers, the children often failed in math, physics, and chemistry, but were good at writing essays. I had read many of the children's essays and felt they were full of thorough observation and rich imagination. I also tested the students in the fifth grade and found that they were unable to solve mathematics questions designed for second grade students. Simply put, Ao Township hunters' children were generally strong in the arts and poorer at sciences.

Based on observations of young Ewenki students, it appears, indeed, that they are poor at academic subjects but strong at subjects like art and music. I believe that they are poor at these subjects because they can see no value in these subjects. Their parents and grandparents had no exposure to such subjects and so these subjects find no practical expression in the everyday lives of Ewenki people. With no visible culturally accepted and practical value, young children cannot easily develop an interest in these classes. Music and art, on the other hand, are culturally valued among all generations of Ewenki and are able to attract the interest of Ewenki children.

Before the relocation, there was an elementary school and a middle school in the Ao Township. But after moving to the new Aoluguya, only an elementary school was provided. The school principal said that the only reason the township was able to have an elementary school at all was through vigorous fighting with the county government. If they had not fought to maintain their elementary school, all of the children in the township would have been sent to schools in the county seat. Now there were even fewer students at the Ao Township school than before. There were only twenty-nine students registered at the school with a teaching staff of thirty-one. The school teachers joked, "These elementary school students are treated like graduate students; one teacher for each student." However, all of the teachers complained about how difficult it was to teach so few children here. Because both elementary and middle school education are mandatory, the children proceed naturally to middle school no matter what kind of score they got in the elementary phrase. The teachers also added that, for many years, hunter parents were not friendly toward the teachers in the Ao Township, and tended to blame the teachers for their children's poor grades. In fact, many parents allowed their children to skip classes without any excuse. The teachers dared not to prevent this because they were scared of potential threats from the children's parents.

After the relocation, the students graduated from the Ao Township elementary school and went on to the middle school in the Genhe County seat. They generally had poor grades for two main reasons. One reason was probably related to the poor basic education they had received at the Ao Township school. Another reason was likely related to the unwritten policy of the Genhe County middle schools toward Ao Township hunter students. Through several friends who worked for the Genhe County Education Department, I learned that the Genhe middle schools did not count the grades attained by Ao Township Ewenki students in the class average. This was because the Ewenki students' grades, which were quite poor, would lower the class average. Since the teacher's performance was evaluated on the basis of overall class averages, a lower class average would have a detrimental effect on the teacher's career and salary. Thus, the

Ewenki students were treated like sit-ins just taking up space—the teachers paid little attention to them. This treatment by the Genhe schools cast a very negative psychological impact on the students from the Ao Township. This was clearly visible in the resentment that the hunter children felt toward education and the fact they so often skipped school.

From the old hunters, who had never received a modern school education, to the elementary school students, who had just began school in the Ao Township, I found it difficult to find evidence that modern school education had any impact on them at all. When observing the Ao Township hunters between the ages of fourteen and forty, it is possible to make some general evaluations regarding the effect of modern school education on them. Most of the Ewenki hunters in this age range generally graduated from the Ao Township school. Prior to 2003, some of them completed nine years of mandatory education at the Township elementary and middle schools, while others attended middle schools in the Genhe County seat. After the relocation in 2003, all middle school students attended school in the Genhe County seat.

After the Ewenki were relocated to Qiqian in 1959, the government began providing a living assistance allowance to encourage the hunters to enroll their children in school. The hunters lived at the old Aoluguya site in 1965 and their children went to a school where they were provided with room and board and had a living allowance of 8 RMB per month. Later in the 1980s, the government increased the living allowance to 16 RMB per month, which has stayed at that rate ever since. The highest education available in the Ao Township was middle school. Most students discontinued schooling after finishing middle school; very few students were able to pass the examinations that would provide them with the opportunity to attend high schools outside the region. Not going to high school meant staying in the Ao Township. Some students repeated grades in the Ao Township school because they could not find any other meaningful things to do as juveniles. Young people who had completed middle school and were eighteen years old had two options available to them—either become a hunter or join the military. Each year the government would distribute a quota to the Ao Township that allowed one Ewenki hunter to join the military. However, over the last several years, owing to the great popularity of joining the military,[5] competition for this opportunity is tough and non-Ewenki people have taken the quota set aside for Ewenki through various means.

All along, the government provided opportunities for the hunters to attend college or technical schools. Over the past thirty to forty years, in the Ao Township there have been over twenty Ewenki who have graduated from colleges and technical schools. Most of these graduates remained in the Ao Township and mainly worked for the government, the veterinarian clinic, the hospital, and the school. Several of them left the Ao Township and worked in other places. To this day, each year the Ao Township offers a certain quota of educational opportunities, funded by the government, for local people. The duration of these education programs ranges from short-term courses that take several months, to long-term courses that can last as long as four years.

Throughout China there is a tremendous emphasis on the value of higher education. Interestingly, even in a small place such as the Ao Township, the staff of no more than thirty employees each holds at least a college-level degree certificate. Even the illiterate cleaning staff member at the township office explained that she only needed to pay 4,800 RMB and three years later would be able to receive a college degree from the Genhe County Party School. The young employees explained that they wanted to obtain higher education in order to secure their current job positions and increase their opportunities for future promotion. Older employees mentioned that obtaining higher degrees helped to raise their salaries and pensions.

Currently, most of the Ewenki hunters no longer have access to government-funded opportunities to receive higher education and training outside of the township. Only the Ewenki people working for the township government would be considered for these opportunities. And only Party members are eligible to pursue degrees from the Genhe County Party School. In the Ao Township, only people who are Party members and have jobs are eligible to apply for the higher education opportunities. Therefore, for the hunter Qinglin, even though he joined the Party during his years in military services, after he returned to the Ao Township and began working as a reindeer herder, he was no longer eligible to apply for an education program that would provide him with a college degree from the Genhe Party School. Most hunters' children had to work as "hunters" after graduating from middle school—they had no official job.

To summarize, the various training and education opportunities, including the possibility for job promotion and future benefits, were only available to people who held official jobs in the Ao Township government. Furthermore, in comparison to employment in other work places, including the school, hospital, and veterinarian clinic, the requirements for the government workers were lower but their benefits were better, and their job position provided them with far better opportunities for education and career development. For these reasons, having an official job with the government was highly desired. Later Dimeiya told me that the only private reason she agreed to promote the relocation was because the township had promised they would find a job for her daughter in the township government office once the relocation had been completed. Despite this promise, in the end, her daughter did not receive employment within the township government.

The hunters did not consider education or achieving good grades in school as something that was very important at all. One of the reasons for this was because they felt that even people with no formal education could still be highly respected and become one of the wealthiest people in the Ao Township. Maruia Suo was a good example of one such person. They believed that spending money to obtain a degree was only necessary to become an official and to obtain increases in salary. Because most hunters had no official job, in their daily lives they could see no value in having a degree at all. This was one reason why for so many years the hunters generally paid little attention to school education. Another reason was that, in the past, when compared to other groups of people who worked at formal jobs, the Ewenki hunters enjoyed an enviable lifestyle. Back then being a hunter was the happiest life one could get, in their eyes. At that time, there were many aimless drifters who came to the old Aoluguya and were more than willing to remain behind to become "hunters." These two factors helped form the hunters' long-term tendency of ignoring education and placing little effort on pursuing higher degrees. However, after the relocation, the hunters' opinion began to change. They felt that sooner or later their traditional way of living would change significantly, and in order to prepare for this it would be better if their children had opportunities to attain higher levels of education. If they were to continue to live as "hunters," more and more of them would become jobless and face poverty with no guarantee of even food and clothing. Even worse, they realized that this kind of life offered no dignity at all. The hunters began to see that people who had higher education and degrees lived more comfortable lives in modern society. This awareness impelled the hunters to pay more attention to their children's schooling.

However, even though the hunters hoped their children might have a better future through better education, the modern school education system did not provide them with any extra assistance. Sometimes it worked against them. During my stay at the Maruia Suo campsite, an incident occurred in the Ao Township: three hunters' children, all new students at a middle school in the Genhe County seat, had stolen money from home and left town without a word to anyone. After 24 hours their parents alerted the authorities. The police department and the parents began a search in Genhe County, but after one week there were still no leads. The children were boys age thirteen, sixteen, and seventeen.

After I left the campsite and returned to the new Ao Township community, I learned more details about this incident. The 16-year-old boy pried his father's locked drawer open and took over 8,000 RMB in cash. He also took from the house several boxes of antlers and several dried reindeer penises (which are valued medicinal ingredients for Chinese materia medica). Someone had seen the boys playing computer games for two days in a game center in downtown Genhe, and then they disappeared. After a few days, the three boys traveled to a small town in Heilongjiang, hundreds of kilometers from Genhe, where they squandered all the money and sold the antlers and penises. When they were penniless, they made a telephone call home and asked the parents to pick them up. Luckily, all three boys were safely found. Two of them were sent back to school but the 17-year-old boy was determined to drop out of school, saying he would rather become a hunter in the mountains than face discrimination at school.

Dimeiya's youngest son was a second-year student at the Genhe County middle school. After learning about this incident, he no longer wanted to go to school. His older sister advised their mother Dimeiya, "Now he does not want to go, so let him be. Do not force him, otherwise he will skip school and learn bad stuff from the other scoundrels. Are those three boys not a lesson?" Dimeiya was quite bitter about this. She had hoped all along that her youngest son would be able to go to college in the future. This was also one important reason that helped convince her to support the ecological migration to the current site near Genhe County—the hope that her son would receive a better education.

This incident sent shockwaves through the Ao Township. From the perspective of the hunters, the incident showed the failure of school education—it demonstrated that children were not interested in school, and they were learning things that they should not have learned. The hunters said:

All of the teachers and students in Genhe are prejudiced against hunters. The teachers do not care about the children from hunter families. How could our children actually enjoy going to school in such a situation? In the past at old Aoluguya, such things never happened. Now our kids have come under the bad influence of the children at the school in Genhe downtown. It is all their fault.

The school teachers in the Ao Township said:

It is understandable that teachers at the Genhe County middle school ignore the students from the Ao Township. They are afraid of the students being wild and lack the guts to impose discipline. In addition, the school system itself is the problem because the grades achieved by Ewenki students from the Ao Township are not counted in the overall class average that is used to evaluate the teacher's performance. Because of the system in place, the teachers are not motivated to care for the students from the Ao Township. At the old Aoluguya the environment was simple and thus the study environment was better. In contrast, there are many fancy distractions in Genhe downtown. The kids in school there lack supervision and so are easily distracted to develop bad habits.

This incident also became an excuse for the hunters to rightfully complain about the relocation and claim the relocation to have been a big mistake.

It is useful to reflect on the type of influence that modern education has had on the hunters. If young people become hunters after graduating from school, the knowledge that they learn in school is almost useless. Yet, at the same time, while going to school they have missed the opportunity to gain knowledge necessary for living in the mountains. Because the school at old Aoluguya was a boarding school, the teachers never used the Ewenki language in school, but rather used standard Mandarin exclusively when teaching. This kind of learning environment and teaching style estranged the children from their people's heritage, traditions, and language. It is no wonder that nowadays young Ewenki Hunters are unable to speak the Ewenki language and are unable to appreciate and identify with the hunting and gathering lifestyle that their parents and grandparents followed.

Besides severing the connection between the Ewenki youth and their heritage, traditions, and language, what other influences have been brought about by modern school education? The direct consequence has been the fracturing of cultural continuity, which has led to the even more serious consequence of a demolished sense of cultural and social identity for the youth, leaving them in a profound state of confusion.

Because the majority of Ewenki youth in the Ao Township cannot pass high school courses and receive opportunities to go to college and receive higher education, then the only choice remaining for them is to become a hunter. And to become a hunter, in this new era since the ecological migration, means that if one owns reindeer, he or she may herd them in the mountains. And for those who do not own reindeer, they can remain jobless in the township and collect social welfare benefits. However, would the students who receive a "modern" education in a "modern" school have any interest in returning to the mountain campsites to live a "primitive" life of a hunter? Because the modern education system considers the lives of hunting and herding people to be "primitive" and "backward" and works to instill this belief in students, how could Ewenki youth possibly choose to live the life of a herder in the mountains?

There is a tremendous difference between young and old hunters in regard to their passion for living a traditional lifestyle of herding and hunting in the forests. If living in the forest involves only hunting for entertainment, then the young hunters are certainly interested and like it. However, if the lifestyle is to involve routine work and long-term living in the campsites in humble conditions, it is hard for them to accept. Old hunters are different. They have a wholehearted love for life in the forest and do not consider this type of life to be "backward" or "primitive." They enjoy the lifestyle in the forest, the day-to-day labor and strong sense of community that leaves them feeling content and happy. The old hunters have trouble understanding why young people these days refuse to go up to the mountain campsites. The only explanation they can arrive at is that the youth have all "become lazy like the Han people." Similarly, young hunters have trouble understanding their elders' passion for forest life in the camps and explain it by saying "the old people are just used to living in the mountains." But closer analysis shows that the reason for the elders' enthusiasm for life in the camps and the youths' inability to accept this lifestyle lies in their different value system. Their different value system has been very much influenced by the degree of modern education they received. Ewenki hunter youths hold modern views that were inculcated in them by the education system.

Old hunters' internal world and conceptualization of their roles in their society is capable of providing them with solace and meaning and is far more stable than that held by the young hunters. This is because old hunters' value system is not subject to being easily shaken or disturbed. Modern young hunters suffer spiritually and emotionally—nearly all of the Ewenki citizens of the Ao Township have experienced this, but for the most part do not understand why. The hunters perceive that the spiritual pains, feelings of disconnection, worthlessness and loss are caused by chaos disrupting their value system. On one side, they have been influenced by modernization—inculcated in the values of modernity, primarily through the school system, and have accepted the value assessment that pits modern lifestyles against backward lifestyles. On the other side, the modern lifestyles they believe must be better than the traditional lifestyles have not brought them any joy and satisfaction. They envy the leisurely and content traditional lifestyle led by the Ewenki elders, but, at the same time, reject the traditional lifestyle as backward and primitive. This confuses the young hunters, leaving them with little sense of what they might do to resolve this. This problem is indicated by the highest rates of death caused by suicide or alcoholism in the last twenty years.

In fact, modern school education is only a catalyst that has torn apart the value system held by young Ewenki hunters. The true root cause lies in the grand historical narrative and value system that underlies "modernization." However, neither Aoluguya hunters nor local government are aware of this point. We will provide a detailed elaboration about this grand historical narrative and its value system in the following chapter.

The Local Government's Placement Measures

Assistance from Both County and Township Governments

County leaders undertook a great deal of thinking, planning and effort in developing a plan to move the Ao Township hunters. When the county leaders visited the mountain campsites to persuade the hunters to move, some of them worried about having no income once they turned in their guns and moved down to face greatly increased life expenses. They asked about benefits the county would provide. The head of the relocation workgroup, the Deputy Mayor of the County, promised that for three years, water, electricity and heating charges would be waived. The government fulfilled the promise.

Right at the beginning of the relocation, the county provided a living allowance of 300 RMB for each hunter household that was moving into a new house. This was to motivate the hunters to move and was not provided to those hunter families that decided to move later after everyone else had already moved. For the first three days following the move, the county government paid for all meals. The government had all of the Ewenki who moved down to the new community gather in the empty Hunter Trading Shop building that had been transformed into a temporary dining hall where they ate. Some hunters commented, "Those three days were joyous! It would be wonderful if things could always be like this!"

Right after the relocation, the county assigned each of the county's work units to provide one-on-one assistance. Coincidently, the county government just happened to be comprised of sixty-two work units, a number that exactly matched the number of Ewenki households that needed to relocate. However, when arrangements were being made, for some reason, one newly established work unit was not counted in, and this left only sixty-one work units on the list to provide assistance. The Ao Township government became the sixty-second work unit that would offer the assistance. Later, by coincidence, I became friends with the Department Head of the work unit that should have been the sixty-second on the assistance list, but had accidentally not been counted in. Feeling fortunate, he said:

> Hey, it was indeed quite a favor to me that the county forgot to count in my work unit and sign us up for this 'good deed' [helping the Ewenki households]. You have no idea. The head of one certain unit was worried to death. His unit was assigned to a household that had a student. When the family was required to pay various tuition charges throughout the year, the Ewenki household called the unit official's home every few weeks. Each time, he had no choice but to quickly take some of his own money to help the family. Providing that kind of assistance was torture. Luckily the county limited the period of assistance to three years. I do not think anybody would be able to stand it if things just went on and on.

As mentioned above, each work unit was responsible for providing assistance to one hunter family. Its main duties were to provide the household with basic living needs, like furniture, bedding, and household goods. During holidays or festivals, each work unit would need to bring an assistance care package to the family that contained items needed for the holiday, like food items and cooking oil. Some units that had more income could even provide money to the family to assist them with their daily living costs. The households and the work units were matched by the township government. Once the match had been decided, each work unit would provide assistance directly to the Ewenki household with no further involvement of the township office. Since the work units' economic status varied, each household received different forms of material assistance. The hunters complained about this arrangement, "This kind of assistance is unfair. The richer work units have all been matched with families who are the direct relatives of township officials!"

After the relocation, the government made some adjustments to the hunters' subsistence allowance. The subsistence allowance that had previously been provided to hunters' spouses was canceled. In the past, their subsistence allowance used to be 30 RMB, 60 RMB, or 90 RMB; now, the qualified Hunters received a monthly allowance of 100 RMB. The Ao Township nursing home, which fell under the direct supervision of the county nursing home, employed only two Ewenki hunter girls as temporary workers, who each received a monthly salary of 300 RMB. The county nursing home funded the Ao Township nursing home based upon living expenses of 150 RMB per month for each resident.

Thirty-Eight Welfare Job Positions

Because the hunters were no longer allowed to hunt, their requests for employment opportunities with income were justified. County officials racked their brains to search for solutions. In Genhe County, a large number of forestry workers had already been laid off since the implementation of the State-owned Enterprises Reform and the Natural Forest Preservation Project in 2000. There were no solutions yet for these people, let alone for the Ewenki hunters who lacked the "skills of modernity"— they lacked advanced education and had little knowledge of modern technology. It was a daunting challenge to make job arrangements for the hunters. But the Genhe leaders still managed to come up with ideas. They managed to create thirty-eight welfare job positions out of the "4050 Re-employment Project"[6] and assigned them to the Ao Township. The main duty of these thirty-eight positions was to clean streets in the Ao Township. Each employee would receive a monthly salary of 200 RMB. In the beginning, the Ao Township government encouraged all the hunters to take employment and emphasized that these positions included medical and pension insurance. As such, Ao Township hunters' treatment was quite good in comparison to the other residents in Sanchejian. Rather unexpectedly, however, these thirty-eight welfare job positions gave rise to quite a storm in Ao Township.

As soon as the township government received the notice of the positions from the Genhe government, it notified the sixty-two households to let them know they could take these jobs cleaning the streets. The timing of these jobs was perfect, as several winter snow storms had completely covered the streets and it was difficult to tell where the roads were. Not only were the main roads blocked, but the lanes between the rows of houses were also piled high with thick snow and ice that made walking very difficult. When they heard that they would receive salaries for cleaning the streets, the people of the Ao Township threw themselves to work without any extra thoughts. Soon the asphalt roads were cleared. This incident made me think about my hometown village in Shandong. Every year when snowstorms hit, the elderly grannies and uncles would voluntarily go out to clear the streets without any payment at all. The Ewenki hunters certainly seemed to be receiving preferential treatment.

In the first several days, there was quite a flurry of snow-shoveling action in the community, involving men and women, young and old. After more careful observation, I noticed that none of the people, in fact, were Ewenki male hunters. Most of them were the non-Ewenki spouses of hunters and some of the others were young Ewenki women. They felt quite satisfied at the prospect of receiving a fixed income of 200 RMB each month.

When the time came to send out their salaries, there was a problem—the township had no idea how to distribute the payment. It hurriedly checked to see who had worked and who had not. Once again the township faced the difficult problem of having too few resources for too many people. Of course, more than thirty-eight people had participated in the snow-removal work, so now the question arose of how to distribute the payment. The township leaders felt that because these thirty-eight positions had been provided to help resolve the hunters' employment concerns, the money, of course, had to be distributed to the hunters. Later, the township made a decision: the job positions were only available to Ewenki Hunters who did not own any reindeer or have any formal employment. Other people could not hold these positions. This announcement caused quite a storm in the Ao Township. People whose family owned reindeer were not allowed to take these positions even if the family had an excess of laborers and not enough reindeer-herding work to keep them occupied. The new rules also excluded hunters' spouses (non-Ewenki) from doing the work. To make matters more complex, the single males who did not have any reindeer tended to disdain this type of street cleaning labor.

In the end the actual work situation was arranged like this: hunters' spouses did the work for the hunters, and single male hunters only

Figure 4.2 New houses in Aoluguya after snowfall

Figure 4.3 Snow removal employment project

undertook street cleaning occasionally, but still received the same salary as those who worked regularly. This led to more complaints, "This is not fair at all. Not doing the work but still taking the money!" To resolve some of the problems, the township threatened to deduct the hunters' salaries to force them to work. But some hunters simply pulled out completely, yet still demanded their salaries. They said with strong conviction, "The money from the county has been issued according to the number of positions. Work or no work we are entitled to the 200 RMB each month. The township cannot be corrupt and keep the money." The township officials responded, "We cannot let them have free money like this. No work, then no salaries!" As a result, for a period of time, those who were receiving the salaries provided by the "4050 Re-employment Project" were almost all Han people—the hunters' husbands or wives. The unemployed hunters then said, "Was not this work arrangement made for hunters? But now the jobs are all taken by ethnic Han people! Where are our jobs? Also, we hunters are supposed to be hunting, so how could you let us just clean streets? Our hands should take guns, not the broomstick!"

After the snow and ice had melted, the street-cleaning work was no longer labor intensive and did not need workers. The township found other positions for the hunters, such as museum narrator and guide, Ewenki language teacher at the Ao Township elementary school, and gardener for the grounds at the Township government building. The salaries for these positions were also drawn from the funds provided by the "4050 Re-employment Project." On average each person received 200 RMB per month.[7]

Reindeer Ownership Transition

Although the reindeer pen-feeding program as planned by the Genhe County government lasted only one week after the relocation, a great deal of human effort and financial resources had been invested. Right after the hunters had moved to the new Aoluguya and began raising the reindeer in pens, the county supplied bean-pellet feed for the animals. However, the reindeer refused to drink the tap water from the municipal water supply, and some of the animals choked to death when eating the bean-pellet feed. As a result, the township mobilized all the officials and employees to help the hunters to gather lichen in the mountains to feed the reindeer. Obviously, this was not a permanent solution. Genhe County's financial status was unable to maintain such a method of feeding the reindeer. Thus, after dealing with news media interviews and broadcasts, the hunters who owned reindeer had no choice but to return to the mountain campsites and live the life of a traditional herder just as they had before. The winter in January 2004 saw more snowfall than previous years. In some places in the mountains, the snow was as deep as one meter. This led to several "white disasters" at the campsites—a danger caused by heavy snowfall that prevented reindeer from digging through thick snow to find lichen. Fortunately, the county government quickly sent over bean-pellet feed and helped them through the crisis.

In March 2004, in order to address the situation regarding reindeer in the Ao Township, the township government proposed to change the policies regarding reindeer ownership. The township sent copies of the draft proposal to the hunters for their comments and advice. The proposal aroused much debate among the hunters. Below is a copy of the government's proposal, which includes a questionnaire form regarding the proposed changes in reindeer ownership.

Implementation Proposal for Changes in Reindeer Ownership (Draft)
1. Guidelines.
This proposal is centered on development, guided by the important ideology of the "Three Representatives," for the purpose of expanding the reindeer population, fully mobilizing and motivating the Ewenki hunters'

production, and bringing rapid improvements in the quality of life for Ewenki hunters.

2. Historical Review.
Before the Liberation, reindeer were the Ewenki hunters' private property. After the Liberation during the People's Commune period, the township government compensated the hunters in exchange for the ownership of reindeer. Since the period of Economic Reforms and Opening, the reindeer have been contracted out to individuals.

3. Current Existing Problems.
(1) Prior to the relocation, the Hunting Service Center served the hunters in the mountains in issues regarding reindeer herding in the Ao Township. Each year the Ao Township Integrated Forest Product Mill provided a 50,000 RMB subsidy for service fees. The Integrated Forest Product Mill was dissolved in 2001 and no longer exists. The township government does not have the funds to pay for these service fees. In accordance with this situation, we will initiate reforms to reindeer ownership. As a result, the Hunting Service Center will be dissolved.
(2) While the Hunting Service Center served the hunters, every year it charged the hunters 30 percent on the profit from antler sales, and 50 percent on the profit from reindeer sales. With the proposed changes in reindeer ownership, the charges are to be canceled and hunters' incomes will increase.

4. Detailed Implementation Steps.
(1) Transfer reindeer ownership to Ewenki hunters in exchange for com-pensation. The Ewenki hunters will then own the reindeer (sales rights, transfer rights, and reindeer product profit rights).
(2) After the reindeer ownership has been privatized, the sales of reindeer must be approved by the township government. Nobody is allowed to cap-ture or slaughter reindeer.
(3) The base number of reindeer is based upon the contract. The transfer fees for each reindeer will be 500 RMB per head. Reindeer can be used as cash payment. The average price for each reindeer is 5,000 RMB. The township will take one from every ten reindeer if the hunters cannot afford the transfer fees of 500 RMB per head. The reindeer taken by the govern-ment will be used for breeding, and for establishing a reindeer preservation project. The goal is to increase the reindeer population.
(4) After the changes in reindeer ownership, the owners will be responsible for all expenses associated with the reindeer. The township government will process antlers for the owners free of charge. The owners are obligated to pay the fuel costs for the vehicles used to transport the animals to the herding sites. The township government will help the owners sell antler products.
(5) The households will receive equal shares of the subsidies provided by the township government. When natural disasters occur, relief funds from

the township government will be allocated according to the headcount of reindeer owned by each household.

(6) The township government will work aggressively to help solve the Ewenki hunters' living and production difficulties. It will support the hunters to raise reindeer, and lead the Ewenki hunters to a well-off life.

(7) After the research survey on this draft is complete, it will be sent to the county government for approval and implementation.

Ao Township People's Government

March 2004

Changes in Reindeer Ownership Research Survey Form

Name		Gender		Ethnic Group		Age	
Do you agree to let individuals own reindeer?							
What other advice and suggestions do you have in regard to changing reindeer ownership?							

The survey forms sent out by the township government were generally not returned. The majority of hunters disagreed with the proposal to change the ownership of the reindeer. Their reasons are discussed below.

The hunters disagreed, firstly, because the proposed changes were unaffordable. Although 500 RMB for each reindeer was indeed inexpensive compared to market prices (market prices per live reindeer ranged from 5,000 to 8,000 RMB), few Ewenki hunters could afford this. This was because the original forest lifestyle of the hunters had given rise to their habit of not preparing any savings or surpluses. Sahlins (2001[1968]) elaborates on this, noting that in modern capitalist societies, the accumulation of assets is considered to be "wealth" and this comes with the assumption that more is better. But this does not apply to hunter-gatherer tribes that live in the conditions of a primitive society. When the animal and plant resources close to the hunting and gathering site are about to be exhausted, the people will move. In other words, roaming and herding are an indispensable part of the hunter-gatherer economy. Only through constant moving is it possible to sustain the community. However, maintaining high mobility cannot co-exist with the accumulation of assets.

To a constantly moving hunter-gatherer tribe, assets would only become burdens. The hunter-gatherer lifestyle is not conducive to accumulation for two main reasons. Firstly, such tribes have relatively low demands for material goods. The living materials they need are conveniently obtained from the natural environment where they live. When game and other sources of food or water are exhausted, they simply move to a different place. Therefore, for hunter-gatherer tribes, there is no need to accumulate food in case of famine. Secondly, constant movement makes it difficult and disadvantageous to carry assets. The ability to carry fewer things and travel lightly enables hunters to roam with greater comfort and convenience. To ensure that they could easily move, the hunters would sometimes intentionally destroy large assets and do things such as discard extra game half way back to camp. For hunter-gatherer tribes, the ultimate goal in life is certainly not the constant accumulation of assets but a sense of freedom from being unburdened by heavy material goods (Sahlins 2001 [1968]: 56–77).

Later, after the Ewenki traditional territory was incorporated into the mainstream economy in China and they began earning income through hunting, they maintained this age-old habit of not maintaining any savings, despite having comparatively high incomes. During the 1950s and 1960s, the Ewenki hunters' income was fairly high compared to the income of the average citizen in China. Because they enjoyed a constant income, they felt little need to save money to prepare for possible hardship in the future. However, in recent years during which their income has greatly decreased, this lack of incentive to save money has prevented them from being able to purchase reindeer.

The hunters disagreed, secondly, because they were unwilling to let the township raise their reindeer. Considering the situation that few hunters could afford the transfer fees of reindeer ownership, the township made an alternative plan that did not require the hunters to purchase reindeer. Instead, the new alternative plan involved the township government taking ownership of one out of every ten reindeer. This mainly served to placate the hunters who had reindeer but no money to turn in the transfer fees. Many of the hunters felt that, "This plan actually intends to seize our reindeer for free because the township knows the hunters cannot afford to purchase the reindeer." The hunters noted:

> In 1996, the nation set aside a substantial fund to enable the Ao Township to bring in reindeer from Russia. A Reindeer Enhancement Station was set up, and at the time a number of strong and excellent reindeer were taken from each hunter household for the purpose of mating with the Russian reindeer. The government promised then that young reindeer born from the mating would be given to the hunters; however, it never happened. Now many years have passed, and the mating reindeer we provided are now dead. These township officials indeed know nothing about raising reindeer. Reindeer cannot be pen-raised at all. Moving down the mountain certainly kills the reindeer. How could we allow these people to keep reindeer when they know nothing!

Thirdly, the hunters disagreed with the plan because they worried that without government assistance they would not be able to ensure the survival of the reindeer. They felt that, at any rate, the reindeer had been the official property of the nation for so many years. The government had covered all the expenses for reindeer production. So all these years, the hunters had herded reindeer at no cost to themselves. In the past, reindeer belonged to the Commune and the government covered their related costs. Later, an Integrated Forest Product Mill was established and it subsidized the Hunting Service Center tens of thousands of RMB each year. The Hunting Service Center served the hunters all around and was supervised by the township government. With the help of the Center, the hunters were able to conveniently commute up and down the mountains, and reindeer could be rescued in a timely fashion when accidents occurred. But now, the government intended to dissolve the Center. Once dissolved, the hunters would be left to do everything on their own, including tasks such as cutting, processing, selling antlers, transporting food from the lowland community up to the mountain camps, moving goods and supplies, and transporting tents. This appeared to be too difficult. The hunters all felt that, with the exception of Maruia Suo's family and campsite, all other hunters lacked the labor, money and the resources necessary to shoulder these responsibilities. The hunters themselves also acknowledged that, for so many years, they had been used to being covered and supported by the government. They worried that once reindeer ownership came back to them they would have to cover all the expenses of going up and down the mountains. On one side, they really could not afford the expenses involved; on the other side, they did not know how to handle the hassles that would be involved. These were the primary reasons why they did not want any change in ownership of the reindeer.

Their basic stance was this: the current ownership system was to be maintained, even if the Hunting Service Center was dismissed, the township government would still be in charge of things. As expected, despite the fact that the hunters disagreed with the proposed change of ownership, the township still quickly dismantled the Hunting Service Center in order to save costs by eliminating the salaried employees of the Hunting Service Center. The township did not remove itself of the obligation to assist the reindeer herders. In other words, although the Hunting Service Center no longer existed to drive the hunters back and forth to the mountain camps, the hunters were able to demand assistance from the government to provide vehicles when needed.

However, the hunters sensed there was a gap in the level of service provided by the township government as compared to the services that had formerly been provided by the Hunting Service Center. They commented:

Services by the township government are not as good as those of the Hunting Service Center. Back then the Hunting Service Center visited the campsites every ten days, to send supplies, and to check if any people or reindeer were sick. Now the township does this poorly. It is already considered quite nice if they visit the sites every half month.

In the past, the Hunting Service Center was in charge of sales. Once we cut the antlers and processed them the antlers were sold immediately. Now the township does not lend a hand with the antler sales. This year, not even one antler was sold!

In the face of these comments, the township leaders argued in their own defense saying:

The goal in changing the ownership of reindeer is to rid the government of this trouble. Under the spirit of the new market economy, the government should not be responsible for the production anymore, so we need to separate ourselves from the production completely. Now, the township government has to lose a lot of money because of the reindeer production. The vehicle rides to and from the mountain campsites, the fuel costs and the long-distance boarding and food costs are all expenses subsidized by the township. The township indeed has little money and everything is funded by the county. By removing government responsibility for the reindeer, we could save the township a large amount of money. In the past when the Ao Township Integrated Forest Product Mill still existed, every year they provided a subsidy of 40,000 RMB to the Hunting Service Center, and a subsidy of 10,000 RMB to the township government. So at that time, it did not matter who had ownership of the reindeer. Now the Integrated Forest Product Mill is gone, and the township government has a very tight budget. The Hunting Service Center was indeed very helpful and it proved to be a great deal of help to the hunters. However, if we had not dissolved the Hunting Service Center, then the salaries for over thirty workers in that unit would have had to have been funded by the township. Anyhow, the township is in charge of the hunters, so it was better to let the Hunting Service Center go in order to save the salary expenses. If the hunters themselves could afford the reindeer production, the township government would have an easy time. Currently, there is no solution to this problem—the hunters disagree with the ownership changes and so their reindeer are still managed by the township. In the end, not only is there no benefit for the township's finances, but all of this is costing the township increased losses.

The township distributed the draft regarding changes in reindeer ownership to all sixty-two households, including the Ewenki hunters who owned no reindeer. Some hunters were firmly against it; some supported it wholeheartedly, while others yet did not know what to think. The hunters who disagreed with the plan were those who currently herded reindeer under contract. In addition to the above-mentioned three reasons why they opposed the township government's proposed changes in ownership, there was one more reason, especially for the kind of family lacking labor: they had long regarded the reindeer as their own private property; if the ownership changed, permitting the ownership transfer inside the ethnic group, and the hunters who currently owned no reindeer were allowed to purchase reindeer at the cost of just 500 RMB per head, then this would present a loss to their current personal accumulated property. People who supported the ownership changes were mainly young hunters and some male spouses who were mainly of the Han ethnicity. They felt, "This is a good proposal. Once reindeer belong to us, we could even make money by selling reindeer meat. Currently antlers make no money at all." But when the old reindeer-loving Ewenki hunters heard statements like this, they were even more vehemently opposed to any changes in ownership.

Because of the significant discrepancy in opinion over the proposed changes in reindeer ownership, the township government did not proceed with the draft completely. The hunters' rejection of the first plan, because they could not afford to purchase the reindeer, led to a new alternative plan that would see the township take ownership of one in ten reindeer. This was also abandoned because the Ewenki herders opposed it. After that, the government adopted an increasingly indifferent attitude toward the mountain campsites. In the past, if the township was unable to send a vehicle to transport the hunters back to the mountains, it would reimburse the hunters the cost of the taxi fare. But now, with the new changes, they would no longer do so. If the township did not have on hand a vehicle to transport the hunters, the hunters had to pay by themselves. When the hunters were able to catch the occasional ride in township government vehicles to the mountains, they regarded themselves as lucky. The government's indifferent attitude forced the hunters to become more independent. After the changes, the Ewenki herders no longer had to discuss issues with the government when they wanted to move their campsites. They simply hired a few vehicles and moved. Each time they moved, they went further north, away from the Genhe County seat. The hunters' return to increasingly remote mountains regions became more obvious.

Over half a year since the relocation, the media's attention on the Ao Township had dwindled. The government turned colder and colder toward the hunters and did not care at all about the hunters' return to the remote mountain campsites. As to Maruia Suo and her campsite, which never relocated, the government no longer attempted to persuade them.

Later, although Maruia Suo did not relocate at all, the county and township officials held a meeting and formulated their message for publication—that all of the hunters had relocated from the mountains and that the "ecological migration" was successfully completed.

Attracting Commercial Investments

In early 2004, timbers were piled up high in front of the Hunter Trading Shop's doors. This unopened store was being turned into a small wood product processing factory. By June, there was much more noise emanating from the Ao Township—the sound of factory machines. One day in August, I arrived at the small factory, which had just begun operation. The warehouse was about thirty square meters in size, and inside were ten workstations where eight women were busy cutting long, thin logs. A middle-aged woman, who was not working, led me into a side room. Upon learning that I was from a university in Beijing and was doing research here, she hurried off to find her husband—the factory boss. They brewed a pot of black tea and recounted how they set up this small factory.

The small factory was named "So and So Wooden Products Manufacture," with the names So and So being a combination of the boss and his wife's first names. The boss' last name was Wang, and he worked as a wood crafts teacher at a technical high school in the Genhe County seat. The two of them were of Han ethnicity and they lived in downtown Genhe. Mr Wang said:

> My intention of setting up this small factory was to have a base from which I could offer training practicum for my wood crafts students. I chose a site at the Ao Township because I want to contribute something to the Ao Township, and to help with the hunters' employment problems. I have deep feelings for the Ao Township because I used to live in the old Aoluguya and worked there. In 1989, I worked at the old Ao Township ethnic school where they set up a wood crafts factory that I managed. Later

Figure 4.4 Small wood product factory

my family moved to Genhe, so now you could say that we have moved back to my 'hometown.' I opened this factory through a special program run by the Ao Township government that aims to attract commercial investments. So this year, we need not pay any fees for renting the building from the township.

The small factory mainly produced round wooden sticks that are used for corn dogs. Mr Wang found a client who exports the factory's products to South Korea. The factory was built in November 2003 and production began on 30 May 2004. Two months after production started, the factory began to make a profit. The estimated annual sales were over 300,000 RMB. In response to my inquiries, Mr Wang provided a thorough introduction to the factory:

This factory is completely privately owned and a total of fifteen people are employed here. Initially, we had eight people from the Ao Township, including hunters' spouses. When the factory was constructed, the township leaders encouraged all jobless hunters to come to try out jobs here. My factory welcomed them with open arms. Many young hunters came and gave it a try, but they quit in less than half day, saying the work was boring. The work here is not hard, but it is repetitious and hunters were not interested. Now there is only one female hunter working here, all the others are laid-off employees from the Genhe forestry industry. They are paid by piecework. Those who work hard can earn about 400 RMB each month.

Mr Wang specifically mentioned the support from the township leaders and added gratefully:

The township offered a free warehouse. I only need to pay for the water, electricity, and heating fees. The monthly heating fee is 3 RMB per square meter. For each heating period [about nine months] we only need to pay fees for an eight month period. This is much cheaper than in the county downtown. Also, the township leaders spent a lot of time running back and forth to the county to help my factory obtain tax exception. In the first month the factory operated, I had to pay in taxes alone several thousand RMB. National taxes and local taxes cost over 3,000 RMB while the industrial and commercial taxes amounted to 80 RMB. The tax rate is too high. After I talked to the township about these difficulties, the leaders went to the county to lobby for me. It worked much better than when I myself had gone to talk to the county. Since my small factory operates in the Ao Township, by getting the leaders to talk to the county and ask for more favorable terms, I now only have to pay a combined tax outlay of just over 500 RMB per month. The township party committee head is really helpful!

Mr Wang was very satisfied with setting up the small factory in the Ao Township. However, the hunters disliked it; the township head disliked it too. Because the ecological migration project did not build houses for the employees of the township government, in order to live near her office, the township head lived in a nearby room of the Hunter Trading Shop. It happened to be located right next door to this small wood products factory. Every day, production at the factory filled the air with the sound of screeching saws, whining electric motors, and the din of manufacture. The township head was unhappy about all the noise that disturbed her life, but could only swallow her bitterness. She said, "It took a lot of effort for the Ao Township to draw this business here. We expect it will help to provide employment for the hunters. So it is best to just put up with the noise."

In regard to the preferential treatment that the township government had offered to the wood products factory—using the hunters' shop warehouse for free and enjoying special benefits, such as cheap heating and a low tax rate—the hunters were unhappy. They said:

> That factory has occupied the large space of the Hunter Trading Shop, claiming that it helps the hunters to solve employment problems. If so, then how many hunters work there? We want to sell reindeer antler slices and leather but have no place to do this, yet the township allowed outsiders to use such a large space to open their factory. The place should benefit the hunters; however, the Han people just took it away just like that!

Later, someone told me that a certain Ao Township leader owned stock shares in this wood products factory. No wonder when I asked Mr Wang if this was a jointly owned business he was ambiguous and avoided mentioning who the partner was.

The Development of Tourism

In order to attract new revenue, the government planned to build an Ethnic Tourism Village near the new Aoluguya community, before the arrival of the busy tourism season lasting from July to September. They chose a location about 4 km southwest of the new community in an open patch in the dense woods. Located in the forest about 500 m from the road, a large military tent was pitched. Both inside the tent and around it were full-grown weeds, obviously this "hunters' campsite" was not at all like the real, inhabited hunters' sites. The so-called Ethnic Tourism Village consisted of only two structures—this military tent, and a solitary *cuoluozi*. The township government arranged for one 35-year-old single male hunter,

Asuo, to live in the tent and tend to six reindeer. As long as Asuo lived at the tent, he could receive a salary of 100 RMB each month that came from funds from the "4050 Re-employment Project" for welfare job positions.

In July, the forests were full of all sorts of dancing insects. Asuo lived there all by himself and spent his days drinking liquor, daydreaming, and being bitten by mosquitoes. With long and dirty hair covering his face, Asuo certainly looked dispirited. Later, the township officials said that the location of the Ethnic Tourism Village was too remote and lacked a vibrant and lively air, and so the county decided to move to another site where they would built a larger Ethnic Tourism Village. Consequently, the township called off Asuo's job. This shabby Ethnic Tourism Village only existed for one week. Several officials stated that two main concerns led to the abandonment of this Ethnic Tourism Village: for one, the inauthentic Ethnic Tourism Village did not attract tourists; the other reason was that the township government worried that the dispirited Asuo would hurt the image of the Ao Township.

The township devised yet another scheme to develop tourism: they had the hunters produce handmade crafts that could show the special aesthetic of Ewenki arts and crafts. The township government set up a "Handmade Crafts Production Studio" using a room in the township museum. Hunters who could tailor, carve, sew and make various handicrafts were asked to teach traditional arts and craft skills, like fungus-carving, root-carving, making boxes out of birch bark, and making purses out of leather. The township government planned to display the crafts in the museum for viewing and sale. Asuo was well known for his artistic skill in the production of traditional handicrafts in the Ao Township. He could create a life-like image of a reindeer out of birch bark or animal hides with just a few deft strokes of his tools. He could also carve images of reindeer out of the thick mushrooms that grew among the roots of forest trees. The township head arranged for him to work in the production studio with the sincere hope that this job would encourage him to cut back on drinking and earn some income. However, Asuo did not work diligently in the studio as the township head had hoped, and did not display much desire to earn money and improve his financial standing. Whenever he wanted to buy liquor, he just casually grabbed a small roe deer hide, clipped it into a reindeer, and then he ran over to the township head saying, "I ran out of money for food. Why do not you buy this one, for I do not know who to sell it to." The township head did not know whether she should laugh or cry at this perplexing and heart-rending failure of her efforts. In the end, she took out 5 RMB and bought it.

Figure 4.5 Boxes made from birch bark

The Reindeer Antler Economy

Reindeer Antler Situation at Aoluguya

After the relocation, due to decreases in the reindeer population, and the changes in the reindeer's living environment, Ao Township reindeer antler production was very low. In the summer of 2004, the total production of finished dry antlers hardly amounted to 350 kg. In a good year, the total production could reach well over 1,000 kg; in comparison, the production in 2004 was very poor indeed. The township was not responsible for the sale of the antlers. The hunters brought their share of antlers back home, cut them into slices and sold them directly to the tourists who came to visit Aoluguya. However, there were few opportunities for sales of this type. That year most of the reindeer antlers had not sold, and the hunters had to store them in their homes. The township had subsidized the cost of processing the antlers for the hunters, and had offered to charge the process fees only after the hunters had sold their antlers. But now, the antlers had not been sold and the township had to keep some of the hunters' antlers for the cost of processing. Because the reindeer antlers had not been sold, the hunters lost their main source of income. But the hunters had considerable expenses that accumulated from commuting back and forth to the mountain camps, including fuel charges and various labor costs. The entire situation left both the hunters and the township government extremely distraught and helpless.

Why had the antlers not been sold this year? I asked the hunters and the township leaders. Township leaders said, "Nobody came to buy." But the hunters said, "It is because the Hunting Service Center was dismissed, no one is in charge of antler sales. The former Hunting Service Center head only cares about selling his own reindeer antlers. Who would care about us?" Hoping to understand this more, I also visited the former head of the Hunting Service Center, Ahai, and learned that his household did not make any antler sales either. He said:

> Now those businessmen all complain that the Ao Township antlers are too pricy, so they are not interested in buying at all. The Ao Township antlers are priced at 700 to 800 RMB per kilogram, and at this price it is still barely profitable. Those sika deer antlers are priced at only 400 to 500 RMB per kilogram. Also the sika deer are pen-fed and they are raised on a large scale and you can have as many antlers as you want. To them, the shabby antlers from the Ao Township are not worth buying, considering the high price and low quality. These days, the reindeer population has seriously degenerated, resulting in the premature calcification of reindeer antlers. The antler quality indeed is not as good as the past years.

The Secret of the Reindeer Antler Economy

Later, by chance, I heard a friend talking about the reindeer antler problem and I learned much more about the reasons why the Ao Township reindeer antlers were not selling. This friend had done thorough research on the antler market with the intention of entering into the reindeer antler business but later dropped the idea. He told me the reasons why:

> According to the traditional Chinese Medicine Pharmacopoeia, reindeer antlers cannot be used as a medicine. Also, worldwide, the only countries that have a market for antlers are mainly in southeastern Asia; Singapore, Malaysia, Thailand, and China. The Western countries do not have any market for antlers. Therefore antler sales are limited to these four countries. Since reindeer antlers are not used in medicines, how did Ao Township reindeer antlers get sold in the past? The truth is, in the past, the merchants who purchased Ao Township reindeer antlers all knew that these antlers should not be used in medicines according to the Chinese Medicine Pharmacopoeia. However, they did not tell the Ao Township hunters about

this. They just made the purchase, then mixed the reindeer antlers with red deer antlers and sold the mixture at the same price as red deer antlers. According to the *Pharmacopoeia*, red deer antlers are allowed in medicines. Because the overall quantity of Ao Township reindeer antlers was low, this type of mixture did not cause any mishaps. Also, because the price of red deer antlers is higher than that of reindeer antlers, the merchants could also make money doing this. Some border merchants used this method of marketing in China to import reindeer antlers from Russia. They imported the reindeer antlers as red deer antlers. Also, antlers were smuggled into China. At the National Customs Office in Manzhouli [port city], if anyone is caught smuggling red deer antlers, he could be convicted for the crime of 'smuggling.' But if someone is caught smuggling reindeer antlers, he could be convicted for the crime of 'smuggling fake pharmaceuticals.' This also indicates that reindeer antlers cannot be used for traditional herbal remedies in China. Even if the government allowed reindeer antlers to be used in remedies, they still could not compete with Russia, because reindeer antlers in China are certainly not as good as those from Russia. In Russia, the reindeer live on the broad tundra where the lichen grows thickly across vast areas of grassland, whereas in China, the reindeer can only find a bit of lichen here and there amidst the rocks in the forest. They do eat not as well as the Russian reindeer, so cannot grow as strong as the Russian reindeer, and so their antlers are not as thick and large as those of Russian reindeer. Consequently, the price of local antlers is not as high as Russian reindeer antlers due to the quality. More so, in Russia, the reindeer population is in the millions—the scale is extremely large, whereas in China reindeer are only raised in the Ao Township, where the reindeer population is barely 1,000 heads. So with regards to both quantity and quality we cannot compete with the Russians. Luckily, reindeer antlers are not used for medicines in our country, otherwise with the entry of China into the WTO [World Trade Organization] the local markets for reindeer antlers would be open to Russia, and the reindeer antlers from Russia would definitely earn a great deal of currency out of us. And our reindeer antler market would be crushed.

This friend continued:

This information can be found from the Internet. How could the officials in Genhe and the Ao Township not know it? Why do they continue with the reindeer antler production? This business cannot make money at all. First of all, there is no market; secondly, even if there was a market, we cannot compete with the Russians. Also, the Ao Township is now famous because of the ecological migration. Everybody knows that reindeer are raised there. The Ao Township still intends to use the 'Aoluguya' brand to sell reindeer antlers, but the question is who would buy them. If it were up to me, the reindeer in the Ao Township have more value for viewing [attracting tourists]. That way would both save labor and money. Who knows what is on the minds of those officials. They only think about production, but nothing about sales. Right now, everything is about the market economy!

Later I went online and did some investigation. I quickly found the stipulation in the traditional *Chinese Medicine Pharmacopoeia* that reindeer antlers cannot be used for medicines.[8]

Prospects for the Reindeer Antler Business

Both the Ao Township head and the Genhe County United Front Work Department deputy director talked to me about the reindeer production overseas. They had just hosted a group of Sami people from Finland. The Sami had seen in news media reports that there was a reindeer-herding ethnic group in China, so they wanted to come to establish friendships. They also sent an invitation to the township head to invite her to attend the World Reindeer Herders' Congress. The township head showed me the photo album presented to her by the Sami people. In the book were photos of reindeer with long antlers, as well as Santa Claus riding on a sled drawn by several strong reindeer. The deputy director commented, "Those people also raise reindeer, and they also use pen-feeding. But unlike our small reindeer pens, they fence in an entire hill. No outsiders are allowed to go in. Only reindeer live in that area. Wow! How freely those reindeer live! They do not cut the antlers off the reindeer either. They raise reindeer not for the antlers, but for their meat." While talking, he pointed to the reindeer slaughter warehouse in the album, "The Ao Township reindeer population is too low. If we ate reindeer meat, in just several days, the entire reindeer population would be gone! Yet these days, we cannot sell the antlers. How can we maintain the reindeer production? The hunters have tough lives!"

Reindeer Ewenki people consider the reindeer to be emblematic of their culture. If reindeer herding could possibly bring income for the hunters, that would be ideal. However, if this is not possible, the Ewenki could still never abandon the reindeer, at least the elderly hunters still living today feel this way. How would the hunters realize that the original goal of "put down your guns, walk out of the forest, and achieve a well-off life" was promoted by the government and media propaganda? This presented a tremendous problem and challenge that lay heavy in the hearts of all people who care about the Aoluguya hunters. It may already be obvious, but to speak truthfully, the current reindeer-herding methods will not be able to lead the hunters to escape from the poverty they now face and make the leap to a "well-off" life.

Despite the fact that this seems obvious, the county government focused all of its attention on the development of the reindeer antler economy. But when these plans did not lead to fruition, and the current situation arose as a result, it was not hard to understand the hunters' complaints. They attributed the decline in post-relocation living standards to the ecological migration and considered it a terrible mistake. All of their complaints were about the relocation.

Notes

1. The subtitles of Chapter Four and Five are derived from slogans used by the government and a counter-slogan employed by the Ewenki. The humor and irony of the original expression is difficult to express in English, so an explanation is necessary. The Ewenki hunters invented their own slogan "*chi kang hai shi ben xiao kang* 吃糠还是奔小康" (Leaving the Forest, Now Eating Chaff—Is This the Way to a Well-off Society?) to ironically criticize the local government's slogan "*zou chu shan lin ben xiao kang* 走出山林奔小康" (Out of the Woods toward a Well-off Society). The Ewenki slogan plays on the homophone "*kang*" and substitutes the word "chaff" for "well-off society." It reflects the Ewenki hunters' dissatisfaction with the relocation, which was supposed to propel them to a well-off lifestyle, but in fact left them despondent and impoverished.
2. In China, rural houses regularly have a "*menkan*" (door threshold), which functions primarily to prevent animals and mice from entering the home. In Imperial China, the homes of all government officials had a high *menkan*, which symbolized their power and status. Today, modern urban homes generally are never built with a *menkan*. This modern home had been built with a high *menkan*, and local people understood that it implied that the host must be a high-level official and that anyone entering their home must be somebody of status and power. Should any common person wish to enter the official's house they must bring expensive gifts.
3. The sister-in-law is Bingyuhong's husband's brother's wife, who is an Ewenki and owns more than 40 reindeer.
4. Her brother-in-law refers to her husband's elder brother.
5. In China, especially for young men in rural areas who cannot pass examinations to continue on to high school or college, joining the military presented a very good opportunity to improve one's life. During military service, a young man might receive technical training that would be useful in later life. Upon completion of military service, after returning home, the local government would arrange employment for them in local government in a related department. This system of arranging jobs for former soldiers without rank was abolished after 1999.
6. The 4050 Re-employment Project was designed to provide employment opportunities for laid-off workers in state-owned enterprises. The program targeted women over the age of forty and men over the age of fifty who lacked specific skills but who wanted to re-enter the workforce.

7. In 2004, the average income per person working in the county or township government was 1,000 RMB per month. In the Genhe County forestry industry, the average
income per worker was approximately 400 RMB per month.
8. It is important to note that although reindeer antlers are not considered part of traditional materia medica, they are still considered highly nutritious.

Chapter 5

Aftermath and Future

➤•◄

As I was spending much time in Aoluguya, I became a member of the Ao Township community. As I became more familiar with their lives and culture they no longer explained things that to them seemed commonplace. With my newfound cultural knowledge, when I witnessed their behaviors in certain situations, I no longer experienced shock and surprise as I did initially. Slowly and gradually I discovered that the commonly encountered portrayal of the hunters as living specimens of primitive savages was not at all in accordance with reality. The transformation of their lifestyle had not just taken place overnight, and it was obvious that the transformation was an ongoing process. When I examined the ecological migration in the state discourse of the grand historical narrative and modernization, I was able to better understand the feelings, experiences and reality of the Aoluguya Ewenki migrants. As I achieved this realization, the confusion that I experienced before started to dissolve.

The Aoluguya Ewenki migrants' complex self-identity, the tightly interwoven network of kinship relations, and the thorny economic and cultural predicament they faced, were all issues that haunted me for a long time. After assiduous contemplation, I gradually sifted out from this mass of seemingly trifle daily matters a thread that interconnected many events. It became clear to me that "complaints" had been the main theme in people's everyday conversations. Struggling through one conflict after another and experiencing ongoing feelings of bitterness had almost become the regular condition of daily life for the Aoluguya

Ewenki migrants. The ecological migration in August 2003 was a historical event. Because of the broad media coverage of the event and the fanfare with which it all transpired, even one year after the official relocation day, the impact of the entire event on people's lives remained as strong as it was before. The great number and variety of complaints were indicative of the impact that the relocation had had on people's lives and caused people to engage in ongoing reflection about the relocation. During the months following the relocation, and well after the first year anniversary of the event, new complaints continued to appear regularly. Complaints ranged from the dissatisfaction over the government measures implemented during the relocation, to the rage over the loss of their lawful rights to reside in the forest; from the anger over the ignorant and dishonest reports by the media, to the strong condemnation of outsiders, who continued to greedily exploit the forest; for instance, the petty drifters, who trapped and killed the reindeer. Even by the time I was about to wrap up my fieldwork, the complaints had not subsided.

Because the values embedded in state-promoted slogans like "comprehensive development," "people-oriented development," and "social harmony" have become ingrained in the collective consciousness and were recognized as desirable social values (Fei 2001, 2004), the hunters were able to use these slogans and the values they imbued as tools to challenge the entire legitimacy of the ecological migration. They impelled the hunters to doubt whether this government-initiated relocation could even be considered a true ecological migration.

There was a large discrepancy, sometimes even direct contradictions, between the statements provided by the county and township governments and the hunters' accounts of the same incident. Both levels of government officials stated that the overall situation in the Ao Township before the relocation was not any better than that after the location. They stressed that, in fact, the current living conditions were much better than those prior to the relocation. In the township leaders' words, "It is like the heaven now! The past cannot match indeed!" However, the hunters held very different views on this, saying that this ecological migration led to their impoverishment—"We are almost as poor as beggars." Many hunters said they were "lied to by the township and deceived by the county," and said that they had been unwilling to relocate right from the very beginning. However, as we have seen above, the Party and government had carried out two large-scale relocations in 1959 and 1965 with the intent to permanently settle the Reindeer-Using Tribe. With this in mind, we may ask whether or not the government encountered the same type of problems as occurred during the "ecological migration." What were the recollections of the hunters with regard to the previous two relocations?

And what were the factors that led to the current problematic situation? What was the root cause of the hunters' complaints? As I reflected carefully on the events that emerged during my fieldwork, I eventually began to find answers to these questions.

The country invested tens of millions of RMB to carry out the Aoluguya Ewenki ecological migration project for a small ethnic group with a population of less than 300. This act showed the preferential treatment that the country granted to the ethnic minority. From the perspective of the state and governance, all groups inside the national borders are objects of governance. The stability and development of the country includes providing conditions that enable the citizenry of every ethnic group, to the highest degree possible, to live peaceful and comparatively happy lives. Under the influence of the grand historical narrative, most people, especially in China, believe that it is inevitable that social development progresses from lower stages to higher stages. The grand historical narrative dictates that although social development progresses from low levels to higher levels, governments have the ability to shorten the course of social evolution by implementing planned modernization projects. For example, with regard to planning a new settlement for the Ewenki hunters, the government believed that traditional Ewenki living conditions in the forest were arduous and poor, and that their nomadic hunter-gatherer lifestyle was backward and barbarous. According to the government's perspective, a nomadic lifestyle was not conducive to the development of the Ewenki people, but was contributing to the destruction of the natural environment. As a result, it was necessary for the government to move them out of the forests and guide them to adopt settled lives in permanent residences.

From the perspective of a marginalized ethnic group, when facing the nation state that possesses both a strong determination to modify traditional lifestyles and the ability to mobilize tremendous resources, accepting the will and decisions of the state is the one and only option. The Ewenki migrants today believe that they were forcibly moved from the old Aoluguya, which has become a distant, happy memory; it was a utopian place where the Ewenki lived far happier lives. A cacophony of the machines of modernity has broken the tranquility of the forest; over the years, increasing numbers of outsiders have arrived to plunder the resources of the forest and land, which were used exclusively by the people of the Reindeer-Using Tribe before. This outraged the Ewenki, but they had no idea with whom they should argue. They were left confused and disappointed with the entire situation, which was supposed to bring them progress.

After one year of fieldwork living among the Ewenki, I was slowly able to see that the worldview of planned modernization had fettered my ability to understand the reality I experienced. Living closely with the Ewenki, I was able to understand their lives and their current situation from their cultural perspective. I then reflected on how government policy, planning and implementation had been strongly affected by the pervasive inertia of planned modernization.

Preserve the People or Preserve the Culture?

Today, the social and ecological conditions in which the Reindeer Ewenki live are vastly different from those in the past. If the goal of ecological migration was to protect the sensitive natural environments, or to save the Ewenki hunters from the deteriorated ecological conditions, then it was indeed necessary for the government to undertake the ecological migration. However, if in fact the forest ecosystem was indeed capable of sustaining the hunting-herding lifestyle of the Reindeer Ewenki, the government still persisted in carrying out the ecological migration as the only method by which they could force the Ewenki to abandon their traditional lifestyle, which compels us to reconsider their ideological notions. Although some parties may claim that the ecological migration was undertaken to ensure the survival of the Reindeer Ewenki, my fieldwork research proved that this is entirely unfounded. By reflecting on the tribe's history prior to the 2003 migration, it is apparent that their living conditions had already dramatically changed from their fully nomadic traditional lifestyle prior to the founding of the People's Republic. Prior to the 2003 ecological migration, the living conditions among the Reindeer Ewenki were nowhere near as low or as "backward" as portrayed in the media reports. In fact, their food, clothing and range of community services were far better than those available to the majority of rural communities in China. They owned houses in old Aolugoya in addition to having tents and reindeer in the mountains.

The ecological migration was carried out under a government directive to "preserve the people" to ensure the survival of the Reindeer-Using Tribe. In order to "preserve the people" the government believed that it was necessary to change their lifestyle by means of relocation. But at the same time, the government advocated "preserving the Ewenki traditional culture." Clearly, these goals give rise to a conundrum—how is it possible to change the Ewenki traditional lifestyle whilst preserving their culture?

Regarding the issue of "preserving people" or "preserving culture," the media once exposed different voices from two researchers about the ecological migration. I talked with them in person, so I know what they really wanted to say in the media report, which had made omissions.

Because this ethnic group needs to develop; because this society needs the Ewenki Hunters to develop, and because the government needs the Ewenki to develop [it must develop]. . . All these things are external forces driving the Aoluguya Reindeer Ewenki to develop in a direction [they did not want to go] . . . The Ewenki hunting practices and their reindeer herding practices . . . either they survive or die off . . . [but this will depend on the government. The essence of traditional Ewenki culture will be diffi-cult to maintain.] (Lan Bai, Vice Director, Inner Mongolia Social Sciences Academy, Ethnic Group Institute)

Only when people's lives have some assurance can cultures be passed down. An ethnic group cannot permanently live in one social stage just for the sake of preserving its traditional culture. After ecological migration, we will be able to effectively preserve the Aoluguya Reindeer Ewenki culture by establishing ethnic group museums, ethnic villages, and hunting areas. (Fanzhi Kong, Vice Director of Genhe County People's Council, Aoluguya Ewenki Research Scholar)[1]

To analyze the above two opinions, we need to examine the concepts of "people" and "culture"—that is to say, who are the "people" we want to preserve, and what is the "culture" we wish to preserve? First, we shall examine what "people" means. Every ethnic group has its own develop-mental history. Most ethnic groups will practice exogamy in an attempt to preserve the long-term vitality of their group and ensure a diversified genetic pool. The Reindeer Ewenki marriage practices shifted from an emphasis on endogamy among the tribe's various branches to exogamy; and for many years they intermarried with many other ethnic groups, including Russians, Hans, Mongolians, Hui, and other ethnic groups. Because of their long-standing practice of intermarriage, it is simply impossible to determine Ewenki ethnic identity based on a notion of purity of bloodline. Even if it were possible, any attempt to only protect pure bloodlines would be pointless; the efforts to protect the Ewenki people should certainly not focus on this as the only criteria. Focusing too much on racial purity will not have a positive effect, but enhance racial awareness, which leads to estrangement and strife among people. Therefore, if we wish to engage in discussion about how to preserve "people," the discussion cannot be about ensuring purity of bloodlines. Instead, we must focus on measures to ensure their health and quality of life. If they are a minority group we might also consider increasing their population. It is also important to consider that since exogamy has led to mixed bloodlines, the delineation of ethnic group identity is based far more on the recognition of cultural traits and practices than it is on bloodline purity.

Next, we should examine what is meant by "culture." I believe that it includes people's living customs, daily lifestyle, the projection of life values and life views onto one's behavior, and also spiritual views that guide people's behaviors. It could be said that the concept of an ecological system is heavily imbued with cultural implications. Anthropology's role is to provide a clear description of the cultural phenomena and interpret the cultural implications that they embody.

When considering the relationship between "preserving people" or "preserving culture," some commentators believe it is a moot point; culture can be preserved only when people are preserved. They claim, "Only when we help them to break away from their barbarous and primitive lifestyle and living environment can we begin to talk about advances in culture and the development of civilization." This opinion is not entirely without logical merit. Considering that people are the bearers of culture, people are thus the foundation upon which culture rests. However, from the perspective of cultural ecology, it is the mutual interaction between people and their ecological environment that gives rise to cultural formations. All cultures have been strongly affected by the environment in which they live.

The very act of raising the question of whether the protection of people should be emphasized over the protection of culture makes the grave error of separating people from their culture. So, from a cultural perspective, when the Reindeer Ewenki people gave up their original nomadic lifestyle and cultural formations, and the spiritual sense of themselves as connected to their mountain environment, they no longer were "hunters." Instead, they only retained a "political identity" as Ewenki Hunters that allowed them to receive preferential treatment by the government. But in reality they had almost lost the cultural characteristics that defined them as a people.

One of the Ewenki hunter elders expressed this succinctly when he said, "After the relocation it would not be long; once all the old hunters die, our ethnic group will cease to exist." So what do old hunters represent? They are the Ewenki hunters who grew up living a traditional lifestyle in the forests and were never severed from their traditional lifestyle and practices. The old hunters are the last remaining Ewenki who serve as the carriers of the traditional culture and its spiritual merit. They embody the psychological and spiritual understandings that tie together the beliefs and practices that defined the identity of the forest hunter. They are the practitioners of the culture.

As for their spiritual understandings, I am now seriously considering the role of shamanism in Ewenki everyday life (Humphrey and Onon 1996; Heyne 1999). Since the death of the last shamaness in 1997,

Ewenki people have struggled in this ever-changing society. Frustrated with interacting with the government and the reality, they have to find answers or even consolations. Thus, they can easily get lost without spiritual help, especially for this young generation. The comfort of alcoholism is possibly one kind of escape from cruel reality. The booming of shamanism in Russia shows the ideological vacuum left after the collapse of the Soviet Union (Humphrey 2002). The role of religion for maintaining the spiritual world of society is not negligible.

In a similar case, another ethnic group, China's Oroqen, also experienced forced lifestyle changes when they were made to give up hunting in 1996, and since then they have taken up an agricultural lifestyle. At the beginning of the transformation, the Oroqen people experienced tremendous pain, as shown in serious alcoholism and suicides. Upon the completion of the transformation, Oroqen traditional culture (lifestyle, values) disappeared quickly (Ma 2003). It is not my intention to suggest that the Ewenki hunters should unwillingly endure the arduous living conditions in the forest by continuing the traditional lifestyles that they have already rejected. Rather, it is my hope that tribal people who do genuinely desire this lifestyle can get respect from outsiders. Outsiders must not attempt to forcibly change the way of living that Ewenki hunters love so deeply. I also sincerely hope that people will come to accept more generously those who genuinely identify with this lifestyle rather than focusing on whether or not they are pureblood Reindeer Ewenki.

The Reindeer Ewenki, a marginalized and disempowered group, was forced onto a path toward development and modernization. From their journey, I could not help but relate the findings of this study to the situation faced by developing countries worldwide. I also began to reflect on the vast changes that took place in China when it adopted a competitive market economy model as the country was swept along the road to modernization—a change that led to the abandonment of many self-sufficient traditional lifestyles. Perhaps at the very beginning, the Chinese state reacted in response to Western countries' invasion; however, later, the situation changed. The Qing dynasty recognized that China's overall economic underdevelopment and low technology made the country a target for attack, and in order to maintain independence as a nation the government began to actively learn about Western science and technology. During this process, the Chinese state was forced from a position of passivity to aggressive modernization. The power of the West was clearly displayed, both in terms of its military power and value system. When the peace and development have been well acknowledged as globally advocated themes, equality, respect and mutual communication should be employed as the primary attitudes and methods for the resolution of all social conflicts.

In the face of pressure from powerful external forces, small and weak ethnic groups (or even entire countries) have no option but to integrate into the mainstream. When China chose Western-style industrialization and economic systems as self-defense, the state had to face the problem of how to optimize the integration of national resources. This nationwide effort to integrate national resources spread throughout society and even affected the Reindeer Ewenki. When facing the national crisis, the Ewenki people were mobilized to assist in the national building process. They contributed their knowledge of the local environment and their familiarity with the composition of the landscape to assist with the state's efforts to develop forestry and mining. It was only later, after the juggernaut of industrialization led to massive environmental destruction, deforestation, and the widespread extinction of wildlife, that the Ewenki faced the cruel fact that their traditional way of life was no longer viable. All of humanity faces a similar problem—the irreversible trend toward the extinction of unique cultural forms. Accumulated evidence clearly shows that regardless of whether a society is large and powerful, or weak and small, they have all set off on the road to modernization, guided by a value system that emphasizes maximizing profits.

However, the state's modernization programs for ethnic groups in China significantly differ from the way that the state implemented modernization on a national scale after 1949, when it faced significant external pressure and had few other options. The modernization of the New China was a process of self-strengthening, self-dependence, self-advancement, and self-correction. In contrast, the ethnic minority's modernization was initiated and assisted by the government; it was full of dependence and unwillingness. What kind of influence was imposed on marginalized ethnic groups when the state applied planned modernization strategies? It is the question that my case study intended to address. This study aimed to explain why the state's well-intended repeated investment in programs to improve the lives of micro-communities like the Ewenki Hunters resulted in complaints and conflicts and little progress.

The Discourse Trap of Ecological Migration

The event prior to and following the Aoluguya Ewenki ecological migration is a story of how the state implemented a planned modernization project. From the perspective of academic research, this event provided a unique opportunity to understand how local government employed an out-of-date, habitual understanding of development, and thus lagged behind in their grasp of the new and more progressive national strategy—the Comprehensive Development Concept.

In the early 2000s, the central government introduced new guidelines for national development termed the Comprehensive Development Concept. The term demonstrated that the state had abandoned the extreme modernization ideology that had dominated the previous fifty years. This study of the Aoluguya ecological migration has demonstrated that, although national strategy had changed, in practice, local government still maintained a habitual mindset centered on extreme modernization ideology, which I defined as "planned modernization" in the introduction of this book. For the past fifty years, economic and social development in China has been guided by the ideology of planned modernization.

It is possible that over time the local government's delayed understanding of the national government's new Comprehensive Development Concept will be resolved. As local government undergoes a period of adjustment and adapts to the new policy, the cultural lag they are experiencing will diminish. After some years, the local government's practice will be in accordance with the national Comprehensive Development Concept. If this were to happen, and the development was guided by this new and more holistic developmental ideology, then the old and highly problematic ideology of planned modernization would not likely arise in most cases. It is my hope that, in the future, problems caused by the implementation of planned modernization will cease to exist, but in the meantime this case study about the overall process of the Aoluguya ecological migration clearly demonstrates the risks of the old planned modernization framework.

The nation's ecological migration policies were formulated to conform to the goal of the Comprehensive Development Concept, which places a strong emphasis on sustainable development. The concept of sustainable development arose in response to the destructive effects of modernization, which include increasing environmental degradation and concomitant threats to human survival. In contrast, indigenous people, who are so often regarded as backward by modern civilization, were able to maintain a generally balanced coexistence with their natural environment. Recognizing this, the United Nations action plan for development, Agenda 21, emphasized the role that indigenous people and their communities must play in working toward building a quality environment and healthy economy for all people.

Here I intend to examine how the local government's implementation deviated from the ecological migration policy envisioned by the central government. How did the central government's ecological migration policy narrative differ from the local government's ecological migration project implementation narrative? Using the Ewenki ecological migration case as an example, we will examine this matter from the following two perspectives: the purpose of discourse and the transformation in the meaning of words.

The Purpose of Discourse

The goal of the Chinese government's ecological migration policies is to preserve the natural environment and to protect severely damaged and endangered ecosystems from ongoing human damage in order to allow these ecosystems to recover. It is necessary to specify that, according to Agenda 21, the relationship between indigenous residents and their ecological environment is not an antagonistic relationship of subject and object, but is rather an intersubjective relationship in which both are mutually dependent. With this view in mind, indigenous residents themselves have a specific role to play in maintaining ecological resources. To rephrase this, we can also say that indigenous people are not destroyers of natural environments, but rather contribute effectively to the maintenance of natural environments. Therefore, strictly speaking, according to the national "ecological migration" policy discourse, the human agents of environmental destruction do not include indigenous residents.

However, when the Genhe County government carried out the ecological migration of Aoluguya, they specified the targets of ecological migration as the Ewenki Hunters "who damaged the natural environment." Local government found culpability with the hunters and cited their traditional practices—such as living in wooden-framed *cuoluozi*, burning firewood, and trampling sensitive vegetation while herding reindeer—as behaviors that have caused significant damage to animal populations and forest cover. However, when we examine the historical record, it is clear that before the central government undertook a nationwide program of industrialization, the forest ecosystems in which the Ewenki Hunters had lived for centuries had not been damaged. They had developed a set of cultural practices; a lifestyle, religious beliefs, a value system and an overall worldview that enabled them to live in harmony with their natural environment.

Ewenki cultural practices prevented them from excessively exploiting their ecological resources. The Ewenki lifestyle, their attitudes toward life and death, and the perilous natural conditions on the mountains all helped to limit population growth and prevent the Ewenki from over-stressing their mountain environment. Before widespread industrialization was undertaken in China, only one to two hundred Ewenki Hunters lived in the vast forest covering over 20,000 square km. Judging from the ecological resources that were available to them, they followed a prehistoric hunter-gatherer lifestyle and were indeed an "original affluent society" (Sahlins 2001 [1968]). Then when the state began a nationwide program of industrialization and modernization, fundamental changes occurred to the forest ecosystem in which the Ewenki people lived. In the early years following the establishment of the People's Republic, industrial expansion, forestry and mining took its toll, and as the deforestation started, wildlife habitats began to disappear. Clearly, it was the government's poor development policies—including practices such as excessive logging and over-hunting by the Oriental Red Hunting Brigade in the 1960s and 1970s, combined with the lack of any scientific understanding of ecosystem management—that led to massive ecological damage in the region.

Furthermore, during fieldwork, I learned that the primary motive behind the Aoluguya ecological migration was the financial crisis of the local government—the local government had no money to upgrade the Ao Township's physical infrastructure, which included its outdated power grid, a deteriorating dam, and rickety buildings. When they applied to the National Western Development Ecological Migration Program for funding, it was clear that they were using the funds allotted for ecological migration to resolve their strained fiscal budget. Of course, we cannot deny the local government's well-intentioned efforts to improve the Ewenki Hunters' standard of living. But when well-intentioned efforts give rise to a myriad of complaints, it gives us a good reason to reflect on the situation to see what went wrong. To sum up the above discussion, the two goals that were implied in the local government's discourse concerning ecological migration obviously differed greatly from the national policy discourse.

The Transformation in the Meaning of Words

During fieldwork, I discovered that group stratification had occurred among the Ewenki Hunters. Indeed, the state's planned modernization programs aimed at this ethnic group led to consequences that are impossible to ignore. They have been transformed from a closed and isolated group living in remote areas to a group living in a semi-urban area with much contact with the outside world. Even the Hunters' habitual ways of thinking had undergone a significant change: many of them now agreed with and accepted the state's perceptions and opinions regarding modernization and development. To explain this more easily, I will refer to this group of hunters as the Modern Hunters (Xie 2015).

These Modern Hunters, who now comprise the majority of the hunters in the Ao Township, have accepted the government's assessment of them as primitive and backward. Therefore, when they were told that they had damaged the forest ecology and should be relocated through the ecological migration plan, they were able to accept this as reasonable. When the government offered them modern accommodation, good living conditions, and various forms of compensation, they were very willing to relocate. Most of them did not want to live in the mountains; even the hunters who moved down from the mountains and later returned did so because they had no other choice. They did not want to move back to the mountains but had to ensure the survival of the reindeer. Later, when the government did not honor their promises, the hunters knew how to use the threat of "moving back to the forests" and its implied rejection of modernity as a way to negotiate with the government. For the government, persuading the hunters primarily involved offering them more tempting conditions. In light of this, how was the term "ecological migration" imbued with different meaning when it was used by the local government and Modern Hunters?

The Definition of "Ecological Migration" When Used by the Government

When the government talked about ecological migration to the Modern Hunters, the term implied that the hunters had damaged the natural environment and therefore there was a need to change the hunters' lifestyle; encourage them to "put down their guns and stride out of the forests," live in fixed residences, raise reindeer in pens, and move toward a life of modernity and wealth. To the Modern Hunters, this all seemed acceptable. They had accepted the government's planned modernization propaganda and had not doubted the logic behind the inevitability of evolution from "primitive and uncivilized" to "modern and civilized." This holistic historical view was the mutual foundation upon which the government and the Modern Hunters understood the ecological migration project.

In this case, the local government deliberately twisted the meaning of the national ecological migration policy to blame indigenous people for environmental destruction. When the local government used this term with respect to the Modern Hunters, the aim of the ecological migration was said to be to protect the natural environment, so it was necessary to relocate the hunters, who were to blame for the destruction. For purposes of clarity, we shall deem this usage of the term "ecological migration" as "Implied Meaning #1"—the goal of ecological migration was to preserve the natural environment. However, other situations arose in which the government used the term "ecological migration" with regard to the Modern Hunters, but the implications and meaning of the term had changed significantly.

Another situation we must note is with regard to the location that the government chose for the relocation of the Modern Hunters. If we use the "Ecological Migration Implied Meaning #1" to examine the relocation of the hunters, then it becomes apparent that there was a significant logical error in the government's course of action in light of their stated goals. The premise behind the relocation was that the hunters' lifestyle damaged the forest ecosystem and thus relocating the Ewenki was necessary to preserve the forests of old Aoluguya. But when the government then proceeded to move the Ewenki to new camps in the forest near the new Aoluguya, the conflict between what they said and what they actually did became apparent: the forests of old Aoluguya should be preserved and the Ewenki hunters should be moved out, but the forests of new Aoluguya were seemingly not in need of preservation and so the Ewenki were moved in. This fact completely undermined the premise of the argument that the relocation was necessary for preserving ecosystems. Facing this contradiction, the government had no choice but to change the meaning of the phrase "ecological migration," and it is this altered meaning that I refer to as the "Ecological Migration Implied Meaning #2"—the intention was to improve the hunters' living conditions. Noting this discrepancy, no wonder the migration researcher Jianxiong Ge noted that the relocation of the Ewenki Hunters was not really a case of "ecological migration" but rather one of "survival migration"—the relocation of a people in an attempt to ensure their survival. But in my view, the migration was not in accordance with national ecological migration policy, nor was it a case of survival migration that necessitated the removal of a people from their original living environment.

Discourse Tactics of the Modern Hunters

For the hunters who already accepted the planned modernization views, both Implied Meaning #1 and Implied Meaning #2 were seen as acceptable explanations of ecological migration. When the government changed its definition of Implied Meaning #1 to Implied Meaning #2, the Modern Hunters were unaware of this change in meaning.

In spite of their acceptance of Implied Meanings #1 and #2, the Modern Hunters were not satisfied with their situation after the relocation. Their major complaints were that: 1) the pen-feeding of reindeer did not succeed; 2) the government had not compensated the hunters for income loss as a result of the confiscation of their guns and the prohibition on hunting; 3) after the prohibition on hunting, increasing numbers of hunters were unemployed, and the jobs provided by the government to address this issue were unsatisfactory; 4) The Hunting Service Center had been dissolved, and the income from the sale of antlers had fallen sharply; 5) The hunters were distinctly aware of strong discrimination by outsiders. The discrimination was manifest in the desertion of Ewenki Hunter children in the Genhe school system; it was also manifest when the county government and media conspired to hire actors to masquerade as Ewenki and perform contrived "Ewenki campfire dances." The hunters were unhappy with many other things as well. For example, when the county work units offered aid to them, the local administrative power was unsupervised. There were many questions regarding the fairness and quantity of assistance that was provided. I have especially emphasized the above-mentioned five problems because they directly demonstrate the Modern Hunters' dissatisfaction with the relocation. The hunters were not opposed to the relocation, but were highly dissatisfied with the entire situation after moving to the new Aoluguya.

Facing this range of complaints emanating from the hunters, the local government defended itself by countering, "Your current living conditions are quite good—the Hunters' houses are much better than *cuoluozi* and tents; central heating is much better than burning wood logs; and flushing toilets are much better than outdoor toilets. You should not make excessive demands." The hunters were not happy with the government's excuses. They repeatedly protested, "You made promises back then and now you have failed to keep your promises. We have been deceived." They began to find certain phrases that were useful in presenting their grievances to the government. They argued:

> Back then the government conducted a survey to see if we agreed with the relocation, and worked hard to persuade us. The government promised us they would relocate the entire group, but look what has happened now. Old neighbors are separated. Many people [those who were not Ewenki Hunters] did not get to move here at all. Even for Ewenki, there were no houses constructed for employees and now many of the employed Ewenki live in downtown Genhe. Because they live so far away from us, our strength has been scattered and dispersed. This is why the government ignores the few of us who remain. The entire group should have been moved here together. Do not exhibit us to outsiders as if we were monsters!

The government found it hard to respond to these protests, so they responded vaguely, "In the future, we will carry out the second phase of the ecological migration to build houses for the employees."

Clearly, the Modern Hunters were deeply influenced by the state's modernization ideology and sincerely longed to live a modern urban life. They were highly conscious of the discriminatory educational policies and attitudes of the Genhe schools toward Ewenki hunter students. They were also very sensitive about how other non-Ewenki viewed them and made comments about them. Through their behaviors, it became apparent that the discourse they used to express their dissatisfaction was rooted in the ideological framework of modernization, and they never challenged the ideology of planned modernization. Their complaints were aimed at the government leaders' management skills and failure to fulfill their responsibilities. Because the Modern Hunters failed to identify planned modernization as the source of many of their grievances, the ideology of the planned modernization theory was able to self-repair and thus shifted this kind of criticism into a managerialism maintenance paradigm (Banuri 2001[1990]).

Among all of the people of the Ao Township, only a handful was able to reflect on the situation and provide insights and ideas that transcended the framework of planned modernization. These individuals were generally either traditionally minded elderly people dedicated to preserving old ways or middle-aged individuals, who possessed a clearer sense of their cultural identity. Regardless of the type of discourse proffered by the government, as long as it was aimed at trying to change the Ewenki hunters' lifestyle by moving them from their mountain campsites and pushing them toward "modernity" it was tenaciously rejected by this small minority of several dozen individuals. This group, of whom Maruia Suo stands as a representative, firmly maintained their traditional values system. For purposes of clarity in this discussion, we shall call this small group the Traditional Hunters. The discussion that follows will reflect on the Chinese state's "planned modernization" ideology from the perspective of the Traditional Hunters.

Reflection on Planned Modernization

Planned Modernization and the Traditional Hunters

During both the planning and implementation of the ecological migration project, the Traditional Hunters, who held a deep love and yearning for their forest lifestyle, remained voiceless. They did not voluntarily participate in the relocation project; their desires and opinions were drowned out by the overriding clamor of the government's planned modernization discourse, and their appeals and grievances were ignored. By coming to understand the true opinions and value systems of the Traditional Hunters, I am able to use their perspective, which clearly lies outside of the obstinate thinking of the planned modernization ideology, to reflect on planned modernization itself (Gao 2005).

When I was living at the Alongshan campsite, Maruia Suo once said, "We do not like the outsiders coming and interrupting our normal lives." The "normal lives" that she referred to was a way of life that, in the eyes of modernity, was a "primitive and backward hunting lifestyle." She had maintained a true love and respect for their traditional herding and hunting way of life. She, like all of the old hunters, cherished memories of her childhood: riding reindeer when their campsite packed up and moved, going on hunting trips with adults, singing and dancing together, celebrations, and the freedom to move about without impediment. The rhythms and cycles of everyday life in the mountains were cherished memories that brought great enjoyment to the old hunters and affirmed the value of their traditional ways of life.

Despite recognizing the value of traditional living, when the township government sent working groups to the campsites to conduct questionnaire surveys and persuade them to relocate, the Traditional Hunters did not have any cogent, persuasive or compelling argument for defending their traditional lifestyle in the face of the powerful mainstream modernity discourse. They only managed to formulate statements like "I like staying here (in the forests) and do not want to change (our lifestyle)." Such statements were regarded by the mainstream discourse as lacking modernity enlightenment and as good examples of backward thinking. Although the old Traditional Hunters were unable to articulate their thoughts and feelings, and were unable to persuade the government to recognize their preferences and choices, the hunters continued to value their traditional life ways and silently resist the local government's efforts to relocate them. The fact that the Maruia Suo campsite remained high in the Alongshan region and never moved served as obvious evidence of their resistance.

After the ecological migration, the local government gradually paid less and less attention to the mountain campsites. This gave rise to anger and complaints among the Traditional Hunters, a response which seemingly contradicts their desire "not to be harassed by outsiders." Through analyzing these statements, we can see that what the hunters mean when they refer to "harassment by outsiders" is the disrespectful behavior and attitudes that outsiders hold toward the Ewenki hunters' way of life. The hunters bore no ill feelings toward the students or research scholars who came to study the Ewenki language and culture and participate in their daily lives. From these people, the Ewenki could clearly sense respect and friendliness. Conversely, the Ewenki were quite disgusted and angered by news media reporters, whose rude questions were laden with contempt and bigotry, and by the obnoxious behavior of government officials, whose orders and commands were intent on changing the hunters' lifestyle. The hunters' emotional response was quite understandable despite the fact that these "outside invaders" had no premeditated ill-intentions but whose arrogance and lack of respect easily offended the Ewenki Hunters, who had become highly sensitive throughout the entire relocation event.

The Traditional Hunters felt the disappointment and hopelessness when the local government exhibited less and less interest in the activities at the mountain campsites, and they persistently rejected the government's ongoing attempts to persuade them to move out of the forests. An old hunter provided this account:

> Those who wanted to remove us out of the forests—what on earth were they thinking? Look at the places they live at. Genhe, Moerdaoga, Jinhe, Alongshan, Mangui, who named these places? Did the Ewenki people not name them? We have lived in these forests for hundreds of years; was there anyone else living here other than us? From the day that the People's Republic of China was founded, Ewenki Hunters became the forest patrollers. Wherever thunder hit, wherever the forests caught fire, it was the Ewenki Hunters who trudged hundreds of miles up and down the mountains to notify others and led the fire-fighting teams. Now look at these roads, did not the Ewenki people help carry material on reindeer and guide the workers during the construction? How come they so quickly forget all of this? Who on earth chopped down all the trees in the forests? Who started the forest fires that burned for so many days? Who poisoned and killed the reindeer and roe deer?

Faced with the current situation of living in the forests without any guns, the old hunters were both outraged and concerned:

> These days we do not even have a place to herd reindeer. No matter where we go in the forests now, our movements are restricted or constrained by the Forest Management Station[2] and we have to search for the reindeer in the forests with nothing but our bare fists—we have nothing to guarantee our safety. Do not tell us we have to use bows and arrows to chase away the bears! If we did that, even the poachers would laugh at us. Even they have guns in their hands! Just several days ago, someone shot our reindeer. We heard the gunfire, and later found that our reindeer had been shot and stolen away. Why does nobody prevent this type of thing? So many reindeer have been trapped and killed. Why does nobody even care to ask? Why does nobody care about us?

The hunters in fact strongly longed for assistance from the government. However, would the care and help that they desired really provide any type of solution to their problems? The old hunters commented, "We hope the government will pay more attention to reindeer-raising at the campsites. But the government continually thinks we can only be better off by leaving the forests. What then about the reindeer? Why is it so hard to provide help according to our needs?"

The hunters' heartfelt longing for their traditional lifestyle and the conflicts they faced in day-to-day reality often left the old hunters in an awkward situation, and they were forced to confront the question of whether or not they wanted to be supervised by the government. If they allowed the government to be in charge, the hunters would have to follow the government's plan to press them into permanent settlement and then rely on government welfare payments to support them. Government welfare payments would be necessary because the hunters lacked the work skills to survive in a modern competitive society and thus, without the government's welfare support, they would become a group with no hope of survival.

Conversely, if the hunters did not want government involvement, then it would be impossible for them to be self-sufficient as they were in ancient times—the overall social, political and ecological conditions have changed dramatically since then. Practically speaking, the hunters needed government assistance with many aspects of their lives in the mountain camps. The relocation was not the sole driver or impetus that led to the awkward situation that exists today. However, it is fair to say that the ecological migration, and its concomitant prohibition of hunting, was a fatal blow to the hunters' desire to maintain a traditional way of life.

From a more macroscopic, historical perspective, it can be seen that the Ewenki hunters' situation today was the consequence of implementing the ideology of planned modernization—a fact of which none of the players were cognizant. It did not occur to any of the players that the government's planning was no longer similar to that of the past. In the past, the hunters had a range of choices, whereas today no choice was offered. Only one option was set before them—to leave their old way of life and embrace modernity. There were fundamental differences between the Traditional Hunters and the Modern Hunters. The Traditional Hunters did not readily accept the relocation because they felt that the ecological migration offered them a lifestyle that they did not want, and that it was an ill-conceived government plan doomed to failure. The ideology of planned modernization did not dominate the mindset and worldview of the Traditional Hunters. In contrast, however, the Modern Hunters had fully accepted the planned modernization ideology and so readily agreed to the relocation.

It is necessary to clarify that although the government had consistently pursued development based on a planned modernization ideology since the 1950s, over the following decades, the methods and intensity through which the modernization ideology was expressed and implemented was different. This led to varying degrees of satisfaction among the people who were the recipients of these programs. The previous two resettlement programs, the first in 1959 and the second in 1965, were not as all-inclusive and invasive as the 2003 relocation, and in fact offered far greater room for the Ewenki Hunters to preserve their original ways of life. The state plans and procedures were carried out with more resolute determination during the 2003 relocation, which led to the Traditional Hunters being deprived of their geographic, social and cultural sphere, and led to feelings of loss, anguish, and despondency.

A severe conflict occurred between the changes in the overall social, political and ecological conditions and the Traditional Hunters' refusal to accept the government's planned modernization, which threw the Traditional Hunters into the abyss of pain. If the government adopts a belligerent attitude and is unable to provide necessary assistance, or if the assistance is not appropriate to the hunters' needs, then the end result will almost certainly lead to the extinction of the hunters' traditional cultural sphere and value system. Should the hunter traditional lifestyle fade into extinction, it would be an immeasurable loss to China's cultural diversity. At present, the methods employed to raise reindeer in fenced-in pens has not been successful, and without the traditional methods of herding, the existing domesticated reindeer herds will disappear in China. It is currently widely accepted that the disappearance of any species leads to an overall decreased gene pool and corresponding decreased possibilities for the long-term survival of other species as well.

The disappearance of the traditional production style is parallel to the rapid disappearance of natural species. An example of this is clearly visible as follows. Every year from August to late September, for the last several years, large numbers of outsiders travel to the mountain forests by car and motorcycle to pick wild berries. By evening, their baskets are fully loaded with the delicious wild fruit. The Ewenki hunters' traditional diet consisted largely of animal proteins supplemented by wild berries—primarily red berries[3] and blueberries, which provide an important source of vitamins and other essential nutrients. In recent years, however, increasing numbers of outsiders began to see the wild berries as a valuable product that could be exploited for profits. Many wine-producing industries began to purchase large quantities of wild berries for the manufacture of wine.

The resulting high demand for berries led to an influx of commercial berry pickers into the Aoluguya mountain regions. Soon the total quantity of berries picked by outsiders vastly exceeded the quantity picked by the hunters. The commercial berry pickers showed little consideration for the natural environment at all. Faced with competitors all fighting over the same territory, the commercial pickers used tools to uproot all plants together with soil, and strip the berries as quickly as possible in order to maximize their harvest. Forest vegetation and the berry plants are seriously damaged by their methods. In contrast, the Ewenki hunters carefully picked each berry off the plant without damaging any of the plants or other vegetation.

According to the recent studies,[4] the red berry belongs to the Ericaceous family of plants that are indigenous to northern Taiga in the Arctic vegetative zone. The Ericaceous family of plants includes the red berry, blueberry, and bilberry. In China, the red berry is only found on the northern slopes of the Greater Khingan Range and does not grow in more southerly regions. This ecological zone, in which the red berry is found, is the same biome favored by reindeer. Red berries are an important source of food for bears, rodents, and birds. In recent years, however, this ecological zone in the Taiga has seen a progressive northward recession owing to global warming. With the ecozone conducive to its growth becoming smaller each year, the red berry and other ecosystem flora face the ever-growing threat of extinction.

One of the major contributors to ecosystem destruction in the region has been the methods and tools used by commercial berry pickers, which damage the ability of the plants to recover and reproduce. A society that is based on the maximum exploitation of resources and labor in order to accrue economic gain undoubtedly expedites the global extinction of flora and fauna, and in this localized case, directly threatens the red berry. With the red berry disappearing from this ecosystem, the disappearance of animal species would be another to follow. Thus, the predominance of a one-sided, aggressive and highly exploitative society with an economic foundation in capitalism leads to the destruction of the environment, which in turn leads to the elimination of cultural identities that depend on that environment. This establishes a vicious cycle of ever-increasing environmental damage and the disappearance of weaker cultural formations. As the Ewenki hunters themselves noted, "Everybody comes to the mountains for the gold rush [economic exploitation], but have made a complete mess of the forest. We cannot even find a place to move to."

Certain regulations have to be formalized to limit the berry picker. It has been reported that the investment of multimillion dollars in harvesting mushrooms, herbal medicines, pine straw, etc. in California in the

United States attracted many commercial pickers. The permits have been sold to them by the Forest Service. However, parts of these lands are the backyards of some Native Americans (Middleton 2011). The successful negotiation between the tribe leaders and the government presented feasible solutions for the berry-harvesting conflicts on Ewenki land.

Planned modernization has continuously brought consequences that have demand humanity to undertake serious reflection and soul-searching. Exactly what benefits has this one-dimensional form of modernization brought to humanity as a whole? When ecosystems and cultural systems encounter disaster, does the homogeneity of modernity proffer any timely solutions? Conversely, a wide diversity of cultural forms that embrace multifarious pathways to development would offer humanity a far greater range of potential solutions for mitigating risks or dealing with looming or actual disasters. The true value of cultural diversity cannot be limited to the utilitarian uses that the current economic system affords. Rather, cultural systems bring rich sensual and spiritual enjoyment to people's lives and more importantly serve as a basis for mutual reference, learning, respect, and understanding. A more equal and beneficial coexistence among diverse cultures is tremendously beneficial to the harmonious coexistence of humans and our natural ecosystems.

The preservation of cultural diversity that I have advocated should not be forcibly implemented, nor should the preservation of cultural diversity necessitate the cutting of ties between cultural forms. Rather, the preservation should lead to equal and mutual communication. Although it is certainly not for mainstream culture to tell another marginalized culture "You are inferior. I will change you. I will replace you," this is exactly what has been happening in this march toward modernization around the globe. A far more productive course would be to enhance cross-cultural communication, which would allow the discovery of common understanding and the adoption of the other's beneficial cultural practices. When the local government forced the Ewenki people to abandon their traditional way of life and practices and embrace modernity, this entire process was the one that did not conform to the essence of the Chinese government's expressed Comprehensive Development Concept. The true essence of the Comprehensive Development Concept, in fact, is about preserving cultural diversity and encouraging dialogue among multifarious cultural forms.

In addition, the preservation of cultural multiplicity is not simply about "museumification"—the preservation of a lifeless culture in museums and contrived folk-custom villages. Rather, preservation should be about the conservation of the living conditions that enable the concomitant ways of life to be perpetuated. Humans, their cultures and nature are all closely interconnected; the survival and continuity of each is mutually interdependent—the ties simply cannot be severed. Only by preserving cultural diversity will we have a rich selection of worldviews and practices that can help us find development pathways beyond that of the trouble-laden "planned modernization."

The preservation of cultural diversity demands an inherent respect for the people who live within their respective cultures. When the conditions for maintaining a way of life are preserved—that is to say, when the people and their defining character, practices and beliefs are preserved, indeed the cultural formation will remain vigorous and continue to flourish. Thus, in order to develop sensitive and flexible systems that will contribute to the healthy preservation of cultural formations, it is critical to respect people's freedom to choose the life-ways they desire, and to provide assistance according to their desires. With regard to the state's practice of categorizing and attempting to manage various cultural groups, this is a topic left for discussion elsewhere. Nevertheless, it is worth stressing that the sacrifice of valuable and meaningful cultural groups simply because such cultural groups are difficult to manage, is a shortsighted perspective based on ignorance.

Planning and Governance

The Aoluguya ecological migration demonstrates to us seemingly conflicting phenomena—the project implemented by the government was intended to improve the Ewenki Hunters' lives, but instead caused overwhelming dissatisfaction. The hunters' dissatisfaction can be identified as two major types: (1) dissatisfaction with the post-migration placement; (2) dissatisfaction with the ecological migration itself.

The first type of dissatisfaction was expressed by the Modern Hunters. The Modern Hunters agreed with the ecological migration, but they were unhappy with the placement situation. In response to their grievances about the implementation of the project, the government's reaction was to develop another project to remedy the shortcomings of the first. For example, after the relocation, the housing that the hunters were unhappy about previously was provided. As a solution, the government offered to carry out a second stage of construction.[5] When we examine the history of the migration project, we can see that every time the government carried out planned modernization projects they repeatedly invested large amounts of money in an attempt to soothe people's emotions and dispel grievances. Gradually, the dependency was increasingly strengthened. The root cause of this problem was a change in the usage rights over resources: when the various parties in the society had not yet reached consensus over change in usage rights, it led to resistance, negativity and complaints by the weaker party.

When a system that was formerly in balance is thrown into chaos as a result of new conditions, a new and long-term balance cannot effectively develop because of repeated external stimulus. Because the government maintained obsolete impressions of the ethnic group, which in turn led to new problems, they were forced to continually invest in new projects in order to address an endless stream of problems in an attempt to achieve social balance and stability. Such projects and the investment of money, however, only served to temporarily shift focus away from the true source of the problem, and an indigenous problem-resolution system character-ized by self-determination and independence never truly came into form.

The second type of dissatisfaction stems from the Traditional Hunters. Based on their narratives and our analysis in the preceding chapters, it is fitting to say that the Traditional Hunters' dissatisfaction was not so much about the results after the ecological migration as it was about the ideology of planned modernization in general. From their dissatisfaction, I derived a perspective that enabled me to thoroughly reflect on, analyze and transcend the planned modernization ideology. These insights and conclusions I believe can shed light on the broader issue of how the Chinese state has, for many decades, relied on planned modernization as its pathway to development. In the analysis, I employed two des-ignated concepts—"governance" (Calame 2005[2003]) and "planning" (Scott 2004[1994])—to compare and understand the fundamental differ-ences between the Chinese government's Comprehensive Development Concept and its earlier planned modernization strategy for guiding development.

In the case of the Aoluguya ecological migration, "planning" charac-terized the actions of local government, which led to the current predica-ment in which the hunters have no voice or say whatsoever regarding their own future. When the plans for the migration began to take form, the government did not consult the hunters or hear their concerns. Instead, the local government took it for granted that the hunters would accept the relocation, so the local government made the decision on their behalf to move ahead with the relocation.

When we examine the recent history of the Ewenki hunters and see the gradual transformation of this group from a hunter-gatherer tribe to the present situation, it becomes apparent that the government sin-glehandedly steered them down this path of development. The state's actions have their origin in a grand historical narrative that is firmly rooted in social linear evolutionary thinking. Believing that their efforts would greatly improve the living environment of the Ewenki hunters, the government began designing its plans to transform their lives. Originally, in the 1950s, the government did not force the hunters to abandon their hunting lifestyle, but they did continually, through the medium of the education system, work to instill their value system, rooted in the grand historical narrative, in the hunters.

After the mainstream discourse of walking the path of moderniza-tion to rise out of poverty and become wealthier became popular, the hunters were unable to formulate any expression to refute modernization when it was imposed on them during the process of ecological migration. With nothing to say in their defense, the hunters were left voiceless. Later, when the government conducted survey questionnaires, the ques-tion, "Do you agree with the ecological migration of the entire group," was designed in such a way as to prevent the Traditional Hunters from expressing any form of dissent or their desire to maintain their old way of life. The myriad of problems revealed the simplistic and paternal-istic way in which planned modernization was carried out. The local government's actions, unfortunately, are indicative of quite poor gover-nance and thus are diametrically opposed to the central government's Comprehensive Development Concept, which is founded on principles of good governance.

In this work, the use of the term "planning" has implied the formula-tion of some idealized theory and the concomitant rigid implementation of that theory. The "planning," which attempts to bring about a desired result, tends to completely ignore the subjectivity of the people toward whom the objective of "planning" is directed. In contrast to this rigid "planning" approach, the use of "governance" is proffered as a preferred method for dealing with diverse ethnic groups. But what characterized good governance?

In this case study, from the local government's perspective, they pro-vided considerable assistance to the Ewenki hunters, yet their efforts still led to a great many misunderstandings, grievances, and complaints. The crux of the problem lay in the government's patronizing attitude and lack of any sincere attempt to undertaking meaningful communication with the Ewenki hunters. The solution lies in developing two-way mean-ingful communication based on mutual respect and the government's acknowledgment of the people's right to self-determination and partici-pation in decision-making processes. To achieve this, it is necessary for the government officials to break free from their patronizing attitude and self-conceit; to humbly listen to other people's opinions, especially to the voice of people who are habitually labeled as "backward"; to strive to understand the merit of their opinions. It is also necessary for the ethnic minorities to confidently express their thoughts and bravely voice their opinions. Only by doing so will their opinions come to be recognized, understood and valued by others. True confidence does not arise from the moral superiority that outsiders offered to condemn the misunderstandings and prejudices. Rather, it must arise from the depth of their hearts and from recognition of their self-identity and of the inherent worthiness of their way of life and values system.

One particular issue worth mentioning is that ethnic minorities are often supported by outside parties—very often by academic researchers in the moral superiority—who help the group to vocalize their concerns and express their desires. Sometimes, the problem with this is that the academic activists' high profile can often exert considerable pressure on government officials. In contrast to the academic's good-intentions, this type of pressure is often unhelpful in nurturing equal exchanges and mutual communication between the ethnic minorities and the government.

Achieving Mutual Understanding

Rigid adherence to opinionated views tends to skew our opinion and lead us to ignore the opinions, perspectives and ideas of others. Thus, when one party blindly expends all of its effort to persuade another party to accept its opinion, it becomes difficult for the first party to recognize the limitations of their own opinions. This case study of the Aoluguya ecological migration is a perfect example of this very problem. With the problem clearly delineated, the solution then also becomes clearer—the government representing the ideology of modernization must stop negating cultural traditions that are considered non-modern, and must strive to discover the value of the Ewenki people's culture instead.

It is worth noting that cultures that embody lived experience and knowledge and that reflect a group's particular worldview, can be inherited not only by the members of a particular cultural group, but also by people with other ethnic backgrounds. This is most clearly visible in the continued popularity of ancient oriental cultural traditions that still glow with brilliance after so many centuries, and still attract the attention and appreciation of people all over the world. Despite the vicissitudes of times and changes in environment, many ancient cultures vigorously manifest themselves in the present through people's thoughts, words, and deeds.

The Ewenki hunting culture has quietly undergone many complex changes over the last several decades and especially during the year of 2003. It became the focus of considerable attention as the tribe was relocated under the auspices of "ecological migration." The media portrayal of this event led to a widespread misconception among the general public that the transformation of the Ewenki from a hunter-gatherer tribe to a modern community took place overnight. By identifying the role of planned modernization in this process, we are able to discern why and how the relocation event, which was supposed to improve the lives of the Ewenki, led to tremendous dissatisfaction and suffering in reality. The resolution of these problems remains a task for the government and the Ewenki people to address in the years ahead with all certainty, and it will demand from both sides far greater degrees of mutual respect, care, and tolerance.

After the relocation, the Ewenki hunters faced many predicaments. The biggest conundrum has been that various parties were not able to, reach any consensus about the usage of natural resources. The Ewenki hunters, with a long history of living in the mountains, felt a strong sense of being deprived and mistreated when they were moved out of their traditional ecological setting. They felt, "The forests used to belong only to us. But now the mountains have been quietly taken away from us and we have now been reduced to a people adrift in the forests." Outsiders, including unemployed workers, who come to the forests to make a living by exploiting resources, such as red berries, often complained, "We are all citizens of China. It is unreasonable to let the Ewenki Hunters have exclusive access to the rich resources in the forests. Of course, we should have the rights to pick berries and gather herbs in the forests."

When faced with limited resources, conflicts that arise over issues related to resource access must be resolved by considering the best possible way to ensure long-term sustainability of the resources in light of the need for economic growth and development. Access to resources must be managed regardless of whether the management methods are based on the taboos and way of life of traditional societies or if they are based on the laws and regulations passed by government. However, in actual practice, resistance from both local government and the Ewenki occurred. Democratic decentralization with local accountability can be introduced in order to ensure that policy outcomes work for the best public interests (Ribot 2004). In addition, civic education is necessary to inform Ewenki people of their rights.

For centuries, the Ewenki people had in fact been the "owners" of the forests and their resources, but this was primarily because no other group made claim to these resources. The Ewenki ownership rights were based on traditional usage, and they were not based on any system of state-recognized legal and economic ownership of the land per se. The Ewenki had never received or needed recognition by any other social group. Today, however, there are other ethnic groups in the region, who also make claims on the forest resources, which gives rise to problems regarding resource allocation and the delimitation of property rights. Population growth in the region and the corresponding increased competition for resources will eventually lead to more serious conflicts over resource allocation. As seen in this case study, problems have already begun to appear. However, they can team up with other ethnic minorities to adopt the best political strategy in order to reclaim their rights with the right authorities. In addition, the international cooperation with other reindeer-herding groups in other countries cannot be ignored. The International Center for Reindeer Husbandry (ICR) was held in Aoluguya in 2013, which bestowed on the China Ewenki significant publicity and gave them more advantages for negotiating with the government. Recent governmental and international aid in the project of REDD+ (Reducing Emissions from Deforestation and Degradation and Enhancing Carbons Stocks) can be another opportunity for the indigenous people who lived in the forests (Sikor 2011), so we can predict this is also a good chance for Ewenki people to continue their journey of the recognition and claiming of forest resources.

Achieving a peaceful resolution of current and future conflicts over resource allocation will require diligent negotiation based on mutual respect by all of the involved parties. The success of such negotiations will require that all parties have a comprehensive understanding of the natural ecological systems and have a clear idea of current and future human impact on these systems. Local government, which serves as the mediator between the diverse interest groups, together with scholars, who bear considerable expertise on the issues at hand, should maintain an unbiased stance to promote communication and understanding among all of the involved parties. Assumptions and actions arising from patronizing attitudes and self-conceit—regardless of whether such assumptions and actions are intended to benefit others—will likely lead only to estrangement, grievances, and violent conflicts.

Notes

1. The two quoted passages are from the article "Aoluguya: The Last Shadow of Reindeer-Using Tribe" (Pinyin: *Aoluguya: yige shoulie buluo de zuihou beiying*) in the newspaper Beijing Times (August 20, 2003: A 16–17).
2. The Forest Management Station is operated by the government and is responsible for forest management and fire prevention. Each year, there is a three to four month fire-prevention period in the summer and autumn during which access to the forest is severely restricted. Even the Ewenki face restrictions on accessing areas that they are permitted to use for herding.

3. The red berry (vaccinium vitis-idaea) is also known as the lingonberry or cowberry.
4. Chinese ecologist Shurun Liu discussed his research about the red berry in "*Man and the Biosphere*" (Pinyin: *Ren yu sheng wu quan*), 2006 2, 39.
5. In 2008 and 2009, the Ao Township Hunters' houses were rebuilt into the Finnish style two-story houses on the original foundation under the unified planning of the county government.

Bibliography

Anderson, D. 1991. "Turning Hunters into Herders: A Critical Examination of Soviet Development Policy among the Evenki of Southeastern Siberia." *Arctic* 44(1): 12–22.
———. 1999. "The Evenki of the Lower Enisei Valley" in R.B. Lee and R. Daly (ed.), *The Cambridge Encyclopedia of Hunters and Gatherers*. Cambridge University Press, pp. 142–146.
———. 2000. *Identity and Ecology in Arctic Siberia: The Number One Reindeer Brigade*. Oxford University Press.
Bai, L. 2003. *Northern China—The Departing Reindeer Herds* [Pinyin: *bei zhong guo—na yuan qu de lu qun*]. Kunming: Yunan People's Publishing House.
Banuri, T. 2001[1990]. "Development and the Politics of Knowledge: A Critical Interpretation of the Social Role of Modernization," in Y. Chen and C. Liu (trans.), *Developmental Illusions* [Pinyin: *fa zhan de huan xiang*]. Beijing: Central Compilation and Translation Press, pp. 148–204.
Beach, H. 1981. *Reindeer-Herd Management in Transition: The Case of Tuorpon Saameby in Northern Sweden*. Uppsala University.
———. 1993. *A Year in Lapland: Guest of the Reindeer Herders*. University of Washington Press.
———. 2012. "Milk and Antlers: A System of Partitioned Rights and Multiple Holders of Reindeer in Northern China." in A.M. Khazanov and G. Schlee (ed.), *Who Owns the Stock? Collective and Multiple Property Rights in Animals*. Oxford: Berghahn Books.
Bourdieu, P. 2003[1980]. *Le Sens Pratique* [*Sense of Practice*], trans. Z. Jiang. Nanjing: Yilin Press.
Calame, P. 2005[2003]. *La Democratie en Miettes. Pour une Révolution de la Gouvernance* [*Democracy in Tatters*], trans. L. Gao. Beijing: SDX Joint Publishing Company.
Cao, T. 2003. "Theory and Practice of The Chinese Road [Pinyin: *zhongguo daolu de lilun he shijian*]," in T. Cao (ed.). *Modernization, Globalization and The Chinese Road* [Pinyin: *xian dai hua, quan qiu hua yu zhong guo dao lu*]. Beijing: Social Sciences Academic Press.
Chaoke, D.O. 1992. "The Mysterious Nature Worship of Evenki [Pinyin: ewenke ren shen mi de zi ran chong bai]," *Encyclopedic Knowledge Volume 1* [Pinyin: *bai ke zhi shi*].
Chaoke, Dular Osor and Wang Lizhen. 2002. *Evenki People's Religion, Faith and Culture* [Pinyin: *ewenke de zong jiao xin yang yu wen hua*]. Beijing: Central University for Nationalities Press.
Chaonang. 1981. "Evenki's Hunting Lives [Pinyin: ewenke ren de shou lie sheng huo]," *Traveling Scope* 3 [Pinyin: *lü you tian di*].
Chen, B. 1999. "Evenki Traditional Hunting Methods [Pinyin: *ewenke zu de chuan tong shou lie fang shi*]," *Heilongjiang National Series* 4 [Pinyin: *Heilongjiang min zu cong kan*].

Du, M. (ed.). 1989. *Evenki Folk Stories* [Pinyin: *ewenke zu min jian gu shi*]. Huhhot: Inner Mongolia People's Publishing House.

Eisenstadt, S.N. 1988. *Modernization: Protest and Change*, trans. L. Zhang, Y. Shen, Y. Chen and G. Chi. Beijing: China Renmin University Press.

Escobar, A. 2000[1998]. "Anthropology and Development," in J. Huang (trans.), *Trends in Anthropology* [Pinyin: *ren lei xue de qu shi*]. Beijing: Social Sciences Academic Press.

Evans, P.B. 1979. *Dependent Development: The Alliance of Multinational, State, and Local Capital in Brazil*. Princeton: Princeton University Press.

Ewenki Banner Political Council Literature and History Materials Committee, Hulun Buir League Ethnic Group Affairs Committee Ancient Books Office, Evenki Autonomous Banner Ethnic Group Committee Ancient Books Office. 1993. "Collection of Evenki Historical Materials [Pinyin: ewenke zu li shi zi liao ji]," internal publication.

Ewenki Banner Political Council Literature and History Materials Committee, Hulun Buir League Ethnic Group Affairs Committee Ancient Books Office, Evenki Autonomous Banner Ethnic Group Committee Ancient Books Office. 1996. "Collection of Evenki Historical Materials (Volume 2) [Pinyin: ewenke zu li shi zi liao ji(di er ji)]," internal publication.

Fei, X. 2001. "Create a Global Society of Harmony and Diversity—Keynote Speech at the Mid Session of International Association on Anthropology and Ethnology [Pinyin: chuang jian yi ge he er bu tong de quan qiu she hui—zai guo ji ren lei xue yu min zu xue lian he hui zhong qi hui yi shang de zhu zhi fa yan]," *Thinking* 6:1–5 [Pinyin: *si xiang zhan xian*].

———. 2004. *On Anthropology and Cultural Self-consciousness* [Pinyin: *lun ren lei xue yu wen hua zi jue*]. Beijing: Huaxia Publishing House.

Foucault, M. 1999[1975]. *Discipline and Punish: Birth of the Prison*, trans. B. Liu and Y. Yang. Beijing: SDX Joint Publishing Company.

Fraser, R. 2010. "Forced Relocation amongst the Reindeer-Evenki of Inner Mongolia." *Inner Asia* 12(2): 317–346.

Freeman, M. (ed.). 2000. *Endangered Peoples of the Arctic: Struggles to Survive and Thrive*. Greenwood.

Gadamer, H.G. 1975. *Truth and Method*. New York: The Seabury Press.

Gao, B. 2005. "Anthropological Reflexive Ethnography Study: Six Attempts to One Paradigm [Pinyin: ren lei xue fan si xing min zu zhi yan jiu]," *Thinking* 5: 42–44 [Pinyin: *si xiang zhan xian*].

Geertz, C. 1999[1973]. *The Interpretation of Cultures*, trans. Naribilige. Shanghai: Shanghai People's Publishing House.

———. 2000[1983]. *Local Knowledge*, trans. H. Wang and J. Zhang. Beijing: Central Compilation and Translation Press.

Guobuku and Manduertu. 1960. "Argun Banner Evenki Ethnic Group Social Histories Supplemental Survey [Pinyin: eerguna qi ewenke zu she hui li shi bu chong diao cha]," informal publication.

Hao, S., et al. 1994. "Aoluguya Evenki Ethnic Group Hunters' Current Situation Study—A Follow-up Research after 34 Years (1960–1994) [Pinyin: aoluguya ewenke zu lie min xian zhuang yan jiu—34 nian hou de zhui zong diao cha (1960–1994)]," internal research report. Institute of Ethnology & Anthropology of the Chinese Academy of Social Sciences.

Heyne, F. Georg. 1999. "The Social Significance of the Shaman amongst the Chinese Reindeer Evenki." *Asian Folklore Studies* 58(2): 377–395.

———. 2007. "Notes on Blood Revenge among the Reindeer Evenki of Manchuria (Northeast China)." *Asian Folklore Studies* 66(1–2): 165–178.

Humphrey, C. 1990. "Buryatiya and the Buryats." in G. Smith (ed.), *The Nationalities Question in the Post-Soviet States*. Longman Group Limited.

———. 2002. *The Unmaking of Soviet Life: Everyday Economies after Socialism*. Cornell University Press.

Humphrey, Caroline and Urgunge Onon. 1996. *Shamans and Elders: Experience, Knowledge, and Power among the Daur Mongols*. Oxford University.

Ingold, T. 1976. *The Skolt Lapps Today*. Cambridge University Press.

———. 1980. *Hunters, Pastoralists and Ranchers: Reindeer Economies and their Transformations*. Cambridge University Press.

Inoue, T. 2001. "Hunting as a Symbol of Cultural Tradition: The Cultural Meaning of Subsistence Activities in Gwich'in Athabascan Society of Northern Alaska," *Senri Ethnological Studies* 56: 89–104.

Kalina. 2004. "Research Trends and Values about Reindeer Evenki [Pinyin: you guan xun lu ewenke ren de yan jiu dong tai ji qi jia zhi]," *Journal of Hulun Buir College* 2: 77–79 [Pinyin: *hulunbeier xue yuan xue bao*].

Kolås, Å. 2011. "Reclaiming the Forest: Ewenki Reindeer Herding as Exception." *Human Organization* 70(4): 397–404.

Kong, F. 1994. *The Evenki of Aoluguya* [Pinyin: *aoluguya de ewenke ren*]. Tianjin: Tianjin Ancient Books Publishing House.

———. 1995. "Analysis of Dualistic Phenomena of Reindeer Evenki [Pinyin: shi lu ewenke zu er yuan xian xiang qian xi]," *Heilongjiang National Series* 3: 80–84 [Pinyin: *Heilongjiang min zu cong kan*].

———. 2002. *Culture Change among the Aoluguya Evenki* [Pinyin: *aoluguya ewenke ren de wen hua bian qian*]. Tianjin: Tianjin Ancient Books Publishing House.

Lavrillier, A. 2010. "The Creation and Persistence of Cultural Landscapes among the Siberian Evenk: Two Conceptions of Sacred Space," in P. Jordan (ed.), *Landscape and Culture in Northern Eurasia*. Walnut Creek, CA: Left Coast Press.

Lindgren, E.J. 1930. "North-Western Manchuria and the Reindeer-Tungus," *Geographical Journal* 75: 518–536.

———. 1935. "The Reindeer Tungus of Manchuria," *Journal of the Royal Central Asian Society* 22(2): 221–231.

———. 1936. "Notes on the Reindeer Tungus of Manchuria: Their Names, Groups, Administration and Shamans," Ph.D. dissertation. University of Cambridge.

Liu, X. 2002. "Effect and Problems of Ecological Migration in Northwestern China [Pinyin: xi bei di qu sheng tai yi min de xiao guo yu wen ti tan tao]," *Chinese Rural Economy* 4: 47–52 [Pinyin: *zhong guo nong cun jing ji*].

Lü, G. 1962. "An Attempt on Origin of Ewenki [Pinyin: shi tan ewenke zu de lai yuan]," *National Unity* 5, 6 [Pinyin: *min zu tuan jie*].

———. 1981. *Research of Northern Ethnic Groups' Primitive Society Status* [Pinyin: *Bei fang min zu yuan shi she hui xing tai yan jiu*]. Yinchuan: Ningxia People's Publishing House.

———. 1983. *Ewenki* [Pinyin: *ewenke zu*]. Beijing: Minorities Press.

———. 1986. *Social and Historical Investigation of the Ewenki* [Pinyin: *Ewenke zu she hui li shi diao cha*]. Hohhot: Inner Mongolia People's Press.

Luo, R. 2004. *New Theory of Modernization—The World's and China's Modernization Process* [Pinyin: *xian dai hua xin lun—shi jie yu zhong guo de xian dai hua jin cheng*]. Beijing: Commercial Press.

Ma, G. 2003. "The Surrounding Marginalized Ethnic Groups amid the Conversation between Globalization and Civilization: Hunting and Gathering Groups' 'Autonomy' and 'Distress'—In the Example of Settled Chinese Oroqen Hunters [Pinyin: quan qiu hua yu wen ming dui hua zhong de zhou bian de bian yuan min zu: shou lie cai ji min de 'zi li' yu 'ku nao'—yi ding ju de lie min zhong guo elunchun zu wei li]," in China Social Sciences Research Committee (ed.), *China and Japan under Globalization* [Pinyin: *quan qiu hua xia de zhong guo yu ri ben*]. Beijing: Social Sciences Academic Press.

Manduertu. 1981. "Evenki's Wulileng Commune [Pinyin: ewenke ren de wu li leng gong she]," *Social Science Front* 1 [Pinyin: *she hui ke xue zhan xian*].

Manduertu, Dular Osor Chaoke and Lizhen Wang. (ed.). 1999. *A Volume on Evenki Shamanism* [Pinyin: *ewenke zu sa man jiao juan*]. Beijing: China Social Sciences Press.

Marcus, George and Michael Fischer. 1998[1986]. *Anthropology as Cultural Critique*, trans. M. Wang and D. Lan. Beijing: SDX Joint Publishing Company.

Marglin, S.A. 2001[1996]. "Farmers, Seedsmen, and Scientists: Systems of Agriculture and Systems of knowledge," in Y. Bian (trans.), *Developmental Illusions* [Pinyin: *fa zhan de huan xiang*]. Beijing: Central Compilation and Translation Press.

Meng, H. 2000. *Shamanism in Northern Chinese Ethnic Groups* [Pinyin: *zhong guo bei fang min zu sa man jiao*]. Beijing: Social Sciences Academic Press.

Meng, Linlin and Zhiming Bao. 2004. "Literature Review on Ecological Migration [Pinyin: sheng tai yi min yan jiu zong shu]," *Journal of the Central University for Nationalities* 6: 48–52 [Pinyin: *zhong yang min zu da xue xue bao*].

Middleton, B.R. 2011. "Advocating for Traditional Native American Gathering Rights on US Forest Service Lands," in S. Thomas and J. Stahl (ed.), *Forests and People: Property, Governance, and Human Rights*. Earthscan.

Nagata, H. 1985[1939]. *Reindeer Oroqen* [Pinyin: *xun lu elunchun*], informal publication. Investigation office of Advising, Japanese Manchukuo Public Security Department.

Nash, M. 1979. "Modernization as a Problem: An Anthropological View," *Central Issues in Anthropology* 1: 69–77.

Ning, C. 1992. "Totem's Repentance: About Ceremonies of Evenki Bear-hunting and Bear-sacrificing [Pinyin: tu teng de chan hui: lun ewenke ren de lie xiong ji xiong yi shi]," *Social Science Journal* 2 [Pinyin: *she hui ke xue ji kan*].

Omura, K. 1998. "Construction of Inuinnaqtun (Real Inuit way): Self-image and Everyday Practices in Inuit Society," *Senri Ethnological Studies* 60: 101–111.

Parsons, T. 1966. *Societies: Evolutionary and Comparative Perspectives*. Englewood Cliffs, N.J: Prentice-Hall.

———. 1971. *The System of Modern Societies*. Englewood Cliffs, N.J: Prentice-Hall.

———. 1977. *The Evolutions of Societies*, Jackson Toby (ed.). Englewood Cliffs, N.J: Prentice-Hall.

Popper, K.R. 2002[1957]. *The Poverty of Historicism*. London: Routledge. (Chinese version 1987[1957]. *Lishi juedinglun de pinkun*, trans. R. Du and R. Qiu. Beijing: Huaxia Publishing House.)

Qiu, P. 1980[1962]. *Evenki Primitive Society Status* [Pinyin: *ewenke ren de yuan shi she hui xing tai*]. Beijing: Zhonghua Book Company.

Rabinow, P. 1977. *Reflections on Fieldwork in Morocco*. Berkeley and Los Angeles: University of California Press.

Ribot, J.C. 2004. *Waiting for Democracy: The Politics of Choice in Natural Resource Decentralization*. World Resources Institute.

Sahlins, M.D. 2001[1968]. "The Original Affluent Society," in Y. Qiu (trans.), *Developmental Illusions* [Pinyin: *fa zhan de huan xiang*]. Beijing: Central Compilation and Translation Press.

Scott, J.C. 2004[1994]. *Seeing Like a State: How Certain Schemes to Improve the Human Condition Have Failed*, trans. X. Wang. Beijing: Social Sciences Academic Press.

Shirokogoroff, S.M. 1923. *Anthropology of Northern China*. Royal Asiatic Society (North China Branch).

———. 1966[1929]. *Social Organization of the Northern Tungus: With Introductory Chapters Concerning Geo-graphical Distribution and History of These groups*. Anthropological Publications. (Chinese version 1985[1933]. *Beifang tongusi de shehui zuzhi*, trans. Y. Wu, F. Zhao and K. Meng. Huhhot: Inner Mongolia People's Publishing House.)

Sikor, Thomas and Johannes Stahl (ed.). 2011. *Forests and People: Property, Governance, and Human Rights*. Earthscan.

Siqinfu. 1999. "Chugoku tonak aievuenki hito no shakai keizai henka 1 [Socioeconomic Change among the Reindeer Ewenki of China, 1]," *Social and Environmental Research* 4: 161–170.

———. 2000. "Chugoku tonak aievuenki hito no shakai keizai henka 2 [Socioeconomic Change among the Reindeer Ewenki of China, 2]," *Social and Environmental Research* 5: 173–186.

Siriguleng. 1991. "Historical Changes of Aoluguya Evenki Hunters [Pinyin: aoluguya ewenke lie min de li shi bian qian]," in *Collection of Studies on Evenki* [Pinyin: *ewenke zu yan jiu wen ji*], volume II (part I) (internal publication).

Song, Z. 2001. *The Last Hunters* [Pinyin: *zui hou de bu lie zhe*]. Jinan: Shandong Pictorial Publishing House.

Suritai. 1992. *Primitive Art of Hunting Ethnic Groups* [Pinyin: *shou lie min zu yuan shi yi shu*]. Hohhot: Inner Mongolia Culture Press.

———. 1997. *Research on Evenki Folk Painting* [Pinyin: *ewenke min jian mei shu yan jiu*]. Hohhot: Inner Mongolia Culture Press.

The Chinese National Committee for Man and the Biosphere. 2006. *Man and the Biosphere* 2 [Pinyin: *Ren yu sheng wu quan*].

The Inner Mongolia Minority Social History Investigation Group and the History Research Institute, Inner Mongolia Branch, Chinese Science Academy (ed.). 1960. *Evenki Conditions in Argun Banner* [Pinyin: *e er gu na qi ewenke ren de qing kuang*], internal publication.

The National People's Congress Ethnic Group Committee Office (ed.). 1958. *Social Conditions of the Reindeer Evenki of Argun Banner in the Inner Mongolia Autonomous Region* [Pinyin: *nei meng gu zi zhi qu e er gu na qi shi yong xun lu de ewenke ren de she hui qing kuang*], internal publication.

Tian, X. 1981. "Evenki clothing, food, shelter and transportation [Pinyin: ewenke ren de yi shi zhu xing]," *Practice* 1 [Pinyin: *shi jian*].

Ulturgasheva, O. 2012. *Narrating the Future in Siberia: Childhood, Adolescence and Autobiography among Young Eveny*. Berghahn Books.

Vitebsky, P. 1990. "The Northern Minorities," in G. Smith (ed.), *The Nationalities Question in the Post-Soviet States*. Longman Group Limited.

Wallerstein, I. 1997. *Open the Social Sciences*, trans. F. Liu. Beijing: SDX Joint Publishing Company.

Wang, L. 2000. "Evenki Shamanism and Nature Worship [Pinyin: ewenke zu sa man jiao xin yang yu zi ran chong bai]," *Journal of the Central University for Nationalities* 6: 72–77 [Pinyin: *zhong yang min zu da xue xue bao*].

Wang, M. 1997. *Cultural Pattern and the Expression of People* [Pinyin: *wen hua ge ju yu ren de biao shu*]. Tianjin: Tianjin People's Publishing House.

Wang, Xiaoming and Yongxi Wang. 1988. "Wedding and Funeral Customs of Evenki [Pinyin: ewenke ren de hun sang xi su]," *Heilongjiang National Series* 3 [Pinyin: *hei long jiang min zu cong kan*].

Wen, T. 2004. *Deconstructing Modernization—Collection of Speeches by Tiejun Wen* [Pinyin: *jie gou xian dai hua—Wen Tiejun yan jiang lu*]. Guangzhou: Guangdong People's Publishing house.

Writing Group of Brief History of Ewenki (ed.). 1983. *A Brief History of Ewenki* [Pinyin: *ewenke zu jian shi*]. Huhhot: Inner Mongolia People's Publishing House.

Wureertu. 1998. *Narration on the Ewenki* [Pinyin: *shu shuo ewenke*]. Hohhot: Yuanfang Press.

Wuyundalai. 1998. *Origin of the Ewenki* [Pinyin: *ewenke zu de qi yuan*]. Hohhot: Inner Mongolia University Press.

Xie, Y. 2010. *The Ecological Migration Policy and Its Application by Local Authorities: A Case Study of the Aoluguya Ewenki Ecological Migration* [Pinyin: *Sheng tai yi min zheng ce yu di fang zheng fu shi jian: yi aoluguya ewenke sheng tai yi min wei li*]. Beijing: Peking University Press.

———. 2015. "The Ecological Migration and Ewenki Identity," in Å. Kolås and Y. Xie (ed.), *Reclaiming the Forest: The Ewenki Reindeer Herders of Aoluguya*. Berghahn Books.

Yan, Y. 2000[1996]. *The Flow of Gifts: Reciprocity and Social Network in a Chinese Village*, trans. F. Li and Y. Liu. Shanghai: Shanghai People's Publishing House.

Yang, J. (ed.). 1994. *An Exploration of Modernization Pathways for Northeastern Fishing and Hunting Ethnic Groups* [Pinyin: *dong bei yu lie min zu xian dai hua dao lu tan suo*]. Beijing: Minorities Press.

Yidi. 2003. "Confusion on Ecological Migration [Pinyin: sheng tai yi min de kun huo]," *Cultural Geography* 5: 137–142 [Pinyin: *hua xia ren wen di li*].

Index